KYLIE

Introduction

The Voice: BBC1, 11 Jan 2013

Putting a smile on people's faces is a gift. Kylie has it. She has always had it. She can cheer you up even on a dull, chilly Saturday night in early January, when the nation is emerging with a collective sore head after the excesses of welcoming a new year. It hasn't been good so far, with the news dominated by stories of wretched weather and the misery inflicted by torrential rain and floods. We could all do with a spoonful of Kylie.

She brought her A-game to her first appearance on the BBC1's *The Voice*. She was enthusiastic and exuberant, like a child at a birthday party. During a fast-paced introduction, she told us that she had a fantasy growing up that she would be a singer. She thought everyone had the same ambition and 'sang into a hairbrush'. You could imagine her still doing that, losing herself in the moment just as she had as a little girl. Her fellow judge will.i.am had told her to be natural and she'd taken his advice.

She really didn't need any fanfare. Everyone knows Kylie. She's been part of our lives for so long. It's been more than twenty-seven years since she first bounced onto our TV screens as Charlene Mitchell in *Neighbours*, an unlikely candidate for superstar status. Now, having sold more than 68 million records, she was back in a series for the first time since those bad-hair days.

The show began with an inspired mash-up of Kylie's biggest-selling single 'Can't Get You Out Of My Head' with 'I Predict A Riot', the best-known record from the other new judge, Ricky Wilson. At forty-five, Kylie is ten years older than the lead singer of The Kaiser Chiefs but she didn't look or act it. She and Ricky had an instant rapport throughout.

Kylie is not the oldest on the show, however. Sir Tom Jones is still there and he's seventy-three. According to a show insider, Tom was 'on the cusp' of leaving but was persuaded to stay when he was told that Kylie, who called him 'old snake hips', would be joining for series three, replacing Jessie J.

After showing the audience they'd still got it, the four judges settled into their red chairs for the auditions. It was our chance to study what Kylie was wearing. It was a classic LBD (little black dress). Throughout her career, style and image have been just as important as her music. Her grandmother Millie was an accomplished seamstress and, from an early age, Kylie has displayed an aptitude for dressmaking and an intuitive sense of fashion. That may not have been clear in the eighties, when she adopted so many 'tragic outfits', as she called them, but the platform heels, sweater dresses and perms were all part of growing up – and the rest of the world was making similarly embarrassing choices.

The designer Julian Macdonald tells a revealing story about Kylie's bold fashion instinct. She persuaded him to let her wear an evening gown he had specially made. She wanted it for her performance at the Brits in 2003, when she was going to sing a duet with Justin Timberlake. It was a floor-length black evening gown covered in 50,000 Swarovski crystals – the sort of dress you would wear for an evening at the White House. It was a one-off and Julian already had a buyer prepared to pay big money, but he allowed Kylie to borrow it, provided she gave his creation back to him immediately afterwards. Imagine his surprise when she came on stage in a micro mini that barely covered her famous bottom. She had gone home and

basically cut his dress in half. She sent Julian some flowers and an apologetic note: 'Sorry I was a bit naughty.'

She didn't need to do anything that daring for *The Voice*, but she did have to create the right first impression. She wasn't performing on tour, so anything containing feathers and corsetry would have been inappropriate. She was going to be in living rooms, watched by an audience that had loved her since she'd worn motor oil stained dungarees in *Neighbours*. Any form of hot pants or revealing jumpsuit would have smacked of a woman trying to be too youthful and not accepting the passage of time. So she chose a black dress that you might wear to a smart drinks party or dinner at a fashionable restaurant. It was perfect.

The renowned fashion writer Alison Jane Reid observed, 'Less is so much more. Kylie looks forever young and pretty by keeping it simple: the elegantly sexy bodycon, mid-length black dress and scarcely any bling or theatrical embellishment apart from killer heels. This is grown-up glamour. Kylie looks fabulously sexy. Even her golden hair is kept simple with subtle loose waves.'

Kylie can expect to be scrutinized every week. It is a burden that all women on television have to bear. At least she is the only female judge – unlike on the rival ITV shows *The X Factor* and *Britain's Got Talent*. When her sister Dannii was on the former, for instance, her outfits were forever being compared to fellow panellist Cheryl Cole's in a sort of juvenile frock wars.

Kylie certainly looked the part, but would she let herself down when it was her turn to talk to the contestants? Would the tired old clichés, like 'You nailed it' or 'You made that song your own', spill out when it was her turn to speak? That proved not to be the case, thank goodness.

The first contestant was an insurance manager from Coventry called Lee Glasson, who sang a slow and emotional version of 'Can't Get You Out Of My Head'. It was a nice touch by the producers to show his performance first, because it immediately put Kylie centre stage. He sounded like a cross between the ethereal voices of Antony and the Johnsons and Jeff Buckley, the finest singer of 'Hallelujah'.

Completely changing the tone and tempo of the song was just the sort of thing Kylie herself might have done. She transformed her first UK hit 'I Should Be So Lucky' into a torch song for her *On A Night Like This* tour in 2001 and, less successfully, converted 'The Loco-Motion' into a smoky jazz ballad for the *Kylie Showgirl* concerts in 2005.

She may yet do something similar with her most successful song, but she was impressed enough to describe Lee's voice as 'arresting' and appreciate its 'other-worldly' quality. To chants ringing round the audience of 'Kylie, Kylie', he chose to be on her team ahead of the other judges. She shrieked, 'Oh, my God', and rushed up to give him a hug, even though his choice wasn't the least surprising.

Kylie was attractively self-deprecating. When one hopeful brought her daughter on to the stage to meet the judges and sit in will.i.am's place, she remarked that the little girl was 'probably the only person smaller than me who's going to sit in the chair'. She had already shown the audience the little step that she was using to stop her feet from dangling over the edge.

Kylie is no stranger to talent shows. She has regularly performed on them and helped her sister Dannii during Judges' Houses week on *The X Factor*. In the 2007 final, her show-stopping duet with Leon Jackson of 'Better The Devil You Know' almost certainly dragged that lacklustre contestant over the winning line. In June 2013, she returned to assist Dannii again in the Australian version of the show. She said then, 'This feels normal for us. We're both comfortable in this environment.'

That comfort was revealed on *The Voice*, as she managed to remain natural and unscripted throughout. She avoided bursting into tears or pretending to be annoyed with the other judges. Instead, she brought a *joie de vivre* to proceedings. 'I'm like a Mexican jumping bean because I just get into it,' she said, describing her enthusiastic performance.

She was suitably apologetic when none of the four turned round for a clearly talented sixteen year old called Ryan Green. He was upset about that and some reviewers criticized the judges afterwards, which missed the point. It was good television and made you want to throw a slipper at the screen. Sometimes we forget that these shows are all about TV and not so much to do with actual singing.

One contestant, a mature performer called Sally Barker, could have been turned into a sob story when it was revealed that her husband had died of cancer at forty-two, leaving her to bring up two small children by herself. Nobody mentioned Kylie's battle against the disease, even if we were thinking about it. Sally gave a moving interpretation of 'Don't Let Me Be Misunderstood', and Kylie told her that she had 'a beautiful dove of a voice'.

There was even time for some mild flirtation with Leo Ihenacho, a good-looking black singer who used to be in the chart band The Streets. He had also appeared on *Celebrity Love Island*, so he was hardly just starting out. Kylie blushed and hid behind a chair while he said he had fancied Charlene since he was 'so high'. She babbled away until she said, 'Just shut up, Minogue. Just shut up.' It was all good fun and would give the papers something to write about in the coming weeks, especially as Kylie has been unattached since her five-year relationship with Spanish model Andrés Velencoso ended in 2013.

The early indications are that Kylie will be refreshingly unaffected on *The Voice*. Kevin O'Sullivan, the television critic of the *Sunday Mirror*, thought she put her 'heart and soul' into it. He told me how amusing she had been when they'd had lunch together: 'She's a good laugh but she's always been packaged up by her publicity machine. She's never, to employ a terrible cliché, let the world see the real Kylie. I hope that at her age she has come to the realization that it's all a load of old b******s and she might as well say it like it is and be herself. I know she can be very entertaining if she does that.'

Throughout the show, that seemed to be Kylie's intention. She was strangely uncool, yet cool at the same time. It's a paradox that has served her well in her career. Her close friend, the novelist Kathy Lette, describes her as a 'down-to-earth diva' who is totally lacking in pretension. She added wittily, 'Kylie may have the world's most beautiful bottom, but the important thing is – she never, ever, ever talks out of it.'

It is just the quality *The Voice* needs, as a show that has limped through two series very much the poor relation of the ITV block-busters. The coup that brought in Kylie seemed to have paid an instant dividend when the first show was watched by an audience of 8.4 million. No instalment of the previous series could match that. It was more than 2 million up from last season's launch. The numbers matched the ratings for the last series of *The X Factor* and was com-fortably the most watched programme on the night.

Comments on Twitter suggested the improvement was due to Kylie's impact. The most obvious question, however, was why on earth was Kylie actually bothering with *The Voice*? She is a superstar far beyond the level of mundane television shows. Kevin O'Sullivan, explained, 'It's a career move. Ten years ago *The Voice* wouldn't have even got past her agent. Now, it will probably do wonders for her.'

In 2012, the Official Charts Company revealed the Diamond Dozen, the list of the twelve performers who had sold the most sin-gles in the UK. The Beatles, Elvis, Madonna and Michael Jackson were at the top, but in twelfth place, with sales of more than 10 mil-lion, was Kylie. There were no Rolling Stones or Westlife, no Lady Gaga or Robbie Williams. How has she done it? One of her secrets is that she does the unexpected.

Kylie has always had a rebellious streak. A hint of defiance is a key element of her survival. It goes a long way to explaining why she rev-elled in her relationship with Michael Hutchence, why she ditched

Stock, Aitken and Waterman and why, throughout her astonishing career, she has continued to shock and surprise.

During *The Voice*, will.i.am paid tribute to Kylie's longevity, telling one of the performers that although she had entered the profession at the top, she had sustained her success. 'It's even harder than coming from the bottom,' he said. Yet, Kylie has released only two albums of original material in the past ten years. There's a new generation of potential fans who need to be introduced to her and they will be watching *The Voice* on Saturday nights. It's currently the quickest way to receive instant exposure.

It came as no surprise, therefore, to learn that her new single will be released on 16 March to maximize the advantage of being on the programme. She has written 'Into The Blue' with Kelly Sheehan, one of the brightest new songwriters and recording engineers, who has composed for Rita Ora and Mary J. Blige. Kelly and Kylie, which sounds like a bad eighties duo, are both managed now by Roc Nation, the entertainment company founded by Jay-Z. Working with the most current figures in the music business is another of the reasons that Kylie has survived at the top for so long.

The Voice will undoubtedly provide a promotional boost for the single and the album that follows, as well as enhancing the affection we feel for her. Yes, we all love Kylie – and here's why . . .

PART ONE

Not The Girl Next Door

1

Suburbia

It's easy to see where Kylie gets her very distinctive looks. If you look at photographs of her as a natural, unstyled nineteen-year-old actress, she is the image of her mother, Carol. They could be sisters. They are exactly the same height – a hair over five feet tall – and have a similar slender build, as well as sharing the well-scrubbed look of a girl next door that would become Kylie's ticket to public affection.

Unlike her famous daughter at that age, the teenage Carol was a shy girl with no ambitions for a career in show business. She was a talented ballet dancer, an ability nurtured at her weekly classes in Maesteg, a small former coal-mining town in the Welsh Valleys not far from Swansea and Bridgend.

In the cruel landscape of the Valleys, there was little to inspire one's dreams, despite a proud tradition of rugby and male voice choirs. For a girl like Carol, learning to dance was just about it. Her mother and father, Denis and Millie Jones, wanted something better for their four children than the gloom and austerity of post-war Britain.

Carol Ann Jones was ten when her parents decided to uproot their family for a new life in Australia. It was a momentous decision. This was 1955 and a long time before air travel shrank the world. Their journey to a new land was an uncomfortable six-week voyage on the good ship *The New Australia*. The family were what was known in those days as 'Ten Pound Poms' because that was the cost of their passage to Oz.

The family of six quickly became a family of eight when Millie had two more sons. They started off in Melbourne, before eventually moving north to the peaceful coastal city of Townsville in northern Queensland. These days it's popular with tourists taking advantage of its water sports facilities and its proximity to the Great Barrier Reef. Maesteg was a million miles away from this tranquil, tropical haven where Carol spent her teenage years.

She continued with her dancing and won many local competitions at the Townsville Theatre Royal but decided not to turn professional. She recalled, 'I was a bit quiet. I never really had the drive to go any further. I danced until I was eighteen or nineteen but then I lost interest. I think dancing is a hard life but I loved it while I was doing it.' Part of her lack of ambition may have been due to meeting Ron Minogue, a young bespectacled trainee accountant, at a local barn dance. They fell in love and have been inseparable ever since.

Ron is a fifth-generation Australian but his family originally came from Ireland, an ancestry that, when combined with Carol's Welsh roots, gave Kylie a hotchpotch of nationalities. He was dependable, hard working and a very good bet for a young woman seeking a boyfriend who would be a 'keeper'.

Carol was twenty when she married in 1965. By the time she was twenty-five, she had three young children and the Minogue family had moved to the Melbourne suburbs, where the now-qualified Ron had set about finding a decent job. While the rest of the world was in the middle of the swinging sixties, they were looking forward to raising a family and working their way up in the world.

Kylie Ann, the eldest, was born on 28 May 1968 in the Bethlehem Hospital, Caulfield, one of the city's southern suburbs. Even before

Miss Minogue, Kylie was a popular Australian first name, apparently derived from an Aboriginal word for a boomerang. Kylie was two when her brother Brendan was born; he was followed a year later by the irrepressible Danielle. They were then living in South Oakleigh.

The Minogue family moved around various suburbs of Melbourne, which was a little unsettling for the children when they were growing up. They were always trying to make new friends in an ever-changing sequence of schools. They started off in Scoresby, where many young families were struggling to get a foot on the property ladder. While it would be stretching things to call this frontier living, the area in those days had no proper roads and the amenities, including the sewerage system, left a lot to be desired. Aspirational families like the Minogues would edge closer to the centre of the city as they went up in the world.

A couple of miles away in Moorabbin, Ron was working as an accountant at a thriving local company called Mackay's, a family-run business that had begun selling car parts but had grown to be a major supplier of engineered rubber. Money was tight and Carol worked part time as a tea lady at a nearby hospital to bring in some extra cash.

When Kylie was six, they moved to Deauville Court, Wantirna, an ideal place for small children, where they could ride their bikes and play safely until their mothers called them in for tea. Family life in general was pretty comfortable and carefree. They had a cat, a canary and a much-loved dog called Gabby, a large black 'Bitsa' (bitsa this, bitsa that).

Kylie went off to the local Studfield Primary School, which she enjoyed, even though at first she rarely spoke up in class. Being so small, she was the one who would always be placed in the middle of the front row of school photos, clutching the board with the class number on it. It didn't help that she was no good at running. Invariably, she was the last to be picked when teams were selected for playground games.

Despite this early reticence, the thought of Kylie as a bashful little flower is well wide of the mark. She always thought she was a shy kid until her mother put her right and said she was nothing of the sort. Carol revealed that her eldest was actually a bit of a poser even when she was tiny girl – always doing something expressive with her hands. At this early stage of her life, however, Kylie wasn't dreaming of being a performer; her chief ambition was to get a car like Fred Flintstone's, with her feet poking out the bottom.

One of the reasons why Kylie might have been mistaken for a shy girl was that she preferred indoor pursuits to the traditional Australian outdoor ones. She enjoyed splashing around with the local children in the above-ground swimming pool her father put in the back garden, but while Brendan and Dannii were outside from dawn to dusk, she would be inside reading, sewing or trying to get her small fingers around the fretboard of a violin.

Much of the credit for Kylie's homely side goes to her grand-mother Millie, who was an expert on the Singer sewing machine, as well as a cook who wouldn't have been out of place on *The Great British Bake Off*. Carol is also a talented seamstress and between them they made many of the clothes for their daughters. Their skill rubbed off on Kylie, who thought nothing of running up a dress for a night out when she was a teenager.

The Minogues were fortunate in that all four grandparents played a part in their upbringing. They called Millie 'Nain', a Welsh version of Nan, and she would always tell them stories about the old days in Wales.

Millie's brother had emigrated to Australia at the same time but didn't share her good fortune in their adopted country. After doing well in the building industry in Queensland, he fell ill with malaria while working on a contract in New Guinea and was advised to call a halt to his Australian dream after seven years because the hot climate was bad for his health. He needed the cooler days of South Wales and returned to Maesteg. Kylie kept in touch with her great-uncle Dennis over the years but he was careful to be discreet about his famous relation, mainly to stop kids singing 'I Should Be So Lucky' outside his front gate.

The three-year age gap between Kylie and Dannii meant that there was little competition between them as small children. Kylie was the big sister and Dannii was the annoying younger one, always hanging on to her coat tails. In the house in Wantirna there was no escape for Kylie because they shared a room.

Even though she was younger, Dannii was, if anything, the more precocious of the two girls – perhaps she was trying to keep up. They both had singing and dancing lessons, but have always been at pains to point out that Carol was not a Hollywood-style pushy mother.

Carol confirmed, 'I was never keen on them taking up dancing because I knew how hard it was. But when they started I didn't try and stop them because I had to let them do what they felt was right.

'I wanted them to learn the piano because I think the piano is something that you have for life. As for singing, I can't sing a note. I couldn't even sing in church.'

Fortunately, that wasn't the case with her daughters. Kylie's musical education had begun aged four, when she attended what was hopefully called a rhythm class. A lack of rhythm class would have been a more accurate title, as the group of youngsters bashed around on all manner of instruments, making an awful din. She progressed at primary school to the violin and then to piano, which she enjoyed most.

She revealed herself to be a natural performer when Carol took her to a small annual festival of music and art at yet another suburb: Dandenong, on the southern outskirts of the city. It was a showcase for serious local talent but, as a diversion, there was a piano competition for talented under-eights. Kylie bounced on stage, played 'Run, Rabbit, Run' and carried off second prize. She gave the judges one of her perkiest smiles, even though her feet barely touched the pedals and her hands couldn't spread to an octave. Her mother was convinced it was the toothy grin that claimed the prize.

The earliest audience for the all-singing, all-dancing Minogue sisters were their grandparents, who would babysit whenever Carol and Ron went out for the evening. The girls would treat them to impromptu performances of Abba songs. The Swedish group were massively popular in Australia. *Abba: The Movie* was released for Christmas 1977 and was set against the backdrop of their Australian tour. Kylie admitted, 'I wanted to be Agnetha, the blonde one, when I grew up. We'd put on dresses and dance to Abba records in the lounge, singing into our hairbrushes.'

Kylie's other great favourite besides Agnetha was the most famous Australian pop star of the time, Olivia Newton-John. Like a million other girls, Kylie dreamed of being Sandy from the film *Grease*, singing 'You're The One That I Want' to Danny, played by John Travolta. She later confided that she loved the scene where the prim and proper Sandy is transformed into a leather-clad rock chick – a piece of fiction that strangely would later be mirrored in Kylie's real life. She, too, dramatically changed her image from the virginal girl next door on the arm of Jason Donovan to raunchy babe on the arm of decadent rock star Michael Hutchence. Kylie, at least superficially, fulfilled her childhood fantasy.

Dannii too loved *Grease*, although she saw herself more as bad girl Rizzo, played so brilliantly in the movie by Stockard Channing. Dannii was always the more exuberant of the two sisters, a characteristic easily misconstrued as cockiness, but she had a sensitive and caring side as well. Kylie, likewise, was not as quiet as she might appear from first impressions and was always prepared to give something a go even if it meant rejection. Like most siblings, the two girls were different and similar at the same time. One popular misconception that they had to live with for years was that they didn't get on. They may have had a healthy rivalry but they were always close.

Poor Dannii always seemed to be half a step behind Kylie in the

UK but that was certainly not the case when they were growing up together in Australia. Until Kylie joined the cast of *Neighbours* at the age of seventeen, Dannii was by far the more famous of the two. Kylie actually owed her start in show business to her younger sister's childhood ambition. Using a combination of persistence and nagging, the seven-year-old Dannii had persuaded her parents to enrol her in the renowned Johnny Young Talent School, where she learned to sing and dance with other ambitious youngsters.

While she was there, Carol's elder sister Suzette, an established actress in Melbourne, used her connections to secure Dannii a casting audition with a large independent production company, Crawfords. Carol decided that in order to keep the peace at home she would take all three children along for the afternoon. As it turned out, Dannii was too young for the role they had in mind, so they cast ten-year-old Kylie instead. She was thought perfect for the part by one of the producers, Alan Hardy, who would become an influential figure in the early career of Kylie Minogue.

The show was *The Sullivans*, a popular if dire soap of the seventies set in World War Two. Kylie played Carla, a Dutch orphan, who befriended a group of Australian troops. She sported long, dark brown bushy hair, and if you didn't know it was her you might never have recognized a young Kylie. She had quite a lot of lines to learn and had to faint realistically. Mercifully, she was killed off after a few episodes. That didn't stop *The Sullivans* from being rerun in the late eighties, purely so that a devoted audience could witness Kylie's television debut. Most of the fun of *The Sullivans* is in trying to spot a famous face of the future. Other than Kylie, both Mel Gibson and Sam Neill cut their acting teeth on the show. In fairness, it was hugely popular in its day.

All Kylie could recall of her first audition was that she had to try to speak in a Dutch accent. 'I wasn't very good at it,' she said. Kylie is right that her accent left a lot to be desired. It sounded like a cross between Oz and German: 'Ve have ways of making you talk, mate.'

Her father was more concerned by her normal speaking voice than her Dutch. Not much gets under Ron Minogue's skin but he did get irritated by Kylie's annoying childhood habit of raising her inflection at the end of a sentence. It is a common trait among Australians, particularly women, to rise to a higher pitch when speaking, so that everything sounds like a question. Ron understood that it would not aid his young daughter's acting career to have a pronounced 'Strine twang', as it is called.

Carol, meanwhile, had to ease Dannii's disappointment. Fortunately, that didn't last long because her younger daughter's chance came soon afterwards when, in the same series, they needed a Kylie lookalike to play the part of Carla in a soldier's dream sequence. Dannii was perfect and everyone was happy.

After *The Sullivans*, Kylie landed another inconsequential part in a show called *Skyways*, set in and around an airport. This time she played a girl called Robin, stranded at the airport with her elder brother, Adam, waiting for their pilot father. She sounded very Australian, especially uttering the line 'He's a beaut pilot' when she spoke of her dad.

It was one of those wonderfully naff shoestring dramas. Kylie recalled that there was supposed to be a plane crash: 'You can see the tissue paper on the model plane as they're rocking it. In one scene another character asks me something and you can see that I have absolutely no idea what I'm supposed to do.' The role only required a few weeks' work but did allow for a key event in Kylie's young life: on set at Melbourne airport, she met a goofy child called Jason Donovan, who played Adam. All Kylie remembers is that he was 'really chubby with a bowl haircut'. In his autobiography, *Between the Lines*, Jason recalled meeting her for the first time and described her as being 'pretty chirpy and friendly', which made her sound like a sparrow. Perhaps unsurprisingly, *The Sullivans* and *Skyways* didn't lead to Kylie becoming the most popular child actress in the land.

By now, the family had moved for the last time – to a much bigger house in St John's Avenue in the suburb of Surrey Hills. It needed doing up and was in desperate need of some tender love and care but the Minogue children appreciated the extra space, especially Kylie, who no longer had to share a room with her pesky kid sister. There was a huge garden and outdoor area where her parents enjoyed entertaining their friends. The favourite family treat was a large home delivery from Pinky's Pizza.

The children had to change school again – to nearby Camberwell Primary School. Kylie developed her first crush on a boy in her class called Grant. She was all of a dither when they were seated next to each other for a spelling test. 'I was terribly excited,' she later recalled. 'I was a bit confused about spelling bicycle so Grant and I cheated together – the start of a blossoming romance.'

Ron had in a well-paid job in the accounts department of the local council, so the Minogues were comfortably off, thanks to hard work. They would usually spend their summer holidays staying in a cara-van on Phillip Island, a popular destination ninety miles south of Melbourne. These were old-style family vacations of lazy days on the beach and fish and chips in the evening.

In 1980, however, just before Kylie was due to start senior school, the whole family travelled to Britain for the first time and saw the sights of London. They also went to Maesteg to see relatives, includ-ing Great-Uncle Dennis, who was working as a carpenter there.

Over the years, right up until he died in 2010, Kylie would contact him when she could, usually when she was appearing in concert in Bristol or Cardiff. She would make sure Welsh relations had tickets for her shows. Occasionally, she would visit in person and enjoy long walks with Dennis. He kept a lovely picture in his family album of her giving him a hug near his home in the small village of Cymmer, near Maesteg, with the beautiful Welsh hills behind them.

On their return to Australia, Kylie could only watch in awe as her kid sister became one of the most famous children in Australia. In 1982 Dannii joined the regular cast of *Young Talent Time*, a hugely popular light-entertainment show. The title was a neat play on the name of its producer, Johnny Young, at whose school she had been enrolled. It wasn't long before she became the star of the show, which was a much bigger deal in Australia than *Neighbours*. Cynical pop fans in the UK have no idea how famous Dannii was then. One of the girls who danced on the show observed, 'Dannii was so popular. I can't believe Dannii has not made it as big as Kylie. She was always the favourite on *YTT*.'

Dannii was chaperoned by her mother when the show went on the road. Carol was a permanent fixture in the audience, proudly watching her daughter perform and encouraging her to do her best; she does this for both of her daughters to this day. Dannii's star was shining so brightly that she even started her own clothing label – something that Kylie, a more accomplished dressmaker, had always wanted to do. The Dannii label consisted of her name with two little love hearts above the i's. After she, too, became famous, Kylie would often use a love heart next to her name. When she later brought out her own range of products, they retailed under the 'Love Kylie x' banner.

Kylie's day-to-day life was mundane in comparison to her sister's. She would take the short walk each morning to Camberwell High in a bottle green uniform that she loathed. When she got in from school, she would sit down at the kitchen table and start sorting out Dannii's fan mail. Mostly there would be requests for photographs, so she would select one from a large pile of snaps, write the person's name at the top and underneath sign it 'Love Dannii'. She became very adept at forging her sister's signature.

Her own ambition was burning no less brightly, but she could do nothing at this stage to match her sister's success. Instead, she had to get used to being referred to as Dannii's elder sister. She even started introducing herself as Kylie, sister of Dannii. An early boyfriend recalled, 'There was no hint of jealousy. The impression I got was that they were great mates and that she was quite enthused about it.'

2

An Encounter with Kylie

Kylie freely admits that she went through a wild stage as a teenager, smoking, drinking and giving her parents a tough time. She later said that she'd had a 'really good upbringing'. She felt her parents, Ron and Carol, handled a rebellious girl with hormones flying in all directions in the way most parents would have done: 'I used to think, I'm fourteen or fifteen and I'm old enough to do whatever I want. We used to have terrible fights. Nowadays, I can understand the things they did and I'd probably be the same if I had kids. I thought they were being incredibly unreasonable, and all my friends seemed to have so much more freedom.'

She had found it difficult to make friends when she started at Camberwell High School. She soon settled down, however, largely thanks to her new best friend, Georgina Adamson, who became her teenage partner in crime and a pal for life. Georgie ended up working in a Melbourne store while Kylie travelled the world but she was always there for a laugh and a catch-up when her friend returned home. At school Georgie was the first to stick up for her petite chum and later, when Dannii joined them, she would act as a protector for her as well.

Georgie and Kylie would invariable sneak out of their houses or be caught sneaking back in after an evening at the Golden Bowl, the local bowling alley. Dannii recalled with relish the excruciatingly embarrassing evening for her sister when their mother marched into the Golden Bowl and yelled at Kylie, 'Get home this minute!'

The bowling alley was a great place to meet boys. Although she was hopeless at sports, Kylie proved more than a match for anyone at bowling, once winning a prize of Aus $15 in a ladies' competition. 'I was pretty stoked,' she recalled. She may hate sports, but Kylie is expert at pursuits like bowling and pool, which are normally associated with bars and having a sociable time. One of her later boyfriends, James Gooding, invited her bowling when he met her for the first time, little realizing that it was a quick and easy way to her heart.

The other place for the girls to meet boys was at the Harold Holt Memorial Swim Centre in High Street, Malvern. Holt was a renowned Australian Prime Minister who disappeared while swimming off the coast near Melbourne – not the best choice of name perhaps for a public swimming baths. It was at the pool that Kylie met her first serious boyfriend, an older local boy called David Wood. A group of teenagers, including Kylie and Georgie, would hang around the pool, where the boys would jump off the high board to try and look impressive. David thought Kylie was 'stunning' although quite reserved, which meant it was difficult to break the ice. He had no idea that Kylie had fancied him for ages and failed to ask her out on a date when they eventually got chatting. She saw him as a bit of a rebel and was fascinated by his curly black hair, which seemed to spring out in all directions.

She wasn't getting anywhere, though, until fate intervened when David was put on 'trash duty' for being a nuisance 'bombing' at the pool. Kylie saw her opportunity and went round with him to pick up the rubbish. It led to a first, very romantic kiss, for which she had been practising diligently on the back of her hand. David, who is now a hairdresser, enjoyed a typical teenage on/off relationship with Kylie throughout her schooldays. He was a bit of a Jack the Lad, which led to several rows and bitter break-ups after he failed to pick her up when he said he would.

David has revealed a side to Kylie that she has kept hidden over the years. She is very emotional. 'She doesn't like to expose her emotions – but she can get mad,' he recalled. Future boyfriends would have to cope with that volatile side of Kylie's nature.

Kylie grew up fast as a teenager. Many of the kids, especially the girls, at Camberwell High School were quite advanced for their age. When she was sixteen, Kylie used to work in a video store in Burke Road, Camberwell, on Saturday mornings, to earn a few dollars to spend on clothes or, more often, the material to run up her own creations on the sewing machine at home. She already had a real aptitude for dressmaking, but her interest in fashion stems from that time. She might well have made a successful career out of fashion if acting, and then singing, had not snared her first.

At weekends she would join friends for parties or a night out at the pubs they knew would serve underage drinkers. One, in particular, was a hundred metres from the police station in the Kew district of Melbourne and, on the occasions when the local constabulary popped in to check IDs, it was always amusing to see the number of girls who would have an urgent need to visit the toilets.

Unusually within her circle, the teenage Kylie was into funky black music, like Donna Summer and Prince. Her favourite record, however, was 'Sexual Healing' by Marvin Gaye, one of the most erotic tracks of all time and perennially favourite background music for making love. Kylie clearly has always enjoyed sex. That was the strong impression she gave Paolo Marcolin on the unforgettable night when she became his first lover. She has never revealed the identity of her 'first love', but clearly, at sixteen years and two months, she was experienced in the ways of pleasing a man.

It was a cool August Friday night in the middle of an Australian winter and Paolo was in high spirits. Earlier, he had played in the final match of the schools' football season in the state of Victoria. This was Australian rules football, a game that's best described as a combination of soccer and basketball. It can be very physical, although the participants don't wear all the padding and paraphernalia associated with gridiron. You have to be fit, and Paolo had the physique of a young man who took his sport seriously. His parents were first-generation immigrants from Italy, and he had the advantage, as far as the young female population of Melbourne was concerned, of traditional Latin looks – dark hair and olive skin. Despite his obvious appeal, Paolo had spent his school years more interested in sport than girls and, as a result, was quite innocent for his age of eighteen.

Everyone was on a high this particular evening because Marcellin College, his exclusive Catholic private school in Melbourne's eastern suburbs, had won the match of the season against their archrivals, Assumption College, and, as a result, were unofficial Victorian grammar school champions. Paolo, an attacking wingman, had played a blinding game, so was more than up for the celebrations planned for that night. It was party time. The venue for the festivities was the home of teammate Damian Bonser, who lived just a few doors down from Paolo in the relatively new and up-and-coming district of Templestowe, about five miles from Kylie's house. By the time she arrived with a group of school friends, the beer was flowing. As well as the victorious players, there were supporters and a number of parents at the party: Paolo's mother popped in for a while to toast the team's success.

Paolo settled himself in a chair in the lounge and was chatting to the boys, drinking beer and generally basking in the glory of their win, when he spotted a girl in an armchair across the other side of the room, surrounded by half a dozen eager boys. She was slender, with blonde curly hair and a winning smile. There were only a few girls at the party, so she stood out and caught the attention of most of the boys there, especially Paolo: 'There was a lack of female options, so I bit the bullet and just wandered over to where she was and sat on the arm of the chair.' Paolo started listening to the conversation, hoping he would get the chance to say more than two words to the girl, when he was joined by another friend, Nick, who was one of the biggest and loudest guys in the team. Nick was also very inebriated and leaned on Paolo's left shoulder to hold himself upright: 'His weight started to push me down towards the girl,' recalled Paolo. 'I am basically a shy sort of person and not the sort who hits on women. I turned around and looked at her to almost apologize but, before I could say anything, we started kissing. It all happened so spontaneously.' The spark was instantaneous and obvious to the other suitors, who, disgruntled, moved away to try their luck elsewhere.

By this stage it was past 11 o'clock and the parental presence was thinning out. Paolo was feeling self-conscious snogging the girl because his mates made loud and gormless comments every time they walked past the chair. He suggested to Kylie they went some-where more private: 'She agreed without question, so we got up and went outside into the backyard where there was a fire going in an old drum. It wasn't that cold for an August night – perhaps about twelve degrees – but we kept each other warm by kissing and cuddling. There were a few people walking around, but it was quite dark and there wasn't as much comment as there had been in the living room.

'By this stage my hands were wandering a bit and we were getting even hotter by the fire. Out of the blue, she said to me, "Do you want to go somewhere even more private?" Of course I agreed. It sounded great to me. We walked down the driveway of the house, around the front and up the other side. She had no idea where she was going, but eventually she took me to the opposite side of the house. There were a few people catching taxis, so we walked round the corner to be out of sight – or so I thought. We started kissing again and I remember that I actually told her my name at this point and she said she was called Kylie. Before that I hadn't a clue who she was. The next thing I knew, her hands had gone down and she had undone my fly, got the old fella out, and dropped to her knees. I thought it was pretty amazing for a sixteen year old.'

Paolo found himself in a state of bliss as Kylie went to work: 'She was fantastic and knew exactly what she was doing. I just shut my eyes and let her get on with it.' Alas, his ecstasy was short-lived when he opened his eyes and realized they were in full view of other party guests: 'I don't think they were watching Kylie in action but I'm sure a couple of them would have wondered what was going on in the dark. I felt very conspicuous and more than a little uneasy that we might be spotted.'

He spied a tiny door next to him, grabbed the handle and was relieved when it opened, so he could bundle Kylie inside, away from prying eyes. It wasn't exactly five-star luxury. The room appeared to be a small workshop underneath the front of the house. The first problem was that neither of them could find the light switch and it was very dark inside, with just a small window at the front letting in a chink of light. The young lovers didn't care too much as passion got the better of them. Nor, remembered Paolo, did it matter to Kylie that he had no protection with him. He later discovered, when it came up in conversation, that she wasn't on the Pill.

That was in the future. For the moment, it was important to take off as few clothes as possible because the dingy room was absolutely freezing. Kylie was wearing a skirt, which made things easier, although Paolo had to remove his jeans. They had sex first on the chair: 'I was on top but this wasn't very comfortable so I took hold of her again and we lay on the floor.' Paolo, ever the gentleman, took off his jacket and laid it on the ice-cold floor for Kylie to lie on before they started again. 'It was freezing but I had enough alcohol in my veins for me not to notice. I was really enjoying myself because Kylie was so nice, but then we heard some voices sniggering outside the door.'

Suddenly passion died in a desperate flurry to get dressed – too late: 'The door burst open just as Kylie was putting her panties back on and my mate Nick, the same one who had leaned on me in the lounge, walked in. He just said, "Oh, *here* you are," but I was embarrassed. Fortunately, the darkness hid my red face and I just mumbled,

"Yeah, yeah." But there was enough light showing through the open door for him to see exactly what we had been up to. Kylie was standing behind me, so I couldn't see whether she was as embarrassed as me, but she followed us outside.'

If Paolo had been able to see his teenage temptress properly, he would have noticed how upset she was. He was soon in no doubt: 'All of a sudden she started crying. Real sobs. I didn't know what to do, so I tried to reach out and reassure her but she just brushed me off. She was wailing: "You've just used me." I assured her that wasn't the case and asked for her phone number. That seemed to cheer her up a bit, because she stopped crying, although she was still tearful.'

In his excitement and youthful pride at having had sex for the first time, Paolo let slip exactly what had happened when another teammate came over to ask what was going on. 'I said, "Don't say anything but I just shagged her."' That was all the encouragement the friend needed to announce the fact at the top of his voice. Paolo was aghast: 'There was a balcony where everybody had gathered, and they all must have heard what my mate said. Kylie didn't appear to react, so perhaps she didn't realize what he had said.'

Back inside the house, Paolo found a pen and a scrap of paper so that Kylie could write down her name and phone number. Shortly afterwards, her friends shouted out that they were leaving and that she should go with them. She told Paolo that she had to go to work the next morning. Once more, his sporting mates were less than tactful: one asked if he was going to ask Kylie out; another blurted, 'Don't worry, he's already been there.' Kylie must have heard, because she was standing right next to Paolo. But, after a little goodnight kiss, she was gone, and Paolo returned to drink beer and talk with his friends.

When he went in to school on the following Monday, Paolo discovered his exploits were still the talk of his set. He thought he had better find out a little more about Kylie. He learned that she went to Camberwell High School and that she was the sister of Dannii

Minogue, whom everybody in Australia had heard of because of her starring role in *Young Talent Time*. He discreetly asked around and was pleased to discover that none of his friends, or even acquaintances, had enjoyed a sexual encounter with Kylie. Perhaps she was not what his friends would call an easy lay. Perhaps he was special.

Now that they had had sex, it was time to think about a first date. Playing it cool, Paolo waited until the middle of the week to call. They chatted briefly and Kylie mentioned that she was a fan of Prince, so he asked her if she fancied going to see his movie *Purple Rain* at the Hoyts Midtown cinema the following weekend. He couldn't have come up with a more appealing idea, because Prince was Kylie's pop idol and she was dying to see his first film.

Kylie suggested he take the bus from Templestowe to Camberwell Junction and meet her there. They could then take the tram into the city. By Saturday, Paolo was full of anticipation at seeing his first lover for the second time. Kylie was clearly excited, too, because as soon as she caught sight of him, she ran over and planted a big, exuberant kiss on his lips. They hopped on a tram and spent the thirty-minute journey talking non-stop all about themselves, as people always do on a first date. Kylie told him she had just been hired to appear in a new television series called *The Henderson Kids* and also confided that she helped Dannii reply to her fan mail. 'Kylie had a nice bubbly personality,' recalled Paolo. 'She was very easy to talk to and get along with.'

It was after they had got off the tram and were walking to the cinema that Paolo had his first misgivings. 'I suddenly noticed how tiny she was. I am close on six feet and she was literally a foot shorter than me. I felt very awkward and self-conscious. People have asked me what it was like and the only way I have been able to put it is that it was like taking out my little sister. She was sixteen, but I realized she looked much younger than that because of her size – even though she was so mature for her age in other ways.' Kylie, meanwhile, was happily unaware of her date's growing unease: 'She was saying things like, "I can't wait to introduce you to all my friends." She was being very chatty and I was listening, but at the same time I was thinking, "I'm not sure about this. Do I really want to be with this girl?"'

Paolo has no idea if Kylie was beginning to pick up on his negative vibes at this point, but he was becoming quieter and quieter. They went in to watch the movie together and, just like any other young couple, bought popcorn and enjoyed a little kiss and a cuddle before the film started. There was no groping in the back row! After the movie, they caught the tram back to Camberwell. By this time, Paolo had decided that he didn't want to take things any further with Kylie, and set about trying to let her down gently. He used the old excuse that he would have far too much work to do in the coming months, as he had been neglecting his studies to play football, and he had his Year Twelve exams (the Australian equivalent of A levels in the UK). 'I told her I wouldn't have a great deal of time to socialize, which was actually true. I genuinely didn't have time for a girlfriend, even one as brilliant sexually as Kylie.'

Eventually, poor Kylie got the heavy hint and agreed that this would be their first and last serious date together. 'She had gone from a long-term relationship to a casual fling in half an hour.' The ability to make hard, even painful, decisions is one of Kylie's great strengths, one that has been important to her throughout her life and career. Perhaps this early teenage setback enabled her to identify when it is time to walk away with your dignity intact. Paolo will never know if Kylie was crestfallen or not, as she made the last leg of her journey home by herself from Camberwell Junction. He took a bus, which conveniently passed The Harp pub in Kew where, through the window, he spotted some of his mates drinking. He got off at the next stop to go back and join them until it was chucking-out time.

And that was pretty much it, although he had mentioned that he had a ticket for her to a school social in a couple of weeks' time. It was a typical school disco, at which the girls all talk to each other about boys and the lads all talk to each other about sport. Kylie turned up and Paolo gave her the ticket, but as soon as they went inside they split up and spent the evening with their respective friends. If Kylie was hurt by what had happened, she didn't let on to him. He was pleased to see that she went home by herself and didn't immediately go on to the next likely guy.

The Paolo saga puts to bed much of the myth of Kylie as an innocent girl next door. Her behaviour with him was hardly unusual for teenage girls in Melbourne then. Paolo observed, 'A lot of the girls we all knew at the time were sexually active. Kylie was mature sexually, but we knew of girls of thirteen and fourteen who were having sex with boyfriends. I am not saying they had multiple partners – just with their boyfriends.'

Maybe Kylie saw Paolo as boyfriend material. If so, she was quickly disillusioned, because he wasn't ready for that. Instead, it was an enjoyable fling. And it exposes the lie that Kylie was 'corrupted' by sex Svengali Michael Hutchence, as has been portrayed time and time again. She may even have taught *him* a thing or two between the sheets. His ungallant and oft-reported boast that Kylie was the best f*** in the world doesn't seem quite so incredible. The other intriguing 'first' in the Templestowe knee-trembler was that it was the first time that Kylie took a risk in being discovered in flagrante. It would not be the last.

Paolo now prefers to be known as Paul. He still lives in Melbourne, where he is happily married with two children and has a successful career as a graphic designer, after a brief spell as a personal fitness trainer. He saw Kylie once more when he was twenty and she was the star of *Neighbours*. He was driving home from university and saw her walking down the street before going into the video store where she used to work. He decided against stopping to catch up on old times: 'I don't have any regrets about breaking up with Kylie or missing out on being part of her career, because I just don't think it would have worked.'

3

A Happy Accident

Producer Alan Hardy could scarcely believe his eyes when he was auditioning young actors and actresses for his new show, *The Henderson Kids*. Was this really the same girl who had appeared in *The Sullivans* five years earlier? Budding actress Nadine Garner, who was fourteen at the time, and would become her co-star, observed that sixteen-year-old Kylie was very aware of her femininity and was much worldlier: 'She had a great sense of herself. There was this determination and quiet ambition.' Kylie confirmed that focus in one of her earliest television interviews, saying: 'You always should have ambition and believe there is more to life than what you are doing now.'

She had been patient while her sister swept all before her like a supersonic Shirley Temple. Like a million other aspiring actors, Kylie had to trudge around to auditions, hoping to catch the casting director's eye. Ron and Carol never put her under any pressure to go to these auditions – far from it – and didn't push her brother, who showed no desire for a career as a performer. Brendan had happily joined in when the Minogue children performed 'Greased Lightning' for an audience in their front room and he could be found in his bedroom pretending to be a member of Kiss, his rock heroes, but that was as far as it went. Kylie's motivation was entirely her

31

own. Auditions are potentially soul-destroying but she had an inner self-belief.

One afternoon after school, she saw a newspaper advertisement seeking young actors aged between eleven and sixteen for a new television series. *The Henderson Kids* had a substantial budget for an Australian series – Aus $3 million – and was going to be filmed on location in the countryside around Melbourne. If Kylie landed a role, it would mean time away from school. Now that she was six-teen, she didn't need her mother to hold her hand at the audition. Instead, she put on one of the dresses she had made at home, did her own make-up and presented herself for consideration to Alan Hardy and the director, Chris Langman.

They both were impressed by her naturalness and thought she had the right personality for the part of Charlotte Kernow, one of nine roles that needed to be cast. Langman admitted that they chose her on a whim rather than on any more substantial consideration. They took a chance on Kylie's potential. They were concerned about her high-pitched voice and her tendency to lose her words some-where in her teeth, but they hoped that a voice coach could sort that out.

Kylie was more anxious about the fact that she had to dye her hair a bright shade of red for the role. On the few occasions that she did pop into Camberwell High, she was greeted with general astonish-ment. She once told *Smash Hits* magazine: 'I went to school and my hair was bright red, especially in the sunlight because it had just been done, and, as you can imagine, bright red dye onto blonde hair was pretty shocking. I was so embarrassed. I had to tell everyone that I hadn't done it of my own free will.'

She never felt comfortable as a redhead and couldn't wait to return to her natural dark blonde. She confessed to Paolo Marcolin that she was a 'little worried' about her new role because they wanted to dye her hair. More importantly, she also told him that she saw *The Henderson Kids* as her 'big break'. Perhaps one of the reasons why she moved on so quickly from the Paolo disappointment was that she was excited by this opportunity.

The plot of *The Henderson Kids* was hardly *War and Peace*, but it did allow Kylie to improve her acting skills and she worked very hard on the clarity of her speech and her emotional range. She put an enormous amount of energy into her role, something that, even at this early stage of her career, took its toll physically. She would burst into tears if anyone shouted at her on set and Nadine Garner described her as 'fragile'.

Nadine played the lead role of Tamara Henderson, who, with her brother Steve, was taken in by their uncle after their mother died in a car crash. Their uncle was a policeman in a country town, and the twelve-part series followed their adventures. Kylie's character, known as Char, lived in the town and became Tamara's best friend. She wore bright orange pants, colourful shirts that clashed horribly and spent most of her time chewing pink bubblegum: 'I'm so sick of this stuff, but it's part of my character,' admitted Kylie, making an early concession to complete professionalism. That quality impressed her director, Chris Langman: 'She was always prepared, always on time, always focused and very much aware of her image and her look.' It is an observation of the 1984-vintage Kylie that could fittingly describe her at any point in her career.

Being on the show meant Kylie spent some time away from home when the production went upstate for outdoor filming. She was given about Aus $10 a day for meals. Kylie and her young co-stars were able to bond and make friends. In particular, she and Nadine became close when they discovered they both loved singing. They would sit around between scenes practising their harmonies, and would listen to each other's records and try to copy the tunes. They proudly announced to the rest of the cast that when they were older 'we are going to be great singers'. Alan Hardy didn't forget his on-set impression that the two girls had great voices, and this would be of great benefit to Kylie in the not too distant future

Nadine never pursued a singing career, but she has been one of Australia's most popular actresses for the past twenty years. She even had a part in the early days of *Neighbours* as a character called Rachel Burns. Her international profile rose in 2013 with the broadcast of *The Doctor Blake Mysteries*, in which she co-stars with Craig McLachlan. Craig was also in *Neighbours* at one time, playing Kylie's brother. Ramsay Street really was a small world.

Kylie's wild stage of fighting with her parents, smoking because she thought it made her look tough, and generally playing the difficult teenager didn't last. She became more focused about acting. Her school even noted that she was 'sensible' about juggling acting and studying. *The Henderson Kids* finally gave Kylie the confidence to tell an interviewer not to describe her as Dannii's elder sister. 'Call me Kylie,' she said.

After filming the first series, Kylie was determined not to lose momentum. She immediately starred in one episode of the *The Zoo Family*. She played Yvonne, an abused child, who is given a temporary home by a zoo caretaker. The episode was entitled 'Yvonne the Terrible'. The child lived up to her name by letting all the animals out of their cages and generally wrecking the zoo. At the end of the episode, she had a Damascene moment when she saw a young roo, which had also been a battered infant, return to its mother kanga. Kylie impressed everybody. She would soon be seventeen but convincingly played a twelve year old. She was proving to be as adaptable in her acting career as she would be later as a singer. Gwenda Marsh, her producer on *The Zoo Family*, was convinced that Kylie would be a 'stayer'.

Kylie learned at an early age one of the most important lessons of show business: you are only as good as your last performance. Once again, after *The Zoo Family*, she was back on the audition trail. This time she beat fifty rivals to the leading female role in a six-part miniseries, *Fame and Misfortune*. Kylie had to play a scheming minx called Samantha, which she managed to do successfully, demonstrating that she was developing her acting abilities. Secretly, though, she still hankered after a career as a singer, an ambition sharpened by her energetic sister's continued exposure on *Young Talent Time*.

So strong was Kylie's desire to be a performer that she paid her own money – part of her fee from *The Henderson Kids* – to record two demos for the executives of *Young Talent Time*. She chose 'Dim All The Lights', a 1979 dance hit by Donna Summer, and 'New Attitude' by Patti LaBelle, which featured on the *Beverly Hills Cop* soundtrack in 1984. The choices were quite removed from the Abba and Olivia Newton-John music that the pre-teen Kylie had loved so much. Instead, they reflected an early interest in black disco, which in many ways influenced much of the music the latter day Kylie would produce. Donna Summer was the brazen 'Queen of Disco', whose UK number ones, 'I Feel Love' and 'Love to Love You Baby', were hardly girl-next-door songs. Coincidentally, Donna was to enjoy a career revival under the guidance of Stock, Aitken and Waterman, who would be so crucial in taking Kylie to the very top. The pop world is always a labyrinth of connections. Patti LaBelle had sung the original version of 'Lady Marmalade' in 1974. In 2001, it was a number-one hit for Christina Aguilera, Mýa, Pink and Lil' Kim, whose version was recorded for the film *Moulin Rouge!*, which featured Kylie in a cameo role as the Green Fairy.

During this period of her career, Kylie's verve and drive were for ever being underestimated by people who couldn't see past a little girl trying to overcome her shyness. Kylie had true grit. She certainly needed it when she was called in to a meeting with Alan Hardy, who was putting *The Henderson Kids II* into production. He sat her down and gently explained that she was being dropped because her character, Char, was being written out of the second series. Kylie was bitterly upset, of course, and went away to consider her options.

She was nearly seventeen and ready to leave Camberwell High, having passed the obligatory Higher School Certificate in Art and

Graphics. While away on location she had on-set teachers and had managed to pass a compulsory English exam.

Kylie describes herself as being of average intelligence, much preferring the arts to sciences, which she disliked almost as much as sport. She is being slightly modest. She has an inquisitive mind, which would serve her well when she came into contact with mercurial talents in the future. She is also articulate – a quality she generally keeps hidden when asked repetitively mundane questions by uninspiring interviewers.

She didn't leave school without incident. On the last day, she joined Georgie and another girl on the second floor of the main building, where they found a hose, turned the taps full on, and proceeded to drench everybody walking below. When a teacher arrived to nab the culprits, Kylie ducked and hid while her two friends took the rap.

The suburban side of Kylie was still drawn to what would have been a normal path for a young woman with her background – marriage, children and looking after house and home – and she was seriously considering taking a secretarial course. Perhaps there was always a nagging feeling that her mother had somehow missed out on fulfilling her destiny that deflected Kylie from this career path. Instead, she decided she would stick to acting for the moment and followed the best course of action for a million wannabes – she signed on the dole.

Kylie has often said that much of her career was a 'happy accident'. One of her favourite observations about her success comes from her father, who told her she was lucky she always skipped steps one to eight and went straight to numbers nine and ten. 'Miraculously, I get away with it,' she confessed. It's a nice story but its flippancy masks the hours of hard graft she has devoted to learning lines, practising dance steps until her feet are covered in blisters and plasters, and grappling with difficult melodies so that her performances are never less than completely polished.

She may not have known it at the time, but being killed off in *The Henderson Kids* was a 'happy accident' because her career – indeed her life – might have been entirely different if she had remained on the show. Instead, she was free to go along to an audition for a part in a Melbourne-based soap opera. The casting director for *Neighbours*, Jan Russ, was one of Australia's most respected talent spotters. She remembered seeing Kylie in *The Zoo Family* and thought she was a possible candidate for a new role that had just come up – a tomboy teenager called Charlene Mitchell.

Jan immediately recognized that Kylie had the right look and attitude for the part, acknowledging that the petite teenager had a certain spark, an 'extra charisma' that lifted her above the competition. When she read for the character, Kylie was transformed from a shy girl into a 'wonderful presence'. Jan had no hesitation in recommending her for the role despite competition from forty other girls because, she observed, 'the camera loved her.'

Alan Hardy has always enjoyed telling the story of how he made Kylie famous by killing her off in *The Henderson Kids II*. 'It turned out to be the best thing for her,' he acknowledged.

4

Everybody Needs Good Neighbours

It's hard to imagine now just how huge *Neighbours* was in the 1980s. It was the golden age of the Australian teatime drama. The series was the brainchild of Reg Watson, head of drama for the Grundy Organisation and the man responsible for such kitsch classics as *Prisoner: Cell Block H* and *The Young Doctors*. He had also launched *Crossroads* on an unsuspecting British audience before he moved back to Australia, so he had early experience of wooden sets filled with wooden actors. *Neighbours* was a brilliant idea because it was such a simple one: a story of everyday families and their ordinary lives. Reg had a lot of trouble convincing his bosses that it wasn't as dull as it sounded: 'When I told them about it, eyebrows were raised and thumbs were turned down. They had doubts about a concept that was simply about communication between parents and their children.'

Neighbours, which was originally going to be called *One Way Street*, first hit television screens on Channel Seven in March 1985, when Kylie was just finishing filming *The Henderson Kids*. It was very innocent and non-controversial, and seemed ideal daytime fodder. Sad things would happen in Ramsay Street, Erinsborough, but very few bad things.

Watson was trying to recreate the warm feeling of life in a

Brisbane suburb where he grew up: 'If you were at the beach when it started raining, your neighbour would dash out, take your washing off the line and fold it ready for your return.' One common observation about Kylie's early life is that her upbringing in suburban Melbourne was very *Neighbours*-like. That impression is as wide of the mark as Kylie being some sort of girl next door. It was generally assumed the Minogue family could have lived in Ramsay Street. That's only true up to a point. Yes, theirs was a household that was very normal on the outside, with pets and barbecues, chores and sibling squabbling, yet both Kylie and Dannii led extraordinary lives as child and, subsequently, teenage stars. Show business became such a normal part of their lives that nobody seemed to realize how unusual it was to have two young daughters 'on the stage'. This was nothing like Ramsay Street.

Picture the scene at the breakfast table: over a bowl of cornflakes, or Vegemite on toast, Ron Minogue inquires what his daughters will be doing before he sets off for a day's auditing of the housing department. The reply: 'We're going to be singing "Sisters Are Doin' It For Themselves" on national television.'

This did actually happen in 1986, when Kylie joined her sister for a duet on *Young Talent Time*. They were both teenage girls of the eighties, with big frizzy haircuts and sparkly silver mini dresses. They may not have had the vocal dynamism of Eurythmics and Aretha Frankin, who had recorded the song a year earlier, but it was lively and fun, and left you wishing they would do another number.

Surprisingly, Channel Seven dropped *Neighbours* after six months, but rival Channel Ten picked it up almost immediately and began airing it the following January, with a brief to Grundy that there should be a greater emphasis on younger characters. The target audience was teenage schoolgirls. That was the decision that would give Kylie her chance and would ultimately provide her with a fan base when she sought musical stardom.

Kylie was originally hired for a thirteen-week run, but this was quickly extended when the producers realized that the on-screen chemistry between Charlene Mitchell and Scott Robinson represented a marketing gold mine for the programme. Scott was played, of course, by Jason Donovan. Kylie hadn't set eyes on him since they had appeared together in *Skyways* six years earlier. Off-screen, there was considerable chemistry as well.

When Kylie was young and impressionable, she had a crush on a minor American singer called Leif Garrett. He was a child actor turned teenie heart-throb in the late 1970s who had one decent hit, the disco-lite 'I Was Made For Dancin''. Garrett was blond with perfect, shiny white teeth and a ghastly mullet. When Kylie met up with Jason again, he was no longer a podgy kid. He had transformed into a blond heart-throb with perfect, shiny white teeth and a ghastly mullet. The attraction was inevitable.

Kylie made the first move. She enlisted the help of an old friend, Greg Petherick, who had become close to the Minogue family when he worked as the floor manager on *Young Talent Time*. She trusted his opinion and he was one of the first to hear the demo she had recorded for that show. He had moved on to become a producer at Channel Ten and agreed to act as a go-between to find out if there was any spark of interest from Jason. She was thrilled to discover there was indeed and, as a thank-you for his help, later gave Greg a photograph of herself and her new man Jason on the set of *Neighbours*. She had handwritten a little message and embellished it with love hearts.

Jason had immediately noticed Kylie's superb figure and her lustrous blue eyes, but it would be wrong to assume that it was love at first sight. For the moment he was most concerned with making an impression in the show. His character had been on-screen from the start but played by another actor. When *Neighbours* changed from Channel Seven to Channel Ten, it was decided that Scott would change too – enter Jason.

Like Kylie, Jason had been a child actor, but he came from more of a show-business background. His father is the well-known Australian actor Terry Donovan, who would later play builder Doug Willis in *Neighbours*, and his mother, Sue McIntosh, was a glamorous television newsreader and actress. His parents divorced when he was five and, as a teenager, Jason always remained closer to his father, geographically as well as emotionally. Jason lived at the bottom of Terry's garden in a one-room bungalow, a teenage grunge paradise where he could strum guitar, smoke a joint and dream of being Michael Hutchence.

Kylie's first on-screen contact with Jason was not that promising: she punched him in the face. She had arrived in Ramsay Street to visit her aunt and Jason's character, Scott, mistakenly thought she was breaking in. Soon, though, the camera picked up the attraction between them – something Reg Watson always thought would be a big success with viewers. It 'made' the show. Jason observed, 'There was just a feeling between us that probably happens once in a million times.'

Their first screen kiss was front-page news not just in Australia but also in the UK, where *Neighbours* went on air in October 1986. It became a phenomenon of British television when artful schedulers decided to show it twice a day. Mothers watched the lunchtime episode while it was nice and peaceful at home, then the kids would switch on the early evening repeat when they returned from school. Kylie and Jason didn't appear on British screens until the following summer, but soon they were as popular in the UK as in Australia. They were described as Britain's most idolized teenagers, loved by both young and old.

Meanwhile, the pair had made a decision back home in Melbourne that would have an enormous effect on their future together: they had agreed to a demand from *Neighbours'* bosses to keep their off-screen relationship absolutely secret. Brian Walsh, the promotions manager for Channel Ten, warned them that if their romance became public knowledge, it would ruin the show and their own popularity. The view was that, while the audience loved the fictional love affair between Charlene and Scott, they might not be able to handle Kylie and Jason arguing in the supermarket over which brand of breakfast cereal to buy.

Kylie's decision was almost Faustian in the way it coloured her future life. She was putting her career before her private relationship. She has continued on the same path ever since. She has never abandoned her working commitments for love. She didn't do it even for Michael Hutchence, one of the greatest loves of her life. And she has always kept parts of her life secret from her adoring fans. This air of mystery remains part of her appeal.

Later, in a fairly candid interview after her duet with Jason, 'Especially For You', was the first number one of 1989, Kylie said, 'Everyone believes we are [together] and I suppose it's quite obvious but no one can be 100 per cent sure, can they? If they knew all about us, where we slept, what we did together, and so on, wouldn't it spoil the mystery?'

It certainly would have spoiled the mystery if the public knew that they did it for the first time in a Melbourne Travelodge, which, while a step up from a garden shed, wasn't exactly glamorous. The revelation that Kylie spent most of her time shacked up with Jason at his place might not have helped either. She loved hanging out at Jason's, not having to bother to wear make-up or smart clothes, just being able to relax in her favourite joggers, away from the pressure of being a celebrity. It's the lifestyle she has always liked best and, when not on show, Kylie is barely recognizable as a singing superstar. She is not a fashion icon when she pops out to buy a loaf of bread or have a cappuccino with her friends.

Jason and Kylie were a pretty boring couple. They worked too hard to have the energy to go clubbing every night. Instead, they would pop out to their local Italian or Japanese restaurant. On days off, they would browse the clothes shops before meeting up with friends to enjoy coffee and conversation. If they had a couple of days free, they would drive down to Phillip Island. Kylie had a beautiful old Morris but she hadn't passed her test, so Jason would take the wheel while she sang along to eighties' hits. Jason's favourite was 'Invisible Touch' by Genesis, and he rather touchingly admits that he still thinks of Kylie whenever he hears it.

Jason bought his first house in the Richmond district of Melbourne – not the most upmarket of the city's areas, but it was home. Kylie didn't move in permanently, but at weekends they were like any other ordinary suburban couple, other than the fact that their romance was still a secret.

Kylie is not the first, and certainly won't be the last, star to manipulate a situation to suit the image she wants to convey at any given moment. It literally happens all the time. The commonest 'lie' is the old Hollywood practice of promoting a leading man as the world's greatest heterosexual when he is in fact gay. To a lesser extent, this also applies to women. At least one female superstar has it written into her contract that she can't reveal her true sexuality. It might well ruin the fans' perception of her. Obviously, Kylie isn't gay – far from it – but the principle of misleading the public in order to promote a carefully conceived fantasy remains the same. The character of Charlene Mitchell was a curiously asexual girl next door, far too nice for any steamy shenanigans in the bedroom.

When a British journalist travelled to Australia to report on the *Neighbours* phenomenon, she asked Kylie if she had a boyfriend. Kylie 'confessed' that she hadn't had a boyfriend for two years – roughly the entire time she and Jason had been living in each other's pockets.

With their secret safe, the public continued to lap up the romance between Charlene and Scott. In one memorable episode, Charlene was going to give herself to Scott in a hotel room – a clear case of life imitating art, or the other way round. Everything was going well, until Scott found out that Lenny, as she was popularly known, wasn't a virgin. He stormed out, leaving her crying on the bed.

And then there was the wedding in July 1987. It was episode number 523. In the UK alone, nearly 20 million people watched it on television when it was broadcast there a year later. This was the biggest wedding of the decade after the real-life one of Prince Charles and Lady Diana Spencer. Charlene had been unable to persuade her mother to give the seal of approval to her living in sin with Scott, so she had decided to marry him. Scott had rolled up on his skateboard, still wearing his school uniform, and proposed. Jason said, 'It was a really nice, natural scene. I didn't feel stupid at all. Sometimes you look at a script and you think, "Oh, God! I've got to tell her she's the most gorgeous person in the world and that I can't live without her and here I am on this stupid skateboard trying to drag her out from underneath an oily car engine."'

Kylie and Jason were mobbed at a shopping mall in Sydney while they were filming the wedding-reception scenes. Somehow, 4,000 fans found out where it was taking place and some ended up in hospital as a result of the mêlée. Unsurprisingly, the following day, the newspapers were full of reports of a 'riot'. Kylie complained that the wedding scene itself was very tiring and she had to walk up the aisle some twenty times before everyone was happy. Ironically, despite much speculation over the years, she has never been close to being a bride in real life. Once again, the public confused fact and fiction, and Kylie found people coming up to her in the street, congratulating her on her 'marriage'.

That wedding remains one of the most popular moments in the history of soap, and the pinnacle of Kylie's acting career so far. Charlene and Scott were the most popular couple in Australia, regularly appearing on the cover of *TV Week*. Even the Australian edition of *Time* magazine was caught up in the hype. They featured Charlene and Scott on the front cover, inside a pink heart, with the headline AUSSIE SOAPS CAPTURE THE WORLD. *Time* was trying to make sense of the cult of niceness, in which *Neighbours* played a leading role. It was, the magazine argued, soap as 'social engineering', an antidote to modern melodrama. The characters were the embodiment of comfy armchairs – the unbearable niceness of being.

Jason Donovan acknowledged, 'A lot of people get us muddled up with Charlene and Scott, but we're really quite different.' Kylie wasn't Charlene Mitchell at all. She wasn't a bit like her but, when the cameras rolled, she was transformed into the tomboy who left school to become a car mechanic. Kylie seemed to spend most of her life in a pair of unflattering overalls that completely disguised the fact that there was a future sex symbol underneath. Lenny was a spitfire with a machine-gun tongue, which she would unleash should any man try to patronize her by calling her 'love' or, even worse, 'babe'. As we know from Kylie herself, her lack of height may have been a disadvantage on the sports field, but it was a definite plus when it came to playing young, fiesty types.

As always, Kylie was determined to extract every last drop of opportunity from her five days-a-week exposure in a popular soap. The big advantage the young stars of *Neighbours* had over other familiar television faces was that promoting them was part of the public strategy to rush the programme into the consciousness of the nation's youngsters. As a result, Kylie was out in the community right from the start, with personal appearances at shopping malls and youth centres. It is a tactic well tried and tested in the pop world as a means of raising public awareness. One of the show's directors, Andrew Friedman, told author Dino Scatena, 'Even at the height of her career with the music and the publicity, she was always there; always early, always keen and always willing to learn. She was always aware of her work.'

Kylie wasn't naive enough to think of *Neighbours* as great art. Former pop columnist Peter Holt remembered Kylie telling him that she couldn't wait to move to London. She revealed: 'It opened the showbiz door for me, but I can't wait to get out of it as soon as possible. I never liked soaps, whether home-produced or imported, and, to be honest, in spite of its success, *Neighbours* is a bit rough. It's only the story of three families but everything happens to them! It's all rather implausible and sometimes I have to grit my teeth when I film an unlikely situation. I shudder at the speed it is turned out day after day. The writers are still working on the script when we start filming.

'Of course I am not complaining. *Neighbours* has been marvellous for me. I am just amazed that so many people are attracted to it. The trouble is that it gives a completely distorted view of normal life in Australia.'

Those are hardly the words of a woolly-headed pop puppet. Kylie was completely focused during her time with *Neighbours* and, not for the last time, she demonstrated a willingness to push her body to the limit of its fragile capabilities. As any actor in soaps will testify, it is always a punishing schedule. Her alarm clock would sound an unwelcome greeting at 5.30 a.m., then a quick shower, breakfast on the run, make-up at 6.30 a.m., rehearsals at 7.30 a.m., a fifteen-minute run-through, twenty minutes of filming – all for one minute of the show. It would be an exhausting schedule for an Olympic athlete. And then there was publicity and the recording career she was so desperate to progress.

Jason was right about the differences between his screen character and real life, because when he and Kylie returned home, tired after a day's filming, he would abandon his clean-living, surfer-boy image and pretend he was a rock star. In the future, he would extol the virtues of cannabis, declaring he would rather walk into a room full of dope smokers than one filled with alcoholics: 'It just puts a smile on your face at the end of the day.' In his memoirs, he admits to enjoying a crafty joint at the back of the set after he had finished his scenes for the day. That would have been fine if he hadn't been called back to shoot some more. It didn't go well and after forgetting all his lines and bumping into the furniture rather a lot, he decided that drugs and work didn't mix.

Some observers believe that the issue of drugs became divisive in the relationship with Jason. That didn't appear to be the case with

Michael Hutchence, another serious drug user, a few years later. It wasn't the most destructive element for Kylie and Jason, however; the amount of time they spent apart pursuing their ambitions was much more critical. As Jason would observe, 'I found it really hard to deal with her fame at the time. I was extremely jealous of Kylie.'

In October 1988, a curious interview with Kylie appeared in *TV Week*, in which she admitted how much she missed Jason when she was away from him. She also confessed that she didn't live at home all the time. Nobody told Jason about the interview, which seemed very indiscreet of her, so when he appeared on television three days later to plug a record and denied any relationship with Kylie, he was made to look a complete idiot. Kylie's team insisted that she had never given the interview, so as not to destroy the myth about her and Jason. But, if she did say it, what a sad admission of how she really felt. It didn't sit comfortably on the shelf next to the souvenir magazine from the same year, *Kylie and Jason: Just Good Friends*. Within a year, she and Jason had drifted apart. Perhaps the killer punch was when Jason declared that he hadn't yet experienced true love and was still looking.

For a while, they were happy.

5

Single-Minded

One of Kylie's early storylines as Charlene in *Neighbours* involved Scott and his mate Mike, played by future Hollywood star Guy Pearce, getting together to form a band and make a demo. They ask Lenny to sing backing vocals. And with the delicious irony of art imitating life, they play the demo for a record company boss who thinks the boys are rubbish but loves Lenny's singing.

In August 1986, five months after Kylie had joined the cast, she was approached by Alan Hardy, who had remembered her passion for singing on location with *The Henderson Kids*. He was organizing a special fundraiser for his favourite Australian rules football team, Fitzroy, at the Dallas Brooks Hall in Melbourne. He was delighted that she was enthusiastic, not knowing that she had already been preparing for just such an opportunity with secret musical sessions organized by Greg Petherick.

Several of the cast shared Kylie's dreams of musical stardom: Jason, of course, as well as Guy Pearce and Craig McLachlan. In that rather macho Aussie way, the guys decided to form Ramsay Street's answer to INXS. They thought it might be fun to invite some of the girls along for decoration and occasional vocals, which is how Kylie became involved. They had absolutely no idea that she would soon leave them in the starting blocks while she ran the whole 100 metres.

There was already a *Neighbours* band of older actors, who would enjoy a jam session once a week after filming had finished on a Thursday: Peter O'Brien (Shane Ramsay), Alan Dale (Jim Robinson) and Paul Keane (Des Clarke). Greg Petherick was the Mr Fix-it who would book a downtown rehearsal room for the group to use. He invited Kylie and Jason to join them. Kylie sat quietly, watching, taking everything in, playing a little tambourine, while Jason sang, strummed guitar and did his impersonation of Michael Hutchence. 'It was interesting, to say the least,' said Greg. Jason soon got bored, but Kylie didn't and started to sing along a little. Then one week she asked Greg if he could find a song specifically for her to sing with the band.

He rummaged around in his record collection and produced 'The Loco-Motion', performed by Little Eva (the stage name of a young black singer from Belhaven, North Carolina, called Eva Boyd), a bit of a one-hit wonder. The song was a product of the great songwriting team of Carole King and Gerry Goffin and had been a huge hit in 1962. Little Eva had been earning extra money babysitting for the couple when they realized she had a very recordable voice. They actually wrote and released the single before there was a dance to go with it. Little Eva made one up. Kylie loved the song instantly. Every week she would practise and everyone agreed it was a show-stopper.

For the fundraiser, Alan Hardy asked Kylie to perform the Sonny and Cher classic 'I Got You Babe' with another local actor and musician called John Waters. On the night, Alan recalled, Kylie was very nervous about performing. But one of the outstanding qualities she possesses is the determination to overcome any nerves to give a great performance – the true art of being a star.

The crowd was ecstatic. Someone on stage said, 'Let's do another one,' so Kylie suggested innocently 'The Loco-Motion', even though she already knew that's what they had been rehearsing and were going to perform. The band just happened to know how to play it and Kylie remembered all the words. It was clear the TV favourite could really hold a tune. It was the first time an audience heard Kylie sing 'The Loco-Motion', but within a year it would be the biggest-selling Australian single of the decade. She was a sensation.

The benefit show displayed all the hallmarks of another 'happy accident' for Kylie, but there was nothing accidental about her polished on-stage performance. There is a famous saying in golf: 'The more I practise, the luckier I get.' She had worked to get it right. Now was not the time to step back and admire her efforts. It was a good start but she needed to secure a record deal, and in order to do that she needed to cut a much more professional demo. Once again, she turned to Greg Petherick.

Greg knew just the man to help – an engineer called Kaj Dahlstrom, who ran a small recording studio in Melbourne. They decided that 'The Loco-Motion' was a good place to start, and Dahlstrom laid down a backing track that had a funkier feel than Little Eva's version. There is nothing quite like the thrill of a trip to a studio to make a real record. Kylie was so excited when she made the journey across Melbourne to where the aptly named Sing Sing Studios were situated. The only problem was that when she arrived she realized she couldn't sing in the same key as the backing track, so she had to go away again while Dahlstrom set about changing everything to the higher E minor key. It took him a week and then Kylie came back.

It was all new to her, but she responded well as he nursed her through the song line by line. Many artists – even very famous chart-toppers – have to record their songs line by line because their pitch isn't perfect. But this was Kylie's first go and she would soon make sure she was as professional in this sphere as she was in every other aspect of her career. Pete Waterman, who would guide her early pop progress in the UK, observed, 'She'd be exhausted half the time, but when she had to work, her whole personality would transform and she would light up. We would literally only get an hour at a time to work with her, but we always got things done.'

Dahlstrom hawked the demo around various record companies before there was a glimmer of interest from the Melbourne-based Mushroom Records. Michael Gudinski, the company chairman, sent a memo to two executives asking them to listen to the demo because he thought it was 'kinda cute' and might be worth taking a chance on. The crucial selling point for Mushroom was that Kylie had swiftly become one of the most recognizable faces in Australia. By the time they signed her up in the spring of 1987, Kylie, on the eve of her nineteenth birthday, had been voted Most Popular Australian Actress at the annual Logies, the premier TV awards. Jason wasn't forgotten – he was named Best New Talent. Kylie's award was voted for by readers of the magazine *TV Week*, so it accurately reflected the strength of her following in the country. Afterwards, wearing a bright red leather skirt she had made herself, she admitted, 'I wish I had been better prepared. I was so nervous I forgot to thank all the people in the show.' It was a huge accolade for such a relative newcomer, yet in her moment of triumph Kylie had chastised herself for a lack of professionalism.

The executives at Mushroom were very smart where Kylie was concerned. First, they wanted to introduce a sound similar to the one that had been dominating the British charts. They asked Pete Waterman if he could send someone to Melbourne to work with their engineers. He and his partners Mike Stock and Matt Aitken already had an impressive list of UK hits to their name. Waterman was the glue that joined together the songwriting skills of Mike Stock, the musicianship of guitarist Matt Aitken and the talent of their singers.

Waterman agreed to 'loan' them Mike Duffy, a Canadian employee. The managing director of Mushroom, Gary Ashley, had met up with Waterman at Midem, the international music trading conference held annually in Cannes, and had told him that they had signed up Kylie Minogue. Amusingly, Pete didn't have a clue who she was.

Secondly, Amanda Pelman, who was in charge of Mushroom's promotion, and who was responsible for signing her to the label, realized that the singing Kylie should complement the acting Kylie. There was a ready-made audience of young girls who could identify with the character of Charlene Mitchell and could will her to be successful as a pop star. Pelman wanted a million girls in a million bedrooms to sing 'The Loco-Motion' into their hairbrushes, just as Kylie herself had done when she imagined she was Olivia Newton-John or Agnetha from Abba.

The character Charlene was about to marry Scott. It is no coincidence that the executives at Mushroom were desperate for the first Kylie record to be released in tandem with this episode. This was cold-hearted, dead-eyed opportunism that was practically guaranteed to be a successful strategy. It was no 'happy accident' that Mike Duffy's version of 'The Loco-Motion' was released in mid-July 1987, just two weeks after millions of potential record buyers had watched the wedding of the year. Confusingly, it was called 'Locomotion' when it was first released but changed to 'The Loco-Motion' the following year, matching the title of the original.

Mike Duffy had started work on the track only the previous month, so it had all been a bit of a rush, but they were able to use Kylie's original vocal from the Sing Sing session. Pete Waterman, who had loved the Little Eva version, had encouraged Duffy to have a go at copying the sound of Stock, Aitken and Waterman. He conceded, 'It sounded roughly, very roughly, like one of ours.' Waterman gave him his blessing but was astonished a few short weeks later to be woken at 3 a.m. by an excited Duffy shouting down the phone that 'Locomotion' was number one. He was so surprised he got up and put on the track. Duffy had sent him a final copy but he hadn't got round to listening to it. He played it through: 'It was rubbish, so I went back to bed.'

'Locomotion' was number one in Australia for seven weeks, the biggest-selling record there of both 1987 and the entire decade.

The Australian public had already been suckered into confusing Kylie with Charlene. In the eyes of the record-buying public, it was Charlene, the girl next door with a feisty edge, who was singing 'Locomotion'. Practically anyone on television can have a hit record, whether it's Robson and Jerome or Orville the Duck. Practically nobody, however, builds a singing career on the back of TV success.

It was time for Kylie to step into the international arena and, in order to do that, she needed someone else in her corner. She would always have her father, a rock for all his children, protecting her interests, but Ron Minogue was never going to give up his life in Melbourne to devote himself to the music business. She was fortunate to find a man to stick by her through good and bad times, a former drummer called Terry Blamey.

In January 1986, when Kylie auditioned for her role in *Neighbours*, a new board game called *So You Want To Be A Rockstar* went on sale around Australia. The idea was that each player represented a band and followed its ups and downs from first gig to, hopefully, a number-one album. The game was devised by Simon Young, director of business affairs at Mushroom Records, and his friend Terry Blamey, who was working as the music talent coordinator for the TV programme *Hey Hey It's Saturday* and also managed a novelty act featuring a former Australian rules footballer called Jacko. Blamey had been in bands in the late 1960s but had decided that 'it was more lucrative to be a manager or an agent'. Young and Blamey resolved not to include anything that involved sex and drugs in the board game and just stuck to the rock and roll.

Blamey explained the philosophy of the game: 'You can lie, but then people can lie back to you. You don't have to tell the truth, you can charge whatever you like, you can give things away free, you can hire them, you can lease them, and you can swap them. It is as wide open in terms of bargaining as it is in the real world, but it all comes back to you when you are in a less favourable position. The winner does extremely well. He ends up with a lot of money and a lot of chart success.'

With exquisite timing, barely six months would pass before Blamey took control of Kylie Minogue's career. They have both done extremely well, ending up with lots of money and outstanding chart success – enough to have won any board game easily. Blamey's 20 per cent or so of all things Kylie has made him a multimillionaire. They remained a strong partnership for twenty-five years and he was always fiercely protective of his famous client. Blamey was practically part of the family at Mushroom and was in a strong position to take over the reins of Kylie Minogue's career when she needed personal day-to-day handling of her life. Mushroom had taken her to number one with 'Locomotion', but the label had other artists and she would need something more if the next phase of her career – the international years – was to be a success.

Before he became her manager, Terry Blamey had to get the seal of approval from her father, rather like a hapless schoolboy on a first date. Ron Minogue was naturally cautious, very shrewd and had maximized all the opportunities for both Kylie and Dannii up until this point. He was most definitely not the sort of man who would be seduced by the glamour of the pop business. His feet were so firmly on the ground, he had lead in his boots. From the very outset, he had set up a limited company, Kaydeebee – Kay was for Kylie, Dee was for Dannii and Bee stood for their brother Brendan – to control the finances of his children, and he had a reputation for being thrifty. It was an amusing reminder of when the three children used to squabble over which television programmes they wanted to watch, and a rota for using the remote control was posted in the kitchen: Monday K, Tuesday D, Wednesday B, and so on.

The success of his daughters meant that Ron no longer felt able to commit full time to his job as the Director of Finance of Camberwell Council. He went on to work as a consultant for three days a week, before finally quitting for good in 1989 to devote himself to the family business. Evidence of his financial acumen came to light when it was disclosed that he had managed to secure a car valued at Aus $17,000 for just $2,000 as part of a severance package. He also took three months' pay and a long-service bonus away with him. The car was sold a few months later to a local dealer for an undisclosed price.

Ron has always had a solid contractual arrangement with Kylie who, as a result, has never had concerns of any kind over the money she has earned. She is not at all mean with money but has inherited a natural prudence. She will always go for the bargain in a supermarket – even today, when she is one of the richest women in entertainment. Like Ron, her mother Carol goes on the payroll when Kylie is on tour. She works backstage helping the dancers, a legacy of her own training as a dancer when she was younger. Although Kylie is very close to her mother, she admits she has always been a daddy's girl.

It was essential, therefore, that Terry Blamey pass the Ron test before he could be accepted into the Minogue inner sanctum. Gary Ashley, of Mushroom Records, described Blamey as a 'straight-up guy', and it was this quality that Minogue Senior liked and thought he could work with in the future. The longevity of 'Kylie Minogue Limited', as the team behind the public Kylie might be called, is proof of what a mutually beneficial decision that was. While Ron remained in Melbourne in the 1990s, Terry Blamey upped sticks and moved to London to stay close to Kylie, rather like a sensible elder brother looking after a vulnerable sister. He didn't exactly rule Kylie's life with a rod of iron, but he always enjoyed a reputation as a hard man with whom to do business.

6

A Lucky Break

Kylie had enjoyed her first working trip to London. Terry Blamey had come with her and the two of them had taken a tourist bus to see the sights of the capital and they had queued up like everyone else to look around Madame Tussauds and the Tower of London. The only problem was she hadn't actually done any work. The reason they had flown from the other side of the world during her short filming break from *Neighbours* in October 1987 was to meet with Pete Waterman, but the week had flown by and they had yet to clap eyes on the chart wizard. Instead, they were apparently wasting their last afternoon in the reception area of the unpretentious Vine Yard studio complex behind Borough Tube station, not far from London Bridge.

Kylie was curled up on the sofa, still expecting something to happen before the car arrived to take them to the airport. Fortunately, she had no idea of the bedlam ensuing behind closed doors. Waterman wasn't even in London that day. He was relaxing at his mansion in Newton-le-Willows, Merseyside, when his partner Mike Stock rang up to enquire if a small Antipodean rang any bells – a small Antipodean called Kylie Minogue? Waterman had forgotten to mention that he had agreed to a joint venture with Mushroom Records to help Kylie's recording career. He had never watched

Neighbours, so the whole thing had gone straight out of his head. 'She's in town,' he told Stock helpfully, only to be told that she was actually sitting in reception and had to be on her way back to the airport in a few hours. 'She's expecting to do something with us, now!' Without thinking, Waterman replied, 'She should be so lucky.' The rest, as they say, is history. It's a great story, and one that Waterman never tires of telling.

The biggest-selling record of 1988 was written by fax between London and Merseyside in about half an hour – although Stock doesn't give Waterman much credit for the song. Later in the day, Waterman rang the studio to find out how Kylie's vocal was coming along. Matt Aitken, the other member of the famous Hit Factory triumvirate, came on the line and announced, 'This girl's got a really good voice.' The record done, they promptly forgot all about Kylie Minogue. Pete Waterman had never even met the girl who would take over his commercial life. He had yet to hear the record.

Six weeks later, at the PWL (Pete Waterman Limited) Christmas party at the Natural History Museum in London, a record came on that he didn't recognize: 'I thought it was fantastic, so I ran over to the DJ and asked him what it was. He said, "It's Kylie Minogue, 'I Should Be So Lucky'."' Waterman turned to Mike Stock and told him the track would be a smash. Waterman, who has an uncanny sense of the commercial, was absolutely right. Kylie once compared the Hit Factory to a Hollywood studio. If that's the case, then Pete Waterman is Sam Goldwyn ('I'm willing to admit that I may not always be right, but I am never wrong').

Waterman didn't fully appreciate just how popular *Neighbours* was becoming in the UK, and how everybody wanted to hear 'Charlene's' record. The show was watched regularly by 15 million viewers a day, potentially a huge record-buying market. Waterman confessed that he had absolutely no conception of the 'power of Kylie's presence in the marketplace'. It was an intangible power that she has always possessed.

There is a little of the chicken and the egg about *Neighbours* and Kylie's pop career. Would *Neighbours* have been an enduring commercial success without 'I Should Be So Lucky', or would Kylie have made it as a singer without *Neighbours*? It is probably a bit of both as each helped the other. The exposure given to the record because it was by 'Charlene' was huge – but then Stock, Aitken and Waterman could have turned their grannies into stars. In 1987, before Kylie, they had sold 37 million records worldwide. One of the famous trio reportedly said that Kylie could have burped into the microphone and it would have been a hit.

Stock, Aitken and Waterman were unlikely candidates to have become the British equivalent of Tamla-Motown. They had met in 1984, when none of their careers was particularly soaring. Waterman was a brash yet sociable ex-Mecca ballroom DJ, Aitken a former cruise-line guitarist and Stock used to play in a hotel band – hardly pop royalty. Yet, for a few years, they gelled into the most formidable hit-making team in the world. According to Stock, the confident Waterman had told his partners, 'Stick with me, boys, and I'll show you how to make a hit record.' And he did. Their roster of stars at the time read like a who's who of unhip: Samantha Fox, Sinitta, Sonia, Hazell Dean, Mel & Kim, Rick Astley, Bananarama . . . and now the bubble-haired soap star Kylie Minogue. Their aim was to produce classic three-minute hit singles. It wasn't rocket science. Waterman explained, 'We have taken pop music back to the people who buy records, not the journalists who preach to people.' They set out to appeal to listeners with 'Woolworth's ears'.

It's easy to underestimate the craftsmanship of a Stock, Aitken and Waterman record, and just as facile to suggest they all sound the same. They constructed energetic records around one catchy melody. Music author Spencer Bright recalled, 'Like everyone else at the time, I found Stock, Aitken and Waterman pretty gruesome. But you could not deny the hummability of their music, or their skill.'

And the lyrics were canny. They didn't seek to save the world in three minutes. Instead they focused on key emotions that would appeal to the young, impressionable record-buying public. There are, for instance, an astonishing number of SAW records that have the word 'heart' in the title: Kylie released 'Hand On Your Heart'; Jason, 'Too Many Broken Hearts'; Rick Astley, 'Take Me To Your Heart'; Sinitta, 'Cross My Broken Heart'; Sonia, 'Listen To Your Heart'; Dead or Alive, 'My Heart Goes Bang'; and Cliff Richard, 'I Just Don't Have The Heart'. Besides this simplistic approach, anything that might offend was banned, so there was no sex, no bottoms – and no 'baby', which Mike Stock considered the most clichéd word in popular music. The satirical magazine *Punch* devised a spoof Stock, Aitken and Waterman song for their Winter Special in 1989. They called it 'Your Arms Are In My Heart'.

SAW moved quickly. When the song was done, it was on the shelves of the record shops before you could blink. On Kylie's return to Melbourne from London, the accompanying video was put together equally swiftly. It was filmed at the Channel Seven studios and directed by Chris Langman, who had worked with her on *The Henderson Kids*. It's not great art but perfectly captured the mood of the song. Kylie looked fantastic but in a wholesome, bouncy way, not in a smouldering, sexpot fashion. Even when she is filmed taking a bubble bath, there's nothing steamy about it. The clever thing about this video was that Kylie could have been in Ramsay Street. In these early Stock, Aitken and Waterman videos, there always seemed to be a hop and a skip about Kylie, however beautiful she looked.

The BBC, cashing in on the *Neighbours* bandwagon, was a huge help in letting the nation know that Kylie had made a record. 'Locomotion' may have been number one in Australia, New Zealand and Hong Kong, but that didn't mean a thing in Oxford Street. *Noel's Christmas Presents*, a special featuring Noel Edmonds, sent a film crew out to Australia, especially to film Kylie singing 'I Should Be So Lucky'. This was significant and well-timed exposure, as the single was released on 23 January 1988.

It was the month of the Australian bicentennial celebrations. Kylie was in Sydney as one of the celebrity guests invited to meet Prince Charles and Princess Diana. Charles met her first and gave her the tried-and-tested royal enquiry: 'And what do you do?' Kylie timidly replied that she worked on *Neighbours*, and Charles smilingly told her he would make sure he watched an episode. When it came to speaking to Diana, six feet tall in high heels and then the most famous woman in the world, Kylie was completely tongue-tied. For a minute, she was Minnie Minogue, the little girl from the Melbourne suburbs, and not the performer who was a blink away from international fame.

Three weeks after the single was released in the UK, Kylie was awoken by her mother with the news that there was a phone call from England. She was grumpy at first, fearing it was a British journalist after an early morning scoop. Instead, it was the PWL office congratulating her on reaching number one. It would be the first single in a decade to stay at the top of the charts for five weeks.

During its stay at number one, British music journalist Jane Oddy travelled to Melbourne to have lunch with Kylie and was astonished by how exhausted she looked: 'She was tired out and so thin.' Kylie complained about the effect her punishing schedule was having on her: 'I don't have any friends any more because I am just too tired to chat and I never have time to go out and socialize. I have to cut out anything that's unnecessary, and that means most things apart from eating.' Her parting words to Jane were particularly poignant for a teenage girl: 'One day I'd like to lead a normal life and not be nagged by people about losing weight.'

Kylie was still only nineteen but she was positively an old lady next to the girl she knocked off the number-one spot, sixteen-year-old Tiffany with 'I Think We're Alone Now'. Great things were predicted for the redhead from California, but she managed only two more top-ten hits and was on the chart scrapheap within a year. Her demise is a striking example of just how difficult it is to stay at the top in such a fickle business for one year – let alone more than twenty-five.

These days, 'I Should Be So Lucky' can be viewed objectively as a classic eighties song. Back then, despite huge sales, it didn't make the top-fifty songs in the *NME*'s end-of-year critics' list. Instead, the magazine's number-one record of the year was 'The Mercy Seat' by Nick Cave, who would later be a big supporter of Kylie and have an enormous influence on her professional career.

Not everything in Kylie's carefully planned progress to world domination went smoothly. Younger Kylie fans will have no idea that the woman so loved by the media these days was treated quite shamefully by the press in the early part of her career. The Fleet Street columnist Jean Rook, of the *Daily Express*, was perhaps the chief culprit. Rook was the very worst kind of bullying old dinosaur, coasting by on a reputation that sometimes bordered on parody. Not for nothing was she the inspiration for the satirical Glenda Slagg in *Private Eye* magazine. She targeted poor Kylie, who was completely unprepared for the poison pen of this wrinkly Rita Skeeter.

In March 1988, Kylie flew in to Heathrow to finish the vocals for her first album and to do some publicity, because, after all, she was number one in the UK. To begin with, she was exhausted, thanks to a punishing schedule. When she arrived, she was shocked by the microscopic scrutiny afforded every celebrity by the British press, and this was the start of a lifelong hate affair with the tabloids. To a certain extent, she was the target of innate racism by good old Brits against all things Antipodean. It's not something Australian visitors to the UK expect. It is by no means reserved for the non-white population, but because it is white on white, it is ignored and laughed off.

It was naive of Kylie and her management to think the latest pop sensation and soap star would escape media attention. Kylie asked her manager what she could expect at the airport. Terry Blamey told her to relax and get some sleep because nobody knew she was arriving on that flight. He had taken the precaution of booking the seats only a couple of hours before take-off. Unfortunately, it would have made no difference if he had booked them two minutes before departure – the telephone lines between Melbourne and London were buzzing, and Fleet Street's finest had plenty of time to trickle out along the M4 to wait for their prey. Kylie stepped off the plane in dark glasses, an old pair of scruffy sandals and a wraparound skirt.

It hadn't helped that she was escorted by burly minders the size of Ayers Rock, who weren't exactly the type you would want to invite home for tea with Mother. Minders behaving badly has always been a surefire way to achieve newspaper coverage, as a list of other over-protected female stars, from Madonna to Britney Spears, illustrates. On this occasion, it just irritated everyone. Jean Rook commented, 'Maybe getting off a plane looking as if you've just crawled out of a kangaroo's pouch is Australian style but Kylie Minogue's disappoint-ing arrival at Heathrow was worse than just the sloppily dressed girl next door. She looked like a slept-in Qantas blanket.' That was the kindest bit. She went on to describe her as a 'filthy-mooded funnel-web spider' and suggested that Kylie could take lessons from a real high-flying star, like Joan Collins. Poor Kylie probably didn't have a clue who Joan Collins was.

Rook's assassination coincided with the publication of topless pictures of Kylie in the *Sun*. They had been taken when she was hol-idaying in Bali with Jason Donovan some eighteen months earlier. That had been their first holiday together and, despite the obligatory bout of Bali belly, had been an idyllic one – not something they wanted to look back on through the pages of a tabloid newspaper.

Kylie, it seemed, was already suffering from a media backlash and over-the-top public criticism. There was a great wave of anti-Kylie feeling, with I HATE KYLIE MINOGUE badges and satirical versions of 'I Should Feel So Yucky' and 'I Should Be So Lucky With My Rubber Ducky'. It was time for the shutters to come down.

The negative publicity, combined with the stress of her schedule, was driving Kylie towards a nervous breakdown. Jane Oddy's anxieties about her, it seemed, were not misplaced. An insider at PWL explained, 'Kylie was young and very fragile because she was quite a small little thing, so it was taking its toll. I don't think she'd say we flogged her to death but, in retrospect, we could maybe have cut down a bit. She was very tired and stressed out and would be like, "Do I have to do all this?"' She was homesick and lonely, and would ring home every day seeking comfort from her family. She admitted that she couldn't sleep or eat and was constantly crying.

Pete Waterman added, 'She was a tiny girl and obviously had a huge workload, so she'd be exhausted half the time.' He was understanding when Terry Blamey came to him and said that Kylie had clearly had enough. The two men decided that the best course of action was to put her on a plane back to Melbourne to recuperate with her family. She did absolutely nothing, except enjoy long lie-ins, take Gabby for walks, shop in Chapel Street and meet old girlfriends for coffee in St Kilda.

Terry Blamey refused all interviews, so Kylie could have a proper rest. In any case, she was receiving too much exposure, and speculation that she was anorexic wasn't helpful when she was so fragile. Stories about weight loss or gain are an additional burden for female pop stars, although it was true that Kylie was put on high-energy diets from time to time to stop her from losing the pounds when she was driving herself too hard.

The publicity bandwagon had been temporarily derailed – even requests from Australian media were turned down. One of the first newspapers to gain access again was the *Melbourne Sun*, which had carried 150 stories about Kylie in one year. The editor, Colin Duck, explained that featuring her meant they sold more papers. It was as simple as that, and very much the same strategy that accounted for the enormous coverage the late Princess Diana always received.

'Kylie Minogue Limited' got together and decided that Kylie must never again be caught out by the media. It was very much a necessary evil that had to be controlled as closely as possible. Instead of a wide-eyed, enthusiastic young woman from Melbourne, the image of the new 'corporate' Kylie that was presented to the world was neatly packaged and always immaculate. Behind the smiling face, she may have been feeling the strain, but on the surface she toed the company line by seeming to be the world's most normal girl – as if her star-spangled life had ever been normal. She never courted controversy. She would always say that she was 'tired', 'nervous' at this or that and flash a big toothy smile. She was asked if she would like to live overseas and replied, 'I'll always call Australia home', which didn't answer the question. It wouldn't be long before London was her permanent home.

Kylie is a far better actress than she is given credit for and she is a past master at giving nothing away. Former pop columnist Rick Sky placed her at number one in his list of worst interviewees, although he admitted her beauty was some compensation. 'She was incredibly unforthcoming,' he recalled. 'It made me wonder what a nineteen-year-old girl had to hide. She was quite po-faced and everything I asked her about came to a dead end.' In the beginning, Kylie was worried about spilling the beans about Jason, or that she would be questioned about rumours of anorexia. After a while, it became second nature to give away nothing or, more precisely, exactly as much as she wanted to divulge.

She also had back-up. Andrew Watt, a local Melbourne music journalist, was commissioned by Mushroom to write Kylie's fanzine copy, the soft-focus biography that is requisite for every star. He was also conveniently placed in press conferences to derail things. Should any tough questions be asked about topless photos or weight loss, Watt would put up his hand and ask, most sincerely, 'So Kylie, what's it like working with Pete Waterman?' Soon she became adept at deflecting these questions without her 'plant'.

The control that Kylie, Terry Blamey and Ron Minogue exercised over all things Kylie was edging towards a stranglehold. Sometimes she could come across as bland and unforthcoming simply because she was being careful and didn't want to upset anyone; she needed to stay popular. Starting from these early days, her management has carefully controlled her image and, just as importantly, changes to that image. They have absolute command over her pictures, her music and her merchandise. In effect, Kylie owns all things Kylie. Her bank account swells a little time every time you see a picture of her in a magazine. There is likely to be big trouble if anybody tries to take an unauthorized photo.

These days this approach is common in the pop business and accounts for the plethora of anaemic pop columns that rely on planted stories from a star's 'people' in order to fill the space. Casual pictures are posed and arranged in advance, relationships and love affairs are written as fact when they are clearly marketing strategies for two people who barely know each other. It has reached a ridiculous level of deceit.

Sometimes the real world intruded into Kylie's carefully orchestrated version. On one occasion she went with Pete Waterman to Peter Stringfellow's now defunct Hippodrome nightclub off Leicester Square in London. The story may have become exaggerated in the retelling but one eyewitness said that a drunken mob of jealous girls started calling Kylie names and jostling her. One girl allegedly spat at her, full in the face, as she was sitting down: 'She didn't say a word – just struggled out of her seat and was ushered out.' She learned a valuable lesson that night: nobody cool ever went to the Hippodrome.

Kylie was polarizing opinion. You either loved her non-threatening, happy smiley image or you hated it. Music snobbery is not so overt today. There is a fashion for instant nostalgia fuelled by the theme nights on Simon Cowell's reality shows or on the revival tours of stars well past the age of bus-pass eligibility. As Spencer Bright acknowledged, 'We are less judgmental today of commercial sounds.' Nowadays, a collaboration between Cheryl Cole and Snow Patrol seems a perfectly natural idea; in the late eighties, it wouldn't have happened.

A great deal of the criticism of Kylie was fuelled by jealousy, especially as PWL was an independent label formed specifically to make Kylie records, and independents were traditionally the home of more cutting-edge sounds like The Smiths and, later, Oasis. Waterman explained, 'We were pissing people off incredibly because every record we had released dominated the independent chart. Kylie Minogue was number one in the independent chart! That was unpopular.'

7

A New Sensation

Kylie was already thinking ahead to life after *Neighbours*. When she gave interviews about her new pop success, she admitted that her future on the show was uncertain, even though she still had six months to run on her contract: 'I've done *Neighbours* since I left school. I'd obviously like to do other things. I'd be in London right now if I could, but I have commitments to *Neighbours*.'

It was no surprise when she decided not to sign another deal. The reality was that in eighteen short months, Kylie had outgrown the homespun Aussie soap. Her second single, another chirpy track entitled 'Got To Be Certain', had just missed the top spot in May, so the signs were promising for her debut album. If the release of *Kylie* could be timed to coincide with her farewell to Ramsay Street, then that would be a promotional bonus.

When she eventually left the series in June 1988, those she left behind presented her with a mahogany mirror and a framed montage of her magazine covers. The producers also gave her an open door to come back. In her last episode, Charlene drives away to start a new life in Brisbane, with the understanding that Scott will join her the following year. Theoretically, it meant that Kylie could return to the show if her pop career imploded, but that showed no sign of happening.

By the time the episode was broadcast in the UK in October, her debut album had reached number one. Unusually, it took seven weeks to reach the top, but by the end of the year had sold close to 2 million copies and was the biggest-selling album of 1988. The only track not written by Stock, Aitken and Waterman was 'The Loco-Motion', which was her third UK single release and second to stick at number two. The same thing happened to 'Je Ne Sais Pas Pourquoi' – Pete Waterman's favourite among Kylie's songs – when it became the fourth single from the album in October.

She may not have had four number-one singles in a row – although that's exactly what she did have in Finland of all places – but the statistics for her first year as a pop singer in the UK were impressive. She had completely eclipsed the competition in the Stock, Aitken and Waterman stable. Her first four singles alone generated more than 1.7 million in sales. According to Waterman, Kylie's success was the worst thing that had happened to him: 'I don't mean that against Kylie, but merely that she was so successful that I had to fall in line with that success. I didn't want my company to become one artist, as much as I loved that artist, as much as now history shows what a wonderful artist she is, and how proud I am of her.'

Jason, meanwhile, was beside himself with jealousy. Kylie was living the life he wanted for himself. He wasn't that much into pop, and didn't exactly like her records, but he desperately wanted what she had. In his perfect world, Jason would have been Stock, Aitken and Waterman's big-name rock star. With hindsight, he realized that his girlfriend's success was the beginning of the end of their love affair. He was happy for her to be a number-one artist, but the implications for them as a couple would soon be apparent as the demands on Kylie's time and energy grew. He described it in his book as a 'terrible sinking feeling'.

From the moment Kylie released a record, there was speculation that 'Scott' would do the same. He came over with Kylie on one of her recording trips to London, and Pete Waterman took them out for a Chinese meal. He asked Kylie whether she wanted him to work with Jason. She said yes, and the deal was done. It is quite telling that this was agreed on Kylie's say-so.

The Hit Factory was not a cosy air-kissing organization. Artists could either stay for the bumpy ride or, like Rick Astley, jump ship. This was conveyor-belt business and Kylie Minogue records were continually on the production line. Waterman had great respect for Kylie, but admitted he never got 'that close' to performers personally: 'We work with artists. We don't work with friends. I always think it is too dangerous to get too close to an artist. You'll always get let down because they will shit on you.'

The one exception to that 'no mates' working philosophy was Jason Donovan. Waterman declared, 'He was a mate and he was treated like a mate. We had a genuine affection for the guy.' Jason shared Waterman's passion for cars, and the pair would dash off to Silverstone together to watch the motor racing. Jason was also the beneficiary of a genuine 'happy accident' chain of events. When Rick Astley abruptly exited the stable, he left behind a song that had already been prepared for him. The very next day, when Jason walked in, Waterman said he had found just the song for him, 'Too Many Broken Hearts'. The track became Jason's first solo number one.

When Kylie first came over to London to record, she brought her mother and the two of them lodged in Pete Waterman's flat over the studio. It gave them more privacy and meant that Kylie could relax and not be distracted from her work. He moved out to a hotel. Later, whenever Kylie and Jason were in London at the same time, they would stay together but, just as in *Neighbours* and at Mushroom Records, their true relationship was kept secret. By now it was one of the worst-kept secrets in show business but, amazingly, nobody printed it, even though pictures of the couple holidaying in Bali had been published. A PWL insider explained, 'It was quite bizarre, because everyone knew. They were always holding hands and kissing in the car.'

Contrary to popular belief, it was Jason who had a roving eye, well before Michael Hutchence turned Kylie's head. He was like a kid in a candy store when he first came to London on a promotional tour. The insider observed, 'She [Kylie] was totally into it [their relationship] and I remember him saying that she was really keen and everything. But he was saying, "I'm a young man and I just want to enjoy myself while I'm here – and she wants to get more serious." I think that probably caused friction between them. It was inevitable it wasn't going to last.'

Intriguingly, the decision to keep their relationship secret was just as much to protect Jason's career as Kylie's. For two years, Jason was the ultimate teen-girl fantasy. He was eligible, and every girl studying for her exams or working behind the counter in a store felt she had a chance to go out with him. Fantasy is what it's all about and, unlike Jason, the more streetwise Kylie has never lost sight of that, whether as girl next door or wet dream.

The ultimate fantasy coupling of Jason and Kylie was on their number one 'Especially For You', which is either cheesy and cynical or the best love song ever, depending on whether you like fluffy, cuddly toys or not. This was 'pop noodle' – popular, but not to everyone's taste. 'We didn't want to do it,' said Waterman, fearing it might be considered too tacky. In the end, he was persuaded by public pressure, and because Kylie thought it was a good idea. She described the duet merely as an extension of their working life: 'We'd done everything else together.'

Although it's a duet, there's no doubt that it was a Kylie song. She sang the first verse and took centre stage in the fluffy video, in which they keep missing each other while she goes to an audition. Waterman and Matt Aitken flew to Australia to record the pair's vocals, caught the next flight home and went straight to the studio to work on the mix in time to turn the track into a Christmas hit. It took only three days from start to finish.

During those three days, though, Waterman was cornered by Ron

Minogue, who showed just how tough he was when it came to dealing with the machinations of the pop world. He demanded that
Kylie see some of her hard-earned cash. A startled Waterman had to
write out a cheque to Kaydeebee for a substantial amount on the
spot. Part of that money was speedily put down on an Aus $500,000
dollar house in Melbourne, even though Kylie knew she would
scarcely live there, if at all. Kylie had signed to a five-year contract
with PWL and was a millionaire after the first year.

'Especially For You' failed to become the planned festive number
one: that accolade went to Cliff Richard with 'Mistletoe And Wine'.
But when the Christmas hangovers had cleared and it was time for
New Year's, it was top of the charts for three weeks and sold close to
a million copies. After 'Especially For You', there was nowhere for
their joint professional career to go, unless they wanted to become
a duo like Sonny and Cher. Commercially, they couldn't top the success of that song, and their careers had been intertwined enough as
it was. Privately, the cracks were beginning to appear.

Jason didn't enjoy being in Kylie's shadow. If he didn't get the full
picture before, he certainly did when they both attended Kylie's
twenty-first birthday party in May 1989. The crowd outside
Melbourne's Red Eagle Hotel in Albert Park surged forward to
wish Kylie a happy birthday as she clambered out of a Mercedes in
a semi see-through black dress. The party coincided with yet
another UK number one for Kylie: the supremely catchy 'Hand On
Your Heart'. Understandably, she was the centre of attention, but
Jason was there too. He seemed almost forgotten as he scrambled
out of the back of the car. As soon as someone had escorted Kylie
through the hotel door, a bouncer promptly slammed it in poor
Jason's face.

By this time, Kylie had met Michael Hutchence. The singer had
been in typically worse-for-wear mode when he first encountered
her at a club in Sydney's King's Cross area. She was standing self-
consciously against a wall, surrounded by minders, when he lurched

over and declared, 'I don't know what we should do first – have lunch or f***.' She was completely tongue-tied.

Kylie's association with Michael Hutchence had a cataclysmic effect on her. The popular version of their relationship is that she was a virginal girl next door, giving herself up to be sacrificed on the altar of perversion by the demonic Hutchence. Lurid tales always accompany the Hutchence name. Suggestions abound that he liked three-in-a-bed sex, was more than intrigued by sadomasochism and had a taste for heroin. He certainly confessed to his family that he had tried heroin. As for sexual shenanigans, he would tell the story of how, once when he was on tour, he was presented with a seventeen-year-old nymphet wearing nothing more than a dog collar and lead. For the most part, it is all hearsay and innuendo, mainly third- and fourth-hand – the traditional stuff of rock myths. Hardly any concrete evidence exists of his debauchery. Newspaper articles and books about the dead star are not littered with kiss-and-tell tales supporting the popular view of his lifestyle.

And Kylie was no virgin – in fact, she was already quite an expert. She had enjoyed a relationship with Jason Donovan and flings with other teenage boys. She was, perhaps, developing a taste for the dangerous side of sex, the thrill of getting caught. She was like a naughty schoolgirl with a lollipop in her mouth and the *Kama Sutra* in her satchel. This is not to suggest a fascination with the Marquis de Sade, more a desire to seize the moment when an opportunity for passion arose. Kylie has spoken many times about their relationship but perhaps her most insightful observation is this: 'Michael was not as bad as everyone thought, and I was not as good. We met somewhere in the middle.'

Michael Hutchence was the classic leader of a rock band. He enjoyed taking his pick of girls and narcotics. He had the arrogance and exhibitionism of a born performer but cloaked them in an almost childlike enthusiasm that made him fun to be with. He was twenty-seven when he met Kylie and the most famous rock star in

Australia. Kylie would have been in awe of him regardless of his swaggering, upfront suggestion of sex. She observed, 'I couldn't believe he would talk to me, and I couldn't believe what he'd just said. I was speechless.'

Kylie was still very suburban despite her rapid rise to pop fame. Her acting career had led to abnormal teenage years. Being a young actress, almost a child star, is like being a boy wonder at football: you don't live in the real world but in a strange, timeless environment, in which you are cosseted and protected. Kylie had the qualities of an ingénue. She had intrigued Hutchence. Before he crossed paths with her again, he mentioned her name in an interview in *Smash Hits* magazine: 'Kylie Minogue ... hmmmm ... she's got a horrible voice ... actually I met her once and she was very sweet.'

Hutchence was carrying a great deal of emotional baggage by the time he stumbled up to Kylie in that King's Cross club. This was no shallow Casanova. He was very well read, a pop philosopher, as well as a collector of fine art and beautiful things. Kylie Minogue was very collectable. The club where they met was hosting the party after the annual *Countdown* Music Awards ceremony, the Australian equivalent of the Grammys or the Brits. INXS had already collected a sackful of awards, but Kylie was a musical novice. She had won the TV Logie for Most Popular Actress in Australia for *Neighbours*, but had been invited to this event because 'Locomotion' was the current number one. In contrast, in 1987, INXS had produced one of the biggest albums worldwide, their enduring rock masterpiece *Kick*, which sold more than 8 million copies. Hutchence, never prone to public self-doubt, once boasted to a journalist, 'I am a f***ing great rock star.' And he was. No wonder Kylie was starstruck. But, amazingly, it was Kylie who made Michael Hutchence a celebrity.

8

The Delinquents

While Kylie was growing up, cocooned in Camberwell, Michael Hutchence was already travelling the world, having enjoyed a cosmopolitan and enlightened upbringing. He was born Michael Kelland John Hutchence in Sydney, on 22 January 1960. The name Kelland was after his father, Kell, an international businessman who bore a passing resemblance to the old Hollywood film star David Niven. His glamorous mother, Patricia, was a model, and ran a modelling school in the city. When Michael was four, his father accepted a job as managing director of a firm importing whisky and champagne for restaurants in Hong Kong. It meant a major upheaval for the family.

It was a very urbane expat world in which Michael, his younger brother Rhett and teenage step-sister Tina found themselves. After a nine-hour flight from the January sun of Sydney to the bustling, humid Far East metropolis, the family checked in to the Hong Kong Hilton. Michael Hutchence seemed to spend a good deal of his life in the impersonal environment of an expensive hotel room. The family settled in to a merry-go-round of cocktail parties and afternoon tea – and soul music. Michael recalled, 'There were loads of parties and good music, like James Brown and Aretha Franklin. Mine were hip parents.' When the family moved in to their own apartment, they employed two servants, who would address young

Michael as 'Master'. His mother, meanwhile, found work as a make-up artist on movies being shot in Hong Kong. The actress Nastassja Kinski was the same age as Michael and was a guest at his sixth birthday party when her father, Klaus, was starring in a film called *The Million Eyes of Su-Muru*.

He may not yet have been a 'man of the world', but Michael was certainly a boy of the world by the time the family returned to Sydney in late 1972, when he was twelve. He was more an international citizen than an Australian. He explained in *Spin* magazine, 'I had a problem with Australia. In the first place, I hated it. I had all the same prejudices in my head that the English have about it – hats with corks dangling to keep the flies away and kangaroos. Once I got there I realized it was different, but I couldn't believe the people where I went to school. I just hated the place.' One saving grace was that his best friend at the school was Andrew Farriss, equally shy and even more serious, who would join Michael in finding fame with INXS. The pair would chat for hours, discussing poetry and music.

Michael, already a shy boy with a subtle lisp, retreated further into the world of books and, in particular, poetry, which remained a constant love in his life. He was soon to suffer another upheaval when his parents' marriage, which had been rocky in Hong Kong, collapsed completely, with Patricia leaving for Los Angeles with Michael, now an impressionable fifteen, in tow. Tina and her young son were with them, but Rhett stayed behind with his father. Michael took to life in LA like a duck to water, and began a lifelong enjoyment of girls and marijuana. But, at seventeen, he was back in Sydney and had decided a career in music was for him, especially when he discovered how easy it was to get girls as the lead singer in the band.

He played his first gig on 16 August 1977, the date Elvis Presley died. The band called themselves The Farriss Brothers, an uninspiring name that would eventually be ditched in favour of INXS. As soon as he finished school later that year, Michael was off again, this time to Perth in Western Australia, when Andrew's family relocated there. The rest of the band, including Michael, decided to move there as well – another year, another home.

By the time he reached the age of twenty, INXS had taken off and were playing nightly gigs all across Australia. Michael was living with a girl called Vicky in Sydney. However, he had met another young woman with whom he was to spend seven years. His relationship with Michele Bennett – tall, leggy and brunette – was arguably the most important of his life. They lived together in a two-bedroom ter-raced house Michael had bought in the Paddington area of Sydney. The relationship was very stable and loving, even though he was prone to infidelity. For all his reputation as a great womanizer and hell-raiser, he had a surprising number of stable, important rela-tionships throughout his short life. His friends and family assumed that one day he and Michele would marry.

Michael's legendary status as a serial cheater on the road with INXS owed much to his fear of being alone. Even after their split, he would remain in touch with Michele – including the night he died – ringing her from all over the world to seek reassurance and help to get to sleep. His mother, Patricia, recalled that just hearing Michele's voice would calm him down. In her memoir of her son, *Just A Man*, she also poignantly described how Michael had told her of their split: 'I watched him walking away, looking so lonely and, somehow, had a feeling that he and Michele would never, ever break off their rela-tionship. I was right, they never did. Until the day he died, Michael loved her.'

Intriguingly, in the light of his future break-up with Kylie, infi-delity was only part of the problem with Michele. She wanted to pursue her career as a video and film producer, and he wanted some-one to be with him, pandering to his every need, twenty-four hours a day. That person wasn't Michele Bennett and it certainly wasn't the ambitious Kylie Minogue. It might have been his last love, Paula Yates, but fate cruelly intervened.

After their first unforgettable encounter, it would be another year before Michael and Kylie met again, this time in Sydney towards the end of 1988. The aptly named single 'Need You Tonight' was a number one in the States and reached number two in the UK (only to be outsold a couple of weeks later by 'Especially For You' by Kylie and Jason). Kylie had admitted in a pop profile that INXS was her favourite band, so she was keen to see them in concert before the mammoth *Kick* tour came to an end. She went with Jason to the last night at the Sydney Entertainment Centre and they were both invited to the end-of-tour celebration afterwards at the Regent Hotel. They cruised over to the party in their Honda Civic, only to be overtaken by the band in an enormous limo. Kylie and Jason definitely weren't rock stars yet.

Kylie's career had gone into overdrive since she had first met Hutchence, with her Stock, Aitken and Waterman alliance in the UK triggering enormous press interest. She still wasn't at ease at celebrity functions though. It was as if in some way she didn't have a right to be mingling with so many famous people. The irony of her reticence was that she and Jason, the old married couple from *Neighbours*, would be the only guests recognized in every supermarket in the land – and probably most of the world.

During this second chance meeting, the conversation was more civilized. Hutchence apologized for his derogatory remarks about Kylie's voice and proceeded to turn on the charm like a 200-watt bulb. He wasn't particularly handsome, with the thin frame of a rock star heavily involved in drugs. His intake had markedly increased during the tour, and he was seen knocking back a handful of ecstasy tablets before he went on stage. His face bore the residual pockmarks of bad teenage acne and had led to him unkindly being called 'crater face'. He couldn't compete with the blond surfer-boy looks of Jason Donovan, but few women could resist his doleful eyes, or the feeling he gave them when he was talking to them that they were the centre of the universe.

Kylie has never been a heavy drinker and, while everyone else was overindulging in the substances on offer, she allowed Hutchence to fetch her a Baileys to sip. She wasn't head over heels at this point. This was a rock party and she wasn't totally relaxed. Michael's half-sister, Tina, recalled, 'Wholesome Jason and Kylie looked so out of place amidst the heavy rock and rollers.' Amusingly, she broke the habit of a lifetime to ask Jason and Kylie for an autograph for her young daughter and was deeply embarrassed to discover they were in the middle of an argument. Jason had noticed that there was a 'buzz' between his girlfriend and Hutchence, but he didn't say whether this was the subject of their heated discussion.

The romance between Kylie and Michael so far had been such a slow starter that it resembled the desultory meetings of the film *When Harry Met Sally*. Kylie was asked by a teen magazine to comment on the INXS singer's new shorter haircut the following May: 'I think people really liked his long hair. I'm not really interested in Michael Hutchence, but I'm sure people will get used to it.'

A far more important event in Kylie's life than Michael's haircut began when she won the lead role in her first feature film. At this stage of her career it was still an open question whether Kylie was an actress who sang, a singer who acted or a combination of the two. She began filming *The Delinquents* at the Warner studios on the Gold Coast of Queensland in the spring of 1989. She was fitting it in between promoting her first million-selling album and recording her second, *Enjoy Yourself*. Perhaps that has always been the problem for Kylie as a movie star: there just aren't enough hours in the day to be a superstar at everything.

The Delinquents was adapted from a popular Australian novel of the same name written by Criena Rohan. When the project was first brought to Kylie's attention, David Bowie was on board as executive producer, which would have made for an interesting soundtrack, but he had dropped out by the time filming began.

Kylie was the 'heroine' of the book, a rebellious teenager called Lola Lovell, who was definitely not the sort of girl likely to pitch up in Ramsay Street or, for that matter, Surrey Hills. This was a rites-of-passage movie, set in a small, provincial town in the mid-1950s. The story centred on Lola's love for a young drifter, Brownie Hansen, who was played by the American Brat Pack actor Charlie Schlatter, then one of a number of young Hollywood men who appeared to be on the verge of major stardom but never quite achieved it. He eventually found his level, playing opposite Dick Van Dyck in the popular TV series *Diagnosis Murder*.

The Delinquents was generally thought to have suffered from the influence of its American financial backers, Warner, who diluted the homespun, ethnic feel of the original book. In the film, Kylie had to remove her clothes on a number of occasions, thrash around in the sheets and, more controversially, be taken by her overbearing mother for an abortion when she was fifteen. Kylie was at pains to point out that the book was much more depressing and gritty than the film: 'If we had left it the way it was, it was so depressing you would have wanted to slash your wrists.' She thought the story 'beautiful and very touching'.

This was a totally different project for Kylie, who, unlike her Stock, Aitken and Waterman incarnation, was allowed plenty of freedom to express her own ideas on set. It was a refreshing change to be taking part in something grown-up at the same time as her seventh single, 'Hand On Your Heart', was topping the UK charts. She was being introduced to a world in which her opinion mattered.

The new image that *The Delinquents* provided for Kylie was, perhaps inevitably, too much for the critics, who still imagined her as the girl next door. The *Daily Mirror*, who would grow to love all things Kylie in the future, declared, 'Kylie has as much acting charisma as cold porridge,' which was unnecessarily cruel. Although the film did reasonably well in both Australia and the UK, it was a flop in the USA, which spoiled any prospects of Kylie soon becoming a Hollywood star.

The film is beautifully shot, and has a great soundtrack and period feel. Kylie is far better in it than the original reviews suggested. She wasn't yet a great media favourite – far from it – and, as a result, she wasn't taken particularly seriously.

The obvious change in Kylie's image is interesting because the movie was shot before she became involved with Michael Hutchence. She had taken the decision to distance herself from the 'girl-next-door' Charlene without his influence. She was technically still with Jason, who would fly up from Melbourne to visit her on location when his schedule on *Neighbours* allowed. Their relationship was floundering, however.

Their diaries wouldn't allow them more time together. They met up briefly in Los Angeles, where Kylie was doing some promotional work. Then she had to prepare for the *Disco In Dream* roadshow – four dates in Japan in October 1989. She was performing a set of eight numbers from her first and second albums, beginning with 'The Loco-Motion' and ending with 'I Should Be So Lucky'.

Enjoy Yourself was little more than an extension of her debut album, an example of not fixing something when it isn't broken. In effect, it was another Charlene album. That hit the right note with the public because the album went straight to number one in its first week of release. The critics were less impressed. *Rolling Stone* gave it a pathetic one star. The magazine's critic, Arion Berger, called the record 'inept' and Kylie's voice 'abysmal', which demonstrated that she had a long way to go to gain any sort of artistic credibility.

Only one track, 'Tears On My Pillow', wasn't written by Stock, Aitken and Waterman. This was an old fifties ballad that had featured on the soundtrack of *The Delinquents*, so there was the chance to gain some cross-media publicity. Kylie preferred 'Hand On Your Heart', and told the young audience on *Ghost Train on Sunday* that it was her favourite of her singles to date.

The most important commodity Kylie has had throughout her career is not her voice, her face, her hair or even her famous bottom but her image, of which they are all part. Nothing can be allowed to deflect from the strict control of that image, whether it be her relationship with Jason or the subtle changes in her clothes, her videos or her music. At PWL, they had already noticed that she was beginning to change naturally into a trendier young woman, wearing clothes that suited her more than the jeans and sweater Charlene look.

It wasn't at all helpful to her changing image that, a year after she left *Neighbours*, the Grundy production company released a video entitled *Scott and Charlene: A Love Story*. Kylie rightly considered that she might be typecast as Charlene if this syrup was stuck on the shelves year after year. She decided to take her grievance to court, but was allocated a presiding judge who said he had never heard of Kylie Minogue before the case and that he had fast-forwarded his way through the video because he wasn't prepared to spend an hour and a half watching it. The judge found against her, declaring that it was obviously the success of *Neighbours* that had directly launched her career.

To say she was annoyed is an understatement, and she certainly voiced her opinion on this issue: 'It's not even *Neighbours*. That's not what I was paid a measly fee of money for [Aus $2000 a week] . . . I have spent a lot of time getting away from Charlene. I know some people say, "*Neighbours* made you what you are." But it didn't. It's exploitation.'

Apart from this hiccup, the Kylie bandwagon rolled merrily along, but she needed to sort things out with Jason. Their relationship was doomed when they cooed 'Especially For You' at one another. When Kylie was in Japan, she knew the time was right to make the call to Jason, who was in New York. It didn't go that well, especially when she told him it was over. In his autobiography, he is very honest about his emotions, describing how he was distraught, inconsolable and 'completely destroyed'.

It just so happened that a certain Michael Hutchence was in Tokyo at the time. Jason doesn't know if she was already seeing the rock singer when she finished things, but he could never win a battle against his hero.

9

The Ego Jacket

In late September 1989, Kylie had met Michael Hutchence for the third time. The venue was Hong Kong, where he had a home, a welcome haven to escape the glare of Western fame and indulge his passion for opium. Intriguingly, Kylie had given an interview a couple of weeks before, in which she confided that she needed to meet more pop stars because she wanted to talk to people in the same business. But, she said, she didn't want to swap stories about work: 'Talking about work is so boring!' She was about to get her chance to talk to someone – and there was nothing boring about Michael.

He was a free agent, having just broken up with the svelte American model Jonnie. He had simply walked out, leaving her devastated in New York. Out of the blue, he heard through a mutual friend that Kylie was coming to Hong Kong on her way to her Japanese concerts. He cleared his diary to make sure he was around when she visited.

A dinner date was arranged and Kylie waited patiently in her hotel suite for the singer to pick her up. She waited and she waited. Hutchence had never been on time for anything and he wasn't about to start now. This didn't go down well with Kylie's entourage, who had formed their usual protective shield around her. When Michael eventually showed up, he was greeted by a gallery of angry faces –

Carol, manager Terry Blamey, a personal assistant and four dancers. The atmosphere failed to faze the rock star, who whisked Kylie off to a local restaurant and completely charmed her, despite the meal making her feel queasy. 'From that terrible start, we had a fantastic time,' she said. 'We talked and talked into the night until we literally had to be separated.'

Kylie was just twenty-one, famous but unworldly, and thus fascinated and overpowered by her companion's knowledge and articulate conversation. Hutchence had a view or a witty comment on every subject, and Kylie was a blank canvas on which he could work. This time, she was completely hooked, but, what was more surprising, so was Michael. He found her fun, fresh and genuine in a world full of fakes: 'She's a very underestimated person, she looks absolutely fabulous, she's very honest, she has no pretensions, she's unjaded. The amount of people in her position I've met and I wouldn't want to spend thirty seconds with. There is nothing worse than successful people who are miserable.'

After some sightseeing in Hong Kong, with Michael as the perfect gentleman guide, the Kylie circus moved on to Japan for her gig at the Tokyo Dome in front of 38,000 fans. She was, and remains, an enormous star in Japan, which is the second biggest music market in the world. In commercial terms, making it there is almost as big a deal as cracking America.

After the show, she was back in her hotel room, relaxing with her entourage, when Michael walked in. He had followed Kylie from Hong Kong – a clear indication of his intentions. Everyone decided to go out clubbing. Michael romantically kept trying to hold Kylie's hand like a lovestruck kid and she kept slapping his away playfully. By the end of the evening, however, her resistance had melted. This night marked the start of a relationship that would blossom and flourish, making the year 1990 one of the happiest of Kylie's life. She fell deeply in love with her rock star. For his part, as his mother Patricia once wisely observed, 'Michael loved being "in love".'

Rumours that Michael and Kylie were an item quickly spread throughout the industry. Nobody could believe it. The public perception was that Michael was so cool and Kylie was so uncool. 'It was shocking for everyone,' she admitted, 'including me.' Even their respective families could scarcely believe it at first, dismissing the rumours as pure gossip. By Christmas of that year, however, everyone knew. Already the famous couple had been playing a game of cat and mouse with the world's paparazzi, with photographs of them together being bought and sold for vast sums. Kylie was accustomed to this daily intrusion, but it was new to Michael.

While Kylie's romance with Michael was blossoming, Jason Donovan was being portrayed as some sort of cuckolded fool. This is very unfair on Kylie, as her relationship with Jason had been on a downward spiral ever since the demands of their new fame took their toll. The problem for Jason was that the public wanted to believe the fairytale of their romance, not the reality. He has admitted, 'We broke up and she went out with Michael and it was splashed everywhere. I was the one that copped that. It was a hard time for me, having spent personal time with her and then her moving on to the guy that I wanted to be.'

It is a cruel irony that Jason enjoyed his first solo number one that year with 'Too Many Broken Hearts'. Kylie, too, had a chart-topper, 'Hand On Your Heart', which was a plea to a lover to confess that their relationship is really over. Pop music, so often accused of being shallow, can sometimes provide a poignant commentary on people's real lives.

Kylie and Jason didn't really speak again that year, although they did see each other for the recording of Band Aid II's version of 'Do They Know It's Christmas?' at the PWL studios in London. An eyewitness at the recording observed that they were both in tears: 'It was very awkward because they hadn't seen each other for some time. It was quite emotional.'

Jason barely figured on the ensemble piece, but Kylie sang the first 'starring' verse that had featured Paul Young in the 1984 original. The track appears a little dated now because of the incessant late-eighties drum-machine beat, but it did feature some of the great vocalists of the time, including Lisa Stansfield and Jimmy Somerville. And, of course, Cliff Richard was on it, so inevitably it became the Christmas number one.

By then, Kylie had left the UK, having finished her commitments as the headlining act on *The Coca-Cola Hitman Roadshow* that toured ten ballrooms around the country. She topped a bill that featured lesser lights in the Stock, Aitken and Waterman stable, including Sonia and Sinitta. Her mother, Carol, travelled with her, now in charge of costumes, while Terry Blamey was present, as ever, as co-producer. The only small hiccup came midway through her opening night performance, when Ben Volpeliere-Pierrot, the lead singer with Curiosity Killed the Cat, stumbled uninvited onto the stage and danced and mimicked Kylie for a couple of minutes. He may or may not have been the worse for wear, but she ignored him and carried on with the same set list as her Japan gigs. She may have performed only eight songs, but somehow, with Carol's help, she managed four costume changes, and gave her fans in the UK their first live glimpse of Kylie wearing hot pants – bright red satin ones that were eye-wateringly tight.

During the tour, she was constantly on the phone to Michael, displaying a mixture of excitement and insecurity. In other words, she was a teenager in love, even though she would soon be celebrating her twenty-second birthday. Michael did his share of calling her, and her entourage were getting used to his familiar greeting, 'Hi, Babe', if one of them picked up the telephone when she was busy. When Kylie grabbed the phone, she would always leave the room so that she could talk privately. No one could fail to notice the immediate change that had come over her. She described it as having had her blinkers taken off.

During the next six months she would, under Michael's influence, start reshaping her life and taking control of her own destiny. It was this period, which at the time so many perceived as Kylie firmly going off the rails, that ensured her long-term survival as an artist. Back at PWL in London, they were noticing a complete personality change: 'After she met Michael, you could tell that she was stronger. Before, she might have said if she didn't think something was a good idea, but afterwards she just wouldn't do it.' The Hutchence philosophy was that she was a star, *the* star, and everyone around her was serving her, not the other way round. He described it as wearing an 'ego jacket' – whenever she messed up it was not her fault, it was the person in the jacket.

After finishing up in London, Kylie was able to spend some quiet time with Michael in Hong Kong before they both flew on to his home in Sydney to prepare for Christmas. The romance was already public property – something denied her fans during her relationship with Jason Donovan. Kylie was used to the persistent press scrutiny and had managed it successfully during her time with *Neighbours*. Michael hated it. He was mortified when they were secretly photographed enjoying each other's company in Sydney's Centennial Park. The Australian magazine *Woman's Day* devoted three pages to a set of pictures showing the couple happy and embracing, with Kylie soaking up the sun in a stripy bra top. They also appeared in the *News of the World* in the UK.

The cameras followed them everywhere – taking rides around the city on Michael's Harley-Davidson, going to the movies, or just hanging out in cafés, bars and clubs. Michael would recommend books for Kylie to read, or he would rent classic films like *Casablanca* and *Citizen Kane* for them to watch together in his minimally furnished apartment. Kylie revelled in Sydney's more cosmopolitan culture and, away from the camera shutters, she was having the time of her life. Such was her lover's influence that she broke her personal ban on taking drugs. It wasn't the sort of intake to persuade rehabilitation centres to put out a welcome mat – it amounted to no more than a little dope and the occasional ecstasy tablet – but it didn't stop the now notoriously false rumour spreading that Kylie was rushed to hospital to have her stomach pumped after her experimentation went wrong. She was most displeased, and a few years later stated categorically, 'I was not even in the country at the time!'

Drugs have never played a major part in Kylie's life. She wasn't happy about Jason's consumption and, even under the influence of Hutchence, she never went through an opium-den phase. She did, however, appreciate her lover's point of view concerning freedom of choice. Drugs, and ecstasy in particular, were an essential ingredient of the rock-star lifestyle in the nineties, and in Sydney Hutchence and his friends would indulge before hitting the clubs and staying out most of the night. It was exhausting and repetitive but, as Kylie explained to *Q* magazine, 'I've experimented, yes; some things you can only talk about if you've had experience of them – so I'm thankful for that experience. But I would condemn drugs now. I guess there's a drug for each decade and ecstasy is this decade's drug.'

Those who try to pin down Michael's influence on Kylie to one thing are missing the point. It wasn't just about popping a few pills or a more adventurous sex life. That was part of it – not least when Kylie's luggage revealed a pair of handcuffs in an airport security check. It was a life change. Kylie liked her new friends. She found them more creative and artistic than her previous crowd. This new circle embraced her. They didn't treat her like a miniature Barbie doll or a trophy girlfriend for Michael. They found her bright, fun and a tonic for their jaded palates. As Tim Farriss, INXS guitarist and brother of Andrew, told music journalist Adrian Deevoy, 'Kylie's a lovely girl and Michael really loves her. So if you were thinking of writing anything smart arse about them, prepare to have your legs broken slowly and painfully.'

The rest of the world became aware of the change in Kylie at the Australian premiere of *The Delinquents*. Hutchence was there, looking every inch the dissolute rock star, complete with garishly patterned trousers, a waistcoat for a shirt and a pair of ill-fitting army boots. Next to him was a girl no one recognized – his latest conquest, no doubt. She was petite, fit looking, with a tight 'suicide blonde' wig and a micro dress with a pattern of noughts and crosses. The photographers took her picture in the weary way they reserved for nameless rock chicks until the whisper went round: 'It's Kylie!'

Gone were the bubble haircut, the comfy-denim teenage outfits and the self-effacing cheery smile. This was a sex bomb at a premiere, years before Liz Hurley, Kelly Brook *et al.* used such occasions to get noticed. It was a bold, rebellious statement – not just challenging the public's perception of Kylie but also making the powers that be at PWL sit up and splutter into their morning tea. It was a watershed moment in Kylie's career, and Hutchence gave her the courage to go through with it. Kylie was also, quite clearly, very happy, and chatted with interviewers about the movie, admitting that people were going to be a 'bit shocked' by what they saw. Michael was the perfect escort, careful not to steal her limelight and planting an affectionate little kiss on her cheek to reassure her that it was going well.

This was one of the few times when her private and public life dovetailed neatly together. She wanted everyone to see her and to realize that she was now with Michael Hutchence: a new, independent, grown-up Kylie. Soon their respective careers would mean they would be apart more than they were together. She was preparing for her first real tour, when she would be singing live with a full band instead of using backing tracks. She spent Christmas, as she always preferred to, with her family back in Melbourne, then plunged into rehearsals for her tour's first night at the Brisbane Entertainment Centre. She did drop everything in late January, however, to fly into Sydney for Michael's thirtieth birthday party, which she helped organize in a large warehouse, a favoured venue for rock events. Her sister Dannii had helped her bake a special chocolate

Kylie is three years older than Dannii, but for a time in the early eighties the younger sister was by far the more famous of the two.

Kylie with her younger brother Brendan. He never sought the spotlight like his sisters, but preferred to stay in Melbourne and enjoy a settled family life.

You can see where Kylie gets her youthful sparkle – she and her mother Carol could be sisters.

Kylie poses with Anne Charleston, who played her screen mother, Madge Bishop, in *Neighbours*. Anne praised Kylie's acting, which she said showed great depth and sensitivity.

Bad hair days with Jason Donovan. Their on-screen chemistry turned *Neighbours* into a ratings success when Kylie joined the show in 1986.

By the time Jason and Kylie sang 'Especially For You' at the *Royal Variety Performance* in April 1989, their three-year romance was almost over.

Everyone was shocked by Kylie's new look when she arrived on the arm of rock star Michael Hutchence at the Sydney premiere of *The Delinquents*, in December 1989.

Kylie's relationship with Michael changed her life but they were only a couple for eighteen months.

She was grief-stricken at his funeral at St Andrew's Cathedral, Sydney, in November 1997.

The mid-nineties were a highly creative time for Kylie, as she gained control of her image. With red hair and a little black dress, she is almost unrecognizable at the London premiere of *Muriel's Wedding* in March 1995.

Performing on stage at the Royal Albert Hall with Elton John as Donatella Versace. They sang 'Sisters Are Doin' It For Themselves' at the Stonewall Fund Gala.

Kylie thought Nick Cave was 'wonderful'. Their duet of his murder ballad 'Where The Wild Roses Grow' remains one of her favourite songs.

Kylie and some of her men in the nineties. She had a minor fling with rock musician Lenny Kravitz.

She fell in love with the mercurial French photographer Stéphane Sednaoui.

Kylie always found gallery owner Tim Jeffries good for a laugh.

Actor Rupert Penry-Jones thought he was one of the luckiest men in the world when he went out with Kylie.

Marilyn Minogue? Kylie performed the film legend's song 'Diamonds Are A Girl's Best Friend' at the opening of the Fox Studios, Sydney, in November 1999.

She gave the notorious gold hot pants an outing at G-A-Y, London, in June 2000.

Robbie Williams always found Kylie hot to handle and their duet at the MTV Europe Music Awards in Stockholm in November 2000 was no exception.

Kylie was more sex tiger than sex kitten when she brought the *On A Night Like This* tour to the Hammersmith Apollo in March 2001.

cake, which, candles ablaze, Kylie brought into the room, followed by a boisterous conga line of most of the 200 guests.

Kylie told Pete Waterman that she wanted some time off from recording in the early part of 1990. After the three Australian dates of the *Enjoy Yourself* tour, there was a gap in her diary until the middle of April, when the UK leg began in Birmingham. She stayed in Sydney while Michael and INXS worked on a new album, which would eventually be entitled *X*. Kylie would spend most days hanging around the studio, grasping the opportunity to watch and learn in a way she had never been allowed to do in the studios of Stock, Aitken and Waterman. They took time off to travel back to Hong Kong and holidayed on Great Keppel Island on the north-eastern coast of Australia. Michael couldn't go with her when she travelled with Terry Blamey to Los Angeles to work with some American producers on tracks for a new album. She dedicated one of the songs, called 'Count The Days', to the lover she was missing so much.

Kylie is a very proud artist and didn't like the implication that she was a puppet under the control of Stock, Aitken and Waterman. Her success might have turned anyone's head, but she didn't suddenly think she could do better without them. Many artists' careers have gone downhill fast when their ego has outstripped their talent. Her professional routine with The Hit Factory was leaving her frustrated and unsatisfied as an artist, however. She would turn up at the studio and they would play her the backing track, print out the lyrics and then Mike Stock would go through it, showing her the cues. She went straight in front of the microphone and did her vocal in one take, or perhaps two. She observed, 'I just wanted to be a bit more involved, and it reached the point where I wasn't happy any more about being told to go and "have a cup of tea till we call you".'

The problem for Kylie was how to break the chains binding her to PWL. Her situation was reminiscent of the young Judy Garland. The petite Garland was also trapped as a child star, controlled by factories, desperate to throw off the child/woman image that had brought her initial fame. She would also become an icon to a gay community magnetized by her mixture of camp and vulnerability. Kylie threw off the chains in rebellious, aggressive fashion. The blonde wig and micro dress of her 'Hutchence era' were a bold statement of intent. This was consolidated by her increased artistic involvement in her videos and the use of producers independent of Stock, Aitken and Waterman.

Kylie had gone to Pete Waterman and told him that she wanted to write with Matt Aitken and Mike Stock. He told her that wouldn't be possible because the three of them worked as a unit. He said she would have to collaborate with someone else. Waterman acknowledged that Kylie was headstrong about her career, but also described her as his 'star centre forward'. Perhaps The Hit Factory had underestimated just how strong and just how motivated Kylie actually is. These days, a more confident Kylie will happily admit that her career is the most important thing in her life. The pop business is not a game to her. She wasn't just passing the time until she got married.

Mike Stock recognized as early as 1990 that Kylie, with the massive success she had enjoyed in the previous two years, wouldn't be happy with just coming in and singing, then going out to lunch. He predicted, 'She'll want to do it all very soon and we won't be involved any more.'

The change in Kylie was all too apparent when she flew back to the UK in the spring of 1990 to resume the *Enjoy Yourself* tour at the Birmingham NEC in front of more than 12,000 fans. One reviewer described the concert as 'unadulterated exuberance'.

This time there were twenty songs and nearly as many costume changes, including half a dozen different pairs of hot pants for Carol to make sure she had ready for her daughter. One skimpy outfit involved a wraparound Australian flag – seven years before Geri Halliwell's famous Union Jack dress. Kylie was developing her own sense of fashion, not one dictated to her by record company executives.

She had sought out the Australian designing duo Morrissey Edmiston to make her premiere dress for *The Delinquents*. Their small boutique in the Strand Arcade, Sydney, was where Kylie's fun and slightly whacky outfits were created. Their biggest problem was making clothes to fit her ultra-petite figure.

A friend of Michael's, the Sydney-based stylist Nicole Bonython, became her fashion guru, ridding her of such eighties essentials as shoulder pads and earrings the size of Blackpool Tower. In came an appreciation of the finest shoes money could buy. It was all part of Kylie's education that Michael had set in motion.

At the end of the tour, Kylie headed up the motorway from London to the Pier Head in Liverpool for the tenth anniversary tribute concert marking the death of John Lennon. Some of the biggest names in music performed, including B. B. King, Joe Cocker and Roberta Flack. The legendary Lou Reed sang 'Jealous Guy'. Kylie sang a specially arranged disco version of the classic Beatles song 'Help', which certainly had the merit of being different.

The tour linked neatly into the release of her next single, the timeless classic 'Better The Devil You Know'. For the first time, Kylie exercised control over her image. It had never occurred to Kelly Cooper Barr, her first stylist at Stock, Aitken and Waterman, to try to make anything sexy of Kylie. Her instructions were to 'turn her into the next Olivia Newton-John'. Kylie was so small that she struggled to find outfits for her. Most of the time, it seemed, early Kylie wore figure-hugging Lycra, topped off with huge platform shoes and knee socks. She looked a sight, as she would later admit with her references to tragic outfits, but she was about to change all that.

She presented Stock, Aitken and Waterman with the video for the song, which she had filmed in Melbourne, and they had little choice but to accept it. The new raunchy Kylie, wearing her trademark hot pants on screen for the first time, danced seductively in front of gyrating, bare-chested black men. It dripped sex. She also took every opportunity to flash the large silver ring that had been a gift from Michael. It was emblazoned with the letter M.

Kylie had clearly matured into sex on a small stick. The quality that separates her work from the more obvious sexual treadmill of the Miley Cyrus generation is that it always appeared carefree and natural. There was never a hint of, 'Look at me, I'm getting down with a hunky black guy.' Kylie always achieved the near-impossible conjuring trick of being innocent and wild at the same time. The video is also interesting because facially she looked different. She was thinner, with prominent cheekbones. She was looking more like the Kylie we know today and not an adolescent girl who could pass for thirteen.

Surprisingly, considering its enduring popularity, 'Better the Devil You Know' didn't become a number one for Kylie. It was kept off the top spot by Adamski and 'Killer'. That didn't matter in the long run, because the song was adopted by the gay community and has become so popular over the years that it is almost a gay anthem.

Kylie didn't enjoy being hounded about her new relationship and, in order to cheer her up, Pete Waterman invited her to stay at his country mansion, where she was able to indulge her love of horses. One Sunday morning, Kylie's horse shied at a milk lorry and bolted into the distance. Waterman, terrified that his leading artist was in peril, set off in pursuit on his large grey, only to realize that he had lost control of the animal in his furious gallop. Far from being the rescuer, he needed rescuing himself. He was thrown off, catching his foot in the stirrup. He was wearing a riding hat and so was fortunate that only his ego was bruised as he was carted along. Suddenly, Kylie appeared from nowhere and stopped his horse from dragging him any further up the road.

Michael, meanwhile, joined Kylie in London towards the end of the *Enjoy Yourself* tour in the spring of 1990. For the first time, she was calling London home, although the couple were soon off on a romantic holiday, travelling across Europe on the Orient-Express.

Kylie helped Michael choose a villa to buy in the French village of Roquefort-les-Pins, on the Riviera between Nice and Cannes. It was a magnificent 400-year-old farmhouse with five bedrooms. Kylie and Michael would speed up and down the coast on a motorbike without a care in the world. Back in London, they were in danger of becoming a familiar showbiz couple. Michael took Kylie to see John Malkovich in *Burn This*, a theatrical tour de force and one of the West End hits of the year. Eyewitnesses in the audience reported that he spent most of the performance twanging Kylie's bra strap.

There was still time for another infamous story to emerge: this time it was that Michael and Kylie had joined the 'mile-high club' on a jumbo jet when the Australian Prime Minister Bob Hawke was seated a row in front. According to one of Michael's entourage, they had just a blanket to cover their modesty. Kylie is petite, but this is not something that should be attempted in economy seats. The whole incident was given a *Carry On* flavour, with the suggestion that Mr Hawke had turned round and winked at them.

PART TWO

The Little Genius

10

Feeling Down

Kylie's life couldn't have been more perfect – or so it seemed. She now had more control over her career, she was a multimillionairess with an estimated fortune of £10 million, and she was in love. The only cloud on the horizon was that Michael was back on tour, promoting the new INXS album. The tour began in Europe but, over the coming months, would take him all over the world and keep them apart. Kylie could be forgiven for feeling insecure, considering his past reputation.

She was busy publicizing her third album, entitled *Rhythm of Love*. While it was still very much a Stock, Aitken and Waterman production, Kylie received her first songwriting credits on four of the tracks: 'The World Still Turns', 'One Boy Girl', 'Count The Days' and the title track 'Rhythm of Love', which closed the album. She wanted to flex her creative muscles. In addition, the people who made up 'Kylie Minogue Limited' weren't stupid and realized early on that songwriting royalties were a goldmine and shouldn't be lining The Hit Factory pockets.

Her co-writer on 'Count The Days' and 'Rhythm Of Love' was Stephen Bray, who was best known for his work with Madonna on her most famous tracks of the eighties, including 'Into The Groove', 'True Blue' and 'Express Yourself'. It was indicative of Kylie's desire to follow Madonna's lead that she should have sought out the superstar's collaborator as she began to edge away from her wholesome pop image.

Initially, the comparisons would have been encouraged by Kylie. She looked up to Madonna as a musical icon long before anybody thought of using the same word to describe her own status. While she was still climbing into her mechanic's overalls for another scene as Charlene in *Neighbours*, Madonna had chalked up five number ones and seventeen top-ten hits in the UK.

Pete Waterman could never understand Kylie's enthusiasm for all things Madonna: 'I found it amazing that she was outselling Madonna four to one, but still wanted to be her. Everyone wanted to be Kylie Minogue except Kylie Minogue, who wanted to be Madonna.' His observation was valid at the end of Kylie's first *annus mirabilis* in 1988, when his charge had five top-ten singles, while Madonna failed to register one. He missed the point, however. Madonna was constantly changing her image to keep her fans fascinated and, more important, buying the merchandise. That was what Kylie sought to emulate.

Rhythm of Love performed disappointingly when it was released in November 1990, making only number nine in the UK album chart. Perhaps the raunchier Kylie sat uneasily with a record-buying public stuck in a Charlene time warp. The second single from the album, 'Step Back In Time', reached only number four despite an imaginative video directed by Nick Egan, the acclaimed visual artist who had worked closely with Michael Hutchence and was later responsible for many Oasis videos. It was an homage to seventies disco, and in some ways sought to reposition Kylie as a dance artist. Again, the public weren't convinced, and she was nominated in several worst categories at the annual *Smash Hits* Reader's Poll Awards.

Far more disappointing, however, was Kylie's first brush with the serious fashion press. She longed to be a cover girl and was very excited when *Vogue* chose her for their December issue. For the photo shoot, she was smuggled into the Raymond Revuebar, home of the famous Soho sex shows. She wasn't exactly hiding under a blanket, but it would have ruined the surprise if the newspapers had been tipped off that she was going in.

The idea of photographing Kylie in a slightly seedy setting was an enterprising one, and she threw herself into a series of poses, wearing an alarming array of golden feathers and 'bling'. Kylie was desperate for it to be a success because the front cover of *Vogue* would be a credible style statement and help her gain international recognition. Everybody was waiting excitedly to see the finished result, especially the choice of cover picture, when the magazine hit the news-stands.

Alas, *Vogue* decided to demote Kylie to the inside, admittedly over eight pages, and use a standard, glossy model picture on the front. One of Kylie's entourage recalled, 'She could not understand why.'

Fortunately, that professional setback didn't interfere with the blissful life she was enjoying in the south of France. She spent Christmas with Michael at the farmhouse and he gave her a Gucci watch as a present. They were joined by fellow musician Chris Bailey and his wife Pearl, old friends from the time when Michael was with Michele Bennett. Kylie cooked for everyone, and did her best to make it a happy, festive occasion, even though it was the first time she had spent the holiday season away from Melbourne and she was missing her family.

What Kylie didn't know was that the famous celebrity photographer Herb Ritts had introduced Michael to the breathtakingly beautiful Danish supermodel Helena Christensen, who was just nineteen. By the time he had crossed the Atlantic for January concert dates in Mexico and the States, he was spending almost as much time on the phone to Helena as he was to Kylie. Rumours of his womanizing – including with singer Belinda Carlisle – and pictures of him with glamorous companions weren't helpful, but it is always a particular fixation that is most dangerous to a relationship. Michael Hutchence, don't forget, loved being 'in love'. Kylie, promoting her new album *Rhythm of Love*, was more independent now than when she first met him. Did she still need him as much as she had a year ago? Was Helena about to become his next 'work in progress'?

In New York, in February 1991, events took a complicated turn, with both Helena and Kylie in town at the same time. Michael's mother Patricia recalled meeting Helena at the INXS concert at Meadowlands, the first time the model had seen the band. The next day, she was expecting Michael to arrive for lunch with Miss Christensen and was stunned when he appeared with Kylie for a distinctly frosty meal. She didn't see Kylie again. Michael ended their intense love affair in a 'Bye, Babe' phone call. Having finished her relationship with Jason by phone, it was an ironic twist that she now suffered the same fate. Michael and Helena subsequently stayed together for five years until Paula Yates arrived on the scene.

Kylie was inconsolable. Her friends offered as much support as they could, but she was heartbroken. Even those who were little more than work colleagues found themselves providing a shoulder to cry on. One who had never had a real conversation with the singer recalled, 'Kylie actually sobbed on my shoulder. It was very unusual for her because she wasn't that kind of person, but for me it was sort of a special moment that she was talking to me 'cause she didn't, she wasn't a natural, she would have her select people she'd talk to and I wasn't one of them, so she was obviously very down indeed for her to talk to me. It just started with "I'm feeling down" and went from there.'

It had all happened so fast. Even in a life as hectic as Kylie's, the relationship with Michael Hutchence seemed to have been conducted at breakneck speed. From the time they first got together to the end was just sixteen months, yet it is still the relationship the media and the majority of her public recognize as the defining one of Kylie's life.

She was understandably fragile as she embarked on a twelve-date *Rhythm of Love* tour to promote her new album in Australia. After the final concert at the Sydney Entertainment Centre, there was a party at The Freezer nightclub in the Darlinghurst district. As usual, there were strict controls over photographers to avoid any 'pirate pictures', as Kylie called them. One freelance photographer sneaked in a pocket camera and started taking pictures of Kylie with an actor called Marcus Graham, who was quite a heart-throb at the time. He's now best known for playing Harvey Ryan in *Home and Away*.

When the photographer left the club, he claimed he was pursued by one of Kylie's minders and a party guest, who, he alleged, pinned him up against a wall, took five rolls of film from him and opened up every one of his cameras. The newspapers were still full of the break-up with Michael, so maybe Kylie was particularly touchy about having her picture taken with another man. Terry Blamey, with masterful understatement, said of the incident, 'We didn't want to create a scene.'

After some more dates in Asia, finishing up in Japan, Kylie could return to Europe to lick her wounds. She didn't want to return to London to be hounded by paparazzi seeking pirate pictures of 'sad Kylie' so, on a whim, she went to Paris armed with nothing more than a few addresses of people who would happily put her up for a while. Among them was a woman photographer, Katerina Jebb, who has been one of her closest friends and collaborators ever since.

Kat, as her friends call her, tells the story of how she met Kylie for the first time when the latter appeared on the doorstep of her apartment bearing champagne. They hit it off immediately, and soon after Kylie arrived with a sleeping bag and moved in. The two women became soulmates. It was a difficult time for them both because Kylie was recovering after Michael, while Kat suffered a serious car accident and had to be hospitalized. Kylie was on hand to help when Kat was allowed to go home. Kylie even managed to persuade her friend to start working again. She suggested Kat take her picture, even though injuries to Kat's arm meant she couldn't hold the camera herself and had to have it placed on a stand.

Over the years, Kat has taken some of the most evocative and intensely erotic pictures of Kylie. She was one of the modish artists of the nineties who found inspiration in Kylie as their muse.

In 2002, many of the pictures featured in the style autobiography *Kylie: La La La*. Kat was also responsible for finding a certain pair of gold hot pants on a market stall that would become the most famous Kylie costume of all time.

Kylie couldn't stay in Paris for ever, although the city has since become her favourite after Melbourne and London. She had to hop back on the Stock, Aitken and Waterman conveyor belt and record her next album, as well as resume her *Rhythm of Love* tour in the UK. The final single from the third album, 'Shocked', made the top ten, but there was a strong suspicion that her star was waning a little.

The song became best known for an amusing guessing game about what Kylie sings in the chorus. The third line, according to the song sheet, is 'I was rocked to my very foundations', but an urban legend quickly grew that she actually sings 'I was fucked to my very foundations'. No matter how often you listen to the track, it's impossible to tell for sure what she is singing.

This was all good fun but it didn't help 'Shocked' to sell more. Her fourth album needed to do better, but unfortunately it did much worse. By the time she opened at the Plymouth Pavilions in October 1991, wearing a succession of outfits specially designed by John Galliano, it had been decided to rename the tour *Let's Get To It*, which would also be the title of her new record.

The costumes left nothing to the imagination. The concert was like a fashion show for a saucy lingerie collection and, if worn today by Rihanna, would have given rise to a series of comments about them being indecent and an oversexualization of women in pop. It began with 'Step Back In Time', for which she wore a see-through plastic jacket that showed off her frilly bra and white knickers underneath. Other costumes included a skirt that was ripped off by her dancers to reveal a minuscule basque and suspenders. Most daring of all was a fishnet body stocking that showed her buttocks during a funky version of 'I Should Be So Lucky'. The look was topped off with a leather cap, and became known as the 'S & M bus conductor outfit'.

Kylie has arguably never looked better. She was positively radiant. This was unashamedly Sex Kylie, the culmination in a period of her development that had begun with *The Delinquents* premiere. The show was high energy and physical, but unfortunately the papers focused on its daring elements rather than on the set of Kylie songs that ended with storming performances of 'Shocked' and 'Better The Devil You Know'.

For the album, Pete Waterman had relented and, for the first time, agreed to share his songwriting credits, which read Minogue, Stock and Waterman. Kylie was listed as their co-writer on six tracks. Matt Aitken had left the all-powerful trio, claiming later that he was burnt out and all the songs were starting to sound the same to him.

Disappointingly, her next single, 'Word Is Out', was her first not to reach the UK top ten – hardly what she was hoping for. The album followed that pattern by peaking at number fifteen. The high-light for many was her soulful duet with the American R & B singer Keith Washington, 'If You Were With Me Now', which was rushed out after 'Word Is Out' and was a big pre-Christmas top-ten hit. It was one of those close and meaningful duets in which the artists never actually meet: Kylie recorded her vocals at PWL in London, while Keith sang his across the Atlantic.

Kylie still had a year left to run on her contract but, when Jason had moved on, she was the last big-name artist remaining with PWL. Pete Waterman later said that they could have signed her sister but Kylie preferred them to pass, so Dannii joined the rival MCA label. She had finally left *Young Talent Time* in 1988 and was now following a similar career path to Kylie. She too joined a popular Australian soap, *Home and Away*, made Terry Blamey her manager, signed to Mushroom Records and moved to London. She never lived with her sister but did stay in her flat when Kylie was touring. They never wanted to be in each other's pockets.

The last few months of Kylie's contract weren't especially memorable. Kylie was desperate to change the public perception of her and so, for a while, it seemed that daggers were drawn between her and her former mentors. By the time she left, however, she had achieved twenty successive hits on the PWL label, including four number ones. Her final release for them, a greatest-hits compilation, became her third chart-topping album. She had, by any standards, had an amazing five years with Stock, Aitken and Waterman. But the success of greatest-hits perhaps endorsed the view that the UK, for the moment, continued to see her as 'The Loco-Motion Girl' and not the mature and talented woman she aspired to be.

She started to immerse herself in the London club scene. She wanted her records to be played in the cooler clubs not the commercial ones. To give her more credibility, she created an alias called Angel K and started releasing white label promo vinyls of tracks that would later become B-sides on some of her more successful singles. 'Do You Dare?' was the B-side for her cover of 'Give Me Just A Little More Time', the old Chairmen of the Board hit, which she took to number two in January 1992 – the most successful track on *Let's Get To It*. 'Closer' was the B-side to 'Finer Feelings', the last release from that album in April.

While the single reached only number eleven, the video was shot in Paris and had the feel of a black and white French film of the forties. More and more, Kylie was laying the foundations for becoming a multicultural performer across a spectrum of the arts. Her last hurrah on the PWL label wasn't great art, however: her version of the old Kool and the Gang hit 'Celebration' only scraped to number twenty, so she had little to celebrate there.

*

Kylie hadn't become a nun after her split with Michael Hutchence. The relationship with him had been an exhausting emotional roller-coaster and she needed a diversion or two that weren't quite so demanding. Not long after she had split from Hutchence, she was seen leaving her new Chelsea apartment with one of her dancers. The couple, scruffy and casual, had managed only a couple of steps down the street when a paparazzo was in their face taking pictures and a statuesque blonde reporter was firing questions. Kylie hared off in one direction, while the dancer bolted the other way.

Running has never been one of Kylie's strengths, and the journalist, despite wearing high heels, soon overtook her and pinned her up against a wall. 'Look,' said the reporter, 'I'm just going to ask you a couple of simple questions, so there's no point in either of us getting out of breath, right!' Poor Kylie had no choice other than to comply, and an article appeared in the *Daily Star*. It was a rare glimpse of the private Kylie, someone who suffered from spots, and couldn't be bothered to do her hair when she was going out to grab the first coffee of the day. And why on earth should she be on show twenty-four hours a day? It was a similar situation to the one that she had found herself in at Heathrow Airport, when she had been mugged by Jean Rook and others. The secret Kylie, when discovered, is like a rabbit trapped in a car's headlamps. She doesn't mind revealing a little of her personal life but it is always on her own terms.

The dancer is one of Kylie's legion of hidden admirers. Sometimes we know about her flings and sometimes we don't. The men in her life seem to fall into two categories: either they are drop-dead gorgeous or they are larger than life. Kylie says the most important qualities she looks for in a man are charisma and humour, a rare combination. 'I'd like him to be artistic, too. I like to be swept off my feet.' There is one other credential shared by at least three of her lovers – they were more renowned for what was between their legs than between their ears.

Zane O'Donnell met Kylie on the video shoot for the single 'What Do I Have To Do', a great gay favourite. O'Donnell was a strikingly handsome and well-built model from South Africa, who was blind in one eye and was best known for showing off his physique in a Levi jeans ad. It is an amusing coincidence that several of Kylie's boyfriends grabbed her attention after they had removed most (or all) of their clothing in front of a camera. Kylie let the cat out of the bag about what attracted her to him when she admitted that they had 'discovered sex'. O'Donnell had a considerable reputation as a ladies' man. He had left his wife Lauren and their young son as his career began to take off. Lauren got something of her own back by declaring, 'The only way to stop him going off with other women is to castrate him.'

His relationship with Kylie was a stormy one: they would split up and then get back together again, declaring undying love. They once separated on Valentine's Day in Paris, where Kylie was filming the video for 'Finer Feelings', her eighteenth UK single in just five years. A confidante observed, 'They spent a long time locked in deep conversations. I believe it was a mutual agreement, but Kylie was very down and almost tearful at times.'

Kylie, who, too often for her own good, can wear her heart on her sleeve when she is involved with someone, was in floods of tears after they had a blazing row at a party given by Pat Cash, in Kingston upon Thames, near London. A friend of Kylie's confided how distraught she was, because she really wanted to make things work: 'She is still very fond of him, but the relationship is just not happening.'

That particular row took place before Kylie flew off for her annual Christmas break in Melbourne at the end of 1992. It was the death knell for their relationship. O'Donnell's career never amounted to much subsequently, and he only became newsworthy once more for discovering God and abandoning advertising jeans in favour of a campaign to attract young people to church.

For someone so careful about her private life, sometimes Kylie can be astonishingly indiscreet. It is as if, every so often, she gets the devil in her and hang the consequences. There was the sexual activity with Paulo Marcolin in a passage next to a house where a party was in full swing; there was the full-blown sex with Michael Hutchence on a plane, in a seat within winking distance of the Australian premier; and then there was Lemonheads singer Evan Dando, with whom she disappeared into a toilet at a party. In 1993, Dando looked like he might follow the Michael Hutchence path to rock-god status. He was flavour of the month after the release of the album *Come On Feel The Lemonheads* – and the classic rock ballad 'Into Your Arms' – and could be seen out and about with Johnny Depp and Courtney Love. Besides Kylie, he shared one other thing with Hutchence: a love of hard drugs. He once admitted that during one binge he had smoked so much crack that his voice was ruined for weeks. Dando was from Boston, but spent a good deal of the nineties in Australia. After an almost ten-year period of relative obscurity, he finally released a solo album in 2003 and, in 2005, put together a new line-up for The Lemonheads.

Kylie has admitted that there is some truth in the Evan Dando story, although they were never boyfriend and girlfriend. They weren't really a one-night stand either – more a one-hour stand. The last time she was asked about it, she blushed and giggled: 'What can I say about it? There was some frivolity.'

If put on the spot by an interviewer, Kylie tends to be truthful about 'frivolity'; therefore, when she is adamant that nothing happened, we can take that as the truth. At various times, she was linked with Chris Evans, Julian Lennon, Jay Kay and Jim Carrey. They were products of media imagination. The last named was particularly amusing. Kylie was once lunching at a fashionable Beverly Hills restaurant when she was asked if she would like to join another table and meet the plasticine-faced film star. She agreed and chatted to Carrey before they air-kissed goodbye in the traditional celebrity way. It was the only time they met, but he instantly became the 'new man in her life'.

Nothing happened with her childhood hero, Prince. In all her early fanzine interviews, she answers the frequently asked question 'Who are your pop idols?' with an acknowledgement of the influence of the petite purple one. He may have been a hero with charisma to burn, but there is no evidence that Kylie actually fancied him, even though she once famously described him as being 'sex on a stick'. In fairness, she never said that she thought he was a sexual lollipop. What she actually said was: 'He's an interesting person and the only person I really admire as a fan. He's so outrageous and different. It's funny. He revolts some people but others think he's sex on a stick.' As a small girl herself, Kylie tends to prefer taller, well-built men – so Tom Cruise need not apply.

She met Prince backstage at one of his London concerts after an introduction from a driver they shared in London. Kylie remained virtually unknown in the US – 'The Loco-Motion Girl' – so Prince didn't wholly realize what a big star she was. 'I don't think he knew much about me,' she confessed. At the time, she was looking for more artistic credibility, following her split from Stock, Aitken and Waterman, so it wouldn't do any harm at all for her to be paired with Prince by the media. She visited him at his London studios, where he playfully suggested she write some lyrics for him.

Although Kylie has always been clear there was never anything between her and Prince, that didn't stop her from fuelling the rumours herself with some typical celebrity behaviour. They spent half an hour chatting at Tramp nightclub in London's West End before leaving separately. Prince set off for his hotel, The Conrad in Chelsea Harbour, in the back of a huge chauffeur-driven limousine. A hundred metres or so down the road, the car pulled up and Kylie darted from the shadows and jumped in. They got out together at his hotel, although, to be fair to Kylie, it was only ten minutes from her home, should she have tired of massaging the man's ego.

She did visit his famous home, Paisley Park in Minneapolis, but again she is adamant she wasn't another conquest. She assuredly didn't want to be on that list. They did, however, enjoy a game of table tennis together. 'He's very good. I consider myself quite good at pool and table tennis, but he slaughtered me. I let myself down there. I remember doing one glorious flying leap and landing in the shagpile.'

Kylie also found the right moment to present Prince with the lyrics she had written to a song, 'Baby Doll', which was pleasant enough without being Lennon and McCartney. Prince took it away and bashed out a melody to go with it, but it has yet to see the light of day on an album.

11

Re-engineering Kylie

Kylie's search for post-PWL credibility ended, for the time being, at the door of a small independent dance-oriented record label called deConstruction. It was typical of Kylie at this point in her career that she chose to ignore the bigger companies. However, deConstruction weren't novices, having successfully cracked the mainstream market with the Manchester group M People. The band was led by the charismatic Heather Small, who boasted a unique voice that launched a thousand karaoke impressions. She is better known today as the subject of a long-running joke on the award-winning comedy series *Miranda*.

Kylie signed for deConstruction in February 1993, the same month that M People broke through with 'How Can I Love You More?', a sophisticated blend of northern soul and dance. Fortunately for Kylie, the label wasn't solely focused on the progress of that hit band, and wanted to start Kylie off on the right track. A sign of their ambition came soon after she signed – when they were taken over by the recording giant BMG – the label suggesting she again team up with the newly fashionable producers and remix kings Steve Anderson and Dave Seaman, who worked under the name of Brothers In Rhythm and whom she had already come into contact with at PWL.

Steve and Dave had joined forces while working for the DMC group after they discovered they shared a love of house music. The company published *Mixmag*, which proudly declared itself to be the world's first dance music magazine. Dave edited the magazine, while Steve was hired by the music arm of DMC to be an in-house producer. Together, they discovered that there was a future in the art of remixing. Dave recalled, 'We hit it off from a musical point of view and did a remix of "Promised Land" by the Style Council that came out on DMC. We had to think of a name very quickly because we were going to press. There was a stack of records in the room and at the front was a compilation one called Brothers In Rhythm, so we thought, "That'll do. Brothers In Rhythm. We will be that." I would like to say that it had some sort of hidden meaning or had some mystery reference of years ago but no, it was as haphazard as that.'

Their first big hit together was called 'Such A Good Feeling', which reached number one in the *Billboard* Hot Dance Club Play Chart in 1991 and was a top-twenty hit in the UK in October when it came to Kylie's attention. While she was still at PWL, they were invited to do a 12-inch remix of 'Finer Feelings', one of her most underrated songs. It's a mesmerizing version, nearly seven minutes long but not a second wasted. The result was so well received that it became the 7-inch radio version as well. It promised a fruitful collaboration in the future.

As soon as Steve and Dave heard that Kylie was joining deConstruction, they were on the phone to label boss Keith Blackhurst to see if it was true. Dave remembered, 'I asked if we could try and do something for her and it went from there. The label arranged a meeting and we had lunch together. She came out to the DMC studios in Slough to meet us and discuss what she wanted to do. We were just very much on the same page. I think at that point of her career her persona was bigger than the music and everybody was kind of willing her to make a more credible record. She had outgrown the pop music she had been making until then.

'I think it's fair to say that she was heading in that direction with songs like "Shocked", but I think half the nation was willing her to make a more mature record.'

Kylie would take a taxi down the M4 from her new Chelsea home many times in the coming months. The first time was to record the demo for a new song that Brothers In Rhythm had written called 'Confide In Me'. Like all the great songs, it came together in the studio in little more than an hour. Dave observed, 'It just all kind of flowed out and slotted into place, which is usually the case with the good stuff.'

Kylie was Miss Professional as usual. She told the taxi to wait, and went in and warmed up while Dave and Steve got everything ready. After just one take she was back out in the taxi and on her way home. Amazingly, it was the original demo that ended up being used on the final recording: 'Obviously, there were embellishments to it and we spent a lot of time on the whole production, but it was still the original one that we were using.

'"Confide In Me" without a shadow of a doubt is the best Kylie track we were involved with. It's the thing I am most proud of professionally – the whole process from start to finish. It's the track that really sort of took her to the next level.'

Having a classic song ready was only part of what deConstruction was calling 'the re-engineering of Kylie'. While her alliance with Brothers In Rhythm was vital to that project, so was her sense of her own style, which was developing through her friendship and working relationship with Kat, who was now her flatmate in her Chelsea apartment. Then, in a Mayfair boutique, she came across the man whom she would refer to as her 'gay husband' and who was, in many ways, the co-creator of her modern iconic status.

William Baker, very camp and very gay, has seen Kylie's boyfriends come and go, but he is always there with a safety pin, some tit tape or a sequin. He is her style guru and the man who converts her whims into reality. His close friends call him Joan, a tribute to his personal icon, Joan Collins. His official title in the Kylie world is 'Creative Director', but she admits that they have such a close relationship that 'they are practically joined at the hip'. He is the kid sister Dannii was often too busy to be.

Manchester-born William met Kylie in 1993, when he was nineteen and working in the Vivienne Westwood store in Conduit Street. Technically, he was still at university – he was an undergraduate studying theology at King's College, London – but he worked part time as the 'Saturday boy' and dreamed of getting a break in the world of design.

Kylie was already revered in the gay community. William had loved the video for the perennial gay favourite 'What Do I Have To Do', in which Kylie does some ironing. He was thrilled at the image of a superstar doing domestic chores. On a whim, he rang deConstruction and asked if she needed a stylist, only to learn that she was abroad. He left his name, number and the name of the shop, and never expected to hear anything more.

Three weeks later, Kylie calmly walked into the store. William couldn't believe it, but boldly seized his opportunity: 'I leapt from behind the counter and bombarded her with ideas, and somehow persuaded her to go for a coffee.' The pair adjourned to a café across the road and Kylie listened intently to his ideas. 'She probably thought I was mad,' he told the Kylie website, *LiMBO*. Fortunately, she thought no such thing. Kylie, though initially reserved, is very astute at sizing people up and knowing who might be useful to her, and the obviously bright, witty and enthusiastic Baker looked a promising addition to 'Kylie Minogue Limited' post-Stock, Aitken and Waterman. So she scribbled her number on a napkin and signed it 'Miss K'.

When William got back in touch, Kylie suggested he might want to meet her great friend, Kat. The two women were very close, so it was a big deal for Kylie to introduce her to William Baker. From that meeting came the idea of a shoot based around a Debbie Harry theme – Harry was the glamorous singer from Blondie whom Kylie had long admired and regularly watched on old videos. William dashed home and raided his boyfriend's old punk-era wardrobe for costumes for Kylie. He settled on a pair of ripped tights and a sleeve-less Marilyn Monroe T-shirt that had once belonged to a girl who had worked at Andy Warhol's New York Factory in the early seventies. Kylie loved the resulting pictures, which were arty enough to fit into the overall strategy of her mid-nineties creativity, and they appeared in a small limited-edition book that accompanied the release of her first deConstruction album.

Neither William nor Kat were directly involved with the design and photography of the new album cover, as deConstruction had hired the renowned photographer Rankin and the stylist Katie Grand. In 1992, they had been two of the founders of the magazine *Dazed & Confused*, which was at the forefront of modern style in the nineties. It was very cool, and perfect for the new Kylie. They whisked her off to Los Angeles to photograph her in a parking lot in a variety of outfits, including the one that would become the final cover. Kylie was pictured barefoot, with her hair brushed back behind her ears. She wore a dark suit and Clark Kent glasses that she might have borrowed from her dad. In the photograph for the front, she is licking her lips and crouching low, like a leopard sizing up her prey. It was startling different from Kylie's former flesh-flashing shots.

Her long-running romance with the camera was further con-firmed when Bert Stern took a set of pictures at Universal Studios in Los Angeles that would fill twenty-one pages in the January 1994 edi-tion of Australian *Vogue*. Stern, who had taken some of the most famous shots of Marilyn Monroe, noted that Kylie shared something of the fragile quality of the great film star.

The same month, Dannii got married at the Grand Hyatt Hotel in Melbourne, and Kylie was chief bridesmaid – the closest she has ever come to walking up the aisle herself. A spread of pictures in *Woman's*

Day and *Hello!* confirmed that the couple were Australian showbiz royalty. The groom was Julian McMahon, a former Levi jeans model and her co-star in *Home and Away*. He was also the son of Sir William McMahon, the former Australian Prime Minister, and very well connected.

This was her sister's day, so Kylie didn't mind playing the role of the unattached spinster sister. She helped Dannii decide on the sort of dress she wanted. She arranged the hen night, a girls-only pyjama party in a luxury hotel suite. On the big day itself, she sang 'Fly Me To The Moon' and 'Celebration' at the reception in the Savoy Ballroom. Terry Blamey said, 'I have heard Kylie sing before queens, princes and stadiums full of thousands of people, but tonight was something truly special.' Later, Dannii joined her sister for a rousing version of 'We Are Family'.

The marriage itself lasted no more than fifteen months, before collapsing acrimoniously amid rumours that he was playing less at home and more away. McMahon, who became a well-known face on US television through his role in *Nip/Tuck*, was portrayed as a cad, especially as he had professed undying devotion to Dannii on their wedding day. 'She is my world,' he cried. After the break-up, Kylie was a great support to her sister and they would speak on the phone while Dannii picked up the pieces of her life back in London.

At first glance, the title of the new album, *Kylie Minogue*, appeared to be singularly lacking in imagination, but the idea was that Kylie was starting over and reintroducing herself to the public: this is my name and this is me. All the creative work that had gone into developing Kylie's image would have counted for little if the music didn't have similar substance.

Brothers In Rhythm may have been responsible for the stand-out track, but Kylie was keen to involve a mix of contemporary writers. She co-wrote 'Automatic Love' with the renowned Italian producers

The Rapino Brothers, who were best known in the UK for their radio mix of the Take That breakthrough hit 'Could It Be Magic'. The track was still produced by Steve and Dave, who were also responsible for 'Where Is The Feeling?' and 'Dangerous Game'.

Kylie travelled to New York to hook up with the up-and-coming producer Jimmy Harry, who wrote two songs for her: 'If I Was Your Lover' and the sublime 'Put Yourself In My Place'. Throw in contributions from the Pet Shop Boys and M People and it becomes clear just how determined everyone was to make this a success.

Lenny Kravitz was another premier division act who was asked to contribute. Like Prince, he was a talented and charismatic black artist, but once again there were no artistic sparks between him and Kylie. The song never materialized. There were other sparks, however, and they did have a minor fling. Kylie admitted that 'there was a little bit of truth' in the rumour that they had connected on a physical level. Coincidentally, Kravitz was a good friend of Michael Hutchence and a regular visitor to his French villa. Like all rock stars, Kravitz has a certain wild image to maintain, but he is one of the very few known to have taken his grandfather on tour with him.

Professionally, it would have given the album positive publicity if Prince and Lenny had been involved but, musically, 'Confide In Me' was a good start. The critics were appreciative and it would have made number one in September 1994 if it weren't for the dire 'Saturday Night' by Danish singer Whigfield, a one-hit wonder if ever there was one. As a consolation, 'Confide In Me' made number one in Australia, New Zealand, South Africa, Turkey, Croatia and (as usual) Finland.

The video, directed by Scottish-born Paul Boyd, who had worked with INXS, was distinctly weird – a garishly coloured pot-pourri, in which Kylie, in six different guises, invited us to dial in and confide in her. It was slightly sinister and contained no cute skipping and jumping. It was one of those videos that demanded that you play it again to try to work out what it was all about. The song itself might have appeared mellow and mature on first listen, but on the second and third hearing it became more hypnotic, edgier and trancelike – perfect for the dance club audience that Kylie was trying to reach.

She spent the summer prior to the release of 'Confide In Me' in Queensland and Bangkok, pretending to be a martial-arts expert for her second feature film, *Street Fighter*, starring Jean-Claude Van Damme. The director, Steven de Souza, had seen Kylie on a magazine cover displaying THE 30 MOST BEAUTIFUL PEOPLE IN THE WORLD and for some reason decided she would be perfect for the role.

The film was based on a popular video game. Kylie played a character called Cammy, a British intelligence officer, master of surveillance and lieutenant to Van Damme's Colonel Guile. It was a curious choice of film for Kylie – hardly a major role at a time when she was embarking on a period of much greater personal creativity. This was starlet stuff, although it did have the advantage of being filmed in Australia and Thailand. Kylie had to take martial-arts lessons, in particular kick boxing, in order to make believable the notion of her petite frame as a lethal weapon. She also had to pump iron, resulting in a temporary inflation of her upper torso.

Kylie and Van Damme, who is not much taller than she is, didn't really excite in the film, although it did reasonably well at the box office, thanks to the actor's loyal fans. In the US, it took close to $100 million. One thing that Van Damme did do for Kylie was teach her an exercise for maintaining a pert bottom by squeezing the butt cheeks together. She was very much in awe of the Belgian's backside, which she thought defied gravity – as her own quite obviously still does, even though she always maintains that she doesn't work out.

Quite what Kylie thought she was doing dressed up in battle fatigues, shooting a bazooka, is a mystery. Years later, her revealing comment on the film was, 'It seemed like a good idea at the time.' Kylie remains a film star waiting to happen, which is a pity, because four years earlier, *The Delinquents* revealed the promise of better things ahead.

Kylie is very different from other female pop stars who have tried to move their celebrity up a notch by making a successful movie. She actually *was* an actress and could reasonably have been expected to make some half-decent films. Being a pop star doesn't guarantee movie stardom. Mariah Carey, the Spice Girls and Britney Spears are just three who stalled at their first attempt. In modern times, only Oscar-winner Cher has a portfolio to be proud of, although Jennifer Lopez has made some very watchable films.

And then there's Madonna. By the time Kylie began shooting *Street Fighter*, Madonna had already made eleven films, five of them in the leading role. Perhaps Madonna and Kylie share the same problem: they can never shake off their pop icon status to suspend the audience's disbelief, so essential for a movie. Madonna is always Madonna and Kylie is always Kylie. They are simply too big to be movie stars.

Street Fighter was a distinctly weird choice for Kylie, even if she was following Madonna's lead in taking supporting roles, but she has never professed to have any belief in her acting abilities. She is always complaining in interviews about nerves, insecurities and lack of confidence. Unlike her music career, her movie path had no apparent overall strategy or purpose. The original idea seems to have been nothing more than a desire to make her even more famous and to turn a television star into an international movie star. But *Street Fighter* wasn't even a stepping stone on the Yellow Brick Road. Ironically, considering she was by far the biggest name in *Neighbours*, two other much more minor actors in the soap went on to become major figures in Hollywood: Russell Crowe and Guy Pearce.

The sting in the tale for Kylie regarding her *Street Fighter* experience didn't happen for nearly twenty years, when Van Damme ungallantly revealed they had had an affair while filming. He told the *Guardian* all about it: 'I was in Thailand, we had an affair. Sweet kiss, beautiful lovemaking. It would be abnormal not to have had an affair, she's so beautiful and she was there in front of me every day with a beautiful smile, simpatico, so charming, she wasn't acting like a big star. I knew Thailand very well, so I showed her my Thailand. She's a great lady.'

Kylie hasn't commented on this 'frivolity', but Van Damme doesn't conform to her usual taste in men. When the film came out, she said, 'He's not really my type but on a general fanciable scale, I'd say he was a seven,' which hardly suggests she was bowled over. The Australian former model-turned-actor Mark Gerber certainly did catch her eye when she saw him in the film *Sirens*, which starred Hugh Grant and Elle Macpherson. He bore a passing resemblance to Zane O'Donnell, and had also revealed a prodigious endowment when he stripped off in the movie in his role as a stablehand.

Kylie boldly rang him up after seeing the film, and discovered that he was visiting London. She suggested they go to the launch party of fashion designer Donna Karan's shop in Conduit Street, and they hit it off. When Kylie went back to Australia for a visit, they got together. The romance amounted to little more than a holiday dalliance. They were seen at various social events around Sydney, including gigs for his band Flaming Boa, at which Kylie briefly took on the role of enthusiastic rock chick. But their affair foundered when she left Australia to fulfil more important commitments. Rarely for her, Kylie commented on the relationship: 'It's a long-distance romance and at the moment my career is at the forefront of everything I do. Any relationship is secondary.' These are thought-provoking words indeed.

It's disappointing that Kylie chose to make *Street Fighter* at a time when her own pop videos were so imaginative and inspiringly artistic. The follow-up to 'Confide In Me' was arguably her finest to date. For 'Put Yourself In My Place', she had to perform a striptease in space. Kylie has never been shy about removing her clothes for the sake of her art. The video is one of her favourites, even though she had to bear two days of filming strapped into a series of wires and pullies to give the illusion that she was removing her spacesuit while she floated about weightless. She suffered for her art.

The video, shot in gaudy, almost psychedelic colours, was based on the opening scene of the famous sixties sci-fi film *Barbarella*, which starred Jane Fonda. Quite what this had to do with the song, which was a plaintive appeal to a former lover who had fallen for someone else, is not exactly clear. It could have been about Michael Hutchence, but Kylie didn't write this particular lyric.

While the video would make anyone's list of Kylie's top ten and became one of the most popular of her songs live, the single only peaked at number eleven in November 1994; the album made it to number four. The reviews were generally positive, appreciating that Kylie had moved on to the second stage of her career. Chris True, at AllMusic online, observed, 'From the first notes of the opener "Confide In Me", you know this is not the teen pop queen of old. Kylie wanted to sound grown up, and she pulls it off with ease.'

While Kylie's earlier four albums encourage a feeling of nostalgia if listened to today, *Kylie Minogue* hasn't dated at all. When *Digital Spy* revisited it in 2010, Nick Levine wrote that it had genuine strength in depth: 'Cohesive, classy and – much like KM herself – remarkably unmarked by the passing years.'

12

A Cathartic Moment

While Kylie was understandably miffed at critics and commentators always comparing her to Madonna, she should have been flattered: nobody else was being mentioned in the same breath as the apparently ageless superstar. Some of the comparisons were rather bitchy, in particular one in the now defunct *Sky* magazine: 'When Kylie bares all, she shows us merely that she has nothing to show. Kylie is trying to follow Madonna – she bared all, thus Kylie must. But where Madonna understands the game, Kylie doesn't. Madonna's a tough egg, a control freak who manipulates her own image in order to manipulate us. Basically, Kylie isn't sex.' Just what Kylie had done to provoke such unkind observations about her sex appeal is a mystery, but they would appear absurd.

The two women did have very different sorts of desirability. A Madonna fantasy is what she might do to you; a Kylie fantasy is what you might do to her. Irvine Welsh, the author of *Trainspotting*, wrote a short story in 1994, entitled 'When the Debris Meets the Sea', about four celebrity women who lounge around a Santa Monica beach-house and lust after unattainable Edinburgh manual workers ('schemies', he called them). They are Kylie, Madonna, Victoria Principal and Kim Basinger. At one point, his Kylie fantasizes about replacing the beloved dog of a Scottish removal man, wishing that she were the animal, wearing a collar and tied to his arm. Welsh, who is proud to proclaim himself one of Kylie's original fans, was more than impressed that she didn't attempt to sue him.

Madonna had one important edge over Kylie for many years – a sense of irony. She once said, 'I love irony. I like the way things can be taken on different levels.' She was talking about one of her first hits, 'Like A Virgin', and the fact that it was considered provocative at the time. Kylie didn't reach an understanding with irony until after her unexpected collaboration with Nick Cave in the mid-nineties. Embracing irony was an essential part of her coolification. It's all about maturity and worldliness. 'I'm tough, I'm ambitious and I know exactly what I want.' That is a quote from Madonna, but it could just as easily have come from Kylie, when she became more self-aware, surrounding herself with cutting-edge talents who demanded that she stretch herself personally and artistically.

Kylie was at Michael Hutchence's Chelsea house, not far from her own, one evening when the phone rang. After the trauma of their break-up had eased, the two of them had formed a lasting friendship. Nick Cave was on the line. Cave was a recovering heroin addict and a genuine original in the world of contemporary culture. He was great friends with Michael and phoned him for Kylie's number because he had written a song with her in mind and wanted her to hear it. She knew who he was, because Michael had mentioned him many times, but she didn't know his music. They chatted easily and she promised to listen to a demo he would arrange to send over for her.

They formed an odd-looking partnership. Nick Cave was tall and lanky with long black hair. He was known as the 'Prince of Darkness' or 'King of the Goths', both sobriquets he hated. Kylie was the petite popsicle who was in the process of turning herself into a sex bomb. While she was belting out 'The Loco-Motion' and 'I Should Be So Lucky', he had been in rehab for his heroin addiction and had a reputation as a mercurial and unpredictable character.

What Kylie didn't know was that Nick had written several songs for her over the years but had never contacted her about them because they had never seemed quite right. He explained to *NME*, 'I've known her stuff since she started, and I was always struck by how uncynical she seemed to be about things. Apart from her basic charm, she seemed very open and honest. I saw her and thought I would like to do a song with her, something kind of brooding with her.'

While the rest of the world thought 'Better The Devil You Know' was a classic pop song, Cave discovered hidden poetic meaning in the combination of Kylie's vocal innocence and a dark lyric describing a flawed, abusive love. He thought it a harrowing portrait of humanity, which could be likened to the Old Testament psalms.

If 'Confide In Me' and 'Put Yourself In My Place' gave some impetus to Kylie's search for credibility, then her alliance with Nick Cave gave her the means to challenge public perception. The real Kylie loves to surprise and shock – something she achieved at the premiere for *The Delinquents* on Michael Hutchence's arm and when she stripped for the video of 'Put Yourself In My Place'. She has always had a streak of exhibitionism but, until she fell under the influence of Nick Cave, she had apparently accepted limitations that in reality didn't exist. There were no limits for this new Kylie Minogue.

Cave came from a middle-class, well-educated Australian family and an environment where he was more likely to have Shakespeare as a bedtime story than *Thomas the Tank Engine*. His father was a teacher and his mother a librarian. They sought to broaden their son's horizons beyond the small town of Warracknabeal, about two hundred miles north-west of Melbourne, where he was born. They sent him off to boarding school in Melbourne before eventually moving to the city suburb of Murrumbeena when he was fourteen. Murrumbeena is only about seven miles from Surrey Hills, but Cave is ten years older than Kylie, so their paths never crossed as teenagers.

While at Caulfield Grammar School, he formed a band with friends that would later become The Boys Next Door. He had planned a career as an artist but failed his art college course at a time when he was going through a troubled phase. His father was killed in a car crash when he was nineteen. The same day, his mother was bailing him out of a police station on a charge of burglary. He turned more to music after that. The Boys Next Door released one album before changing their name to The Birthday Party and moving to London in 1980. The band had a brand of hip nonconformity that Hutchence, in particular, sought to emulate. The INXS singer may have been outrageous when he met Kylie, but he was shy the first time he was introduced to one of his heroes. Cave was dangerously cool, a charismatic quality that Kylie finds so attractive in men.

When the band split up, Cave moved to West Berlin, which in the eighties was at the forefront of experimental European culture. By 1984, a new line-up was formed, the now legendary Nick Cave and The Bad Seeds, which may have been a reference to the Parable of the Sower in the Gospel of St Matthew. Cave had been influenced by the Bible throughout his Anglican upbringing. In the eighties, he revealed his gift for poetry in his song lyrics but, in 1989, he expanded his writing to include a novel entitled *And the Ass Saw the Angel*, described by Michel Faber in the *Guardian* as 'an explosion of linguistic brio and Gothic grotesquery, horrifying, funny and tragic'.

Of more significant appeal to a wider audience was the beautiful 1987 Wim Wenders film *Wings of Desire*, which featured two of Cave's songs, 'The Carny' and the pulsating 'From Her To Eternity', performed with The Bad Seeds, who also made a cameo appearance on-screen. The highly acclaimed movie, about an angel who falls in love on earth, remained a favourite of Kylie's after she was first persuaded to see it by Hutchence.

Cave branched into film a year later, when he produced the drama *Ghosts. . . of the Civil Dead*, set in the Central Industrial Prison. He also co-wrote the soundtrack and starred as Maynard, a psychopathic inmate. It is a thoughtful indictment of the way society is controlled.

Everything Nick Cave was involved in challenged the viewer, the listener, the reader and the participant. That is what Michael Hutchence and Kylie Minogue found so appealing. Kylie has freely acknowledged that she is in awe of him. 'I think Nick Cave is wonderful,' she has said simply. She found him 'mild and gentle', making him sound more like a washing-up liquid than a cutting-edge talent.

Spencer Bright observed, 'Cave is aptly named, inhabiting a twilight world somewhere between William Faulkner and William Burroughs. He is an intellectual with a grim take on life and death, filling his songs with apocalyptic characters and incidents. There's tons of murder and lust, revenge and retribution in his songs.'

'Where The Wild Roses Grow' was certainly one of those. He wrote it for his 1995 album, *Murder Ballads*, which featured tracks dealing exclusively with murder. Kylie's song, which had a country feel to it, was a duet, a haunting dialogue between a killer (Cave) and his victim (Kylie). He bludgeons her to death with a rock.

The song was so different from anything Kylie had previously been involved in that Cave acknowledged it 'was a dangerous song for her to sing'. The finished article worked brilliantly, with Cave's Scott Walker-style baritone contrasting powerfully with Kylie's brittle vocal. The video attracted more attention than the atmospheric song, certainly at the *Daily Mirror*. Its headline screamed KYLIE STRIPS IN SATAN VIDEO and, underneath, the sub-heading 'She's fondled by singer Cave'.

It was a little more artistic than that. Kylie is seen floating in a stream in the pale repose of a dead Ophelia. Nick is crouching over her, bloody rock in hand, gently caressing her breast. Kylie loved it, confessing that she did indeed have a darker side to her and much admired the shot of Nick washing the blood off his hands: 'It's very Shakespearean and it adds darkness to it and a beauty. I love the colour of blood.' She didn't bat an eye when he suggested it would be even better if a snake slithered across her body. She found the strange sensation 'quite nice after a while'.

The publicity from the video did the trick and 'Where The Wild Roses Grow' reached number eleven in the charts. It was Kylie's biggest hit in the UK between July 1995 and July 2000, when 'Spinning Around' announced she was back. It did even better in Australia, peaking at number two. Over the years, Kylie has often referred to the track as her favourite among all her recordings.

Murder Ballads received outstanding reviews when it was released in February 1996 and reached number eight in the UK album charts. *Rolling Stone* magazine thought the duet with Kylie was the album's zenith, 'underscoring the link between sex and death'. She also featured on the album's finale, a cover of the Bob Dylan song 'Death Is Not the End', in which she sang a verse along with other artists, including Shane MacGowan and PJ Harvey. It's the only song in which no one gets killed. Nick explained, 'It's on there because we murdered it.'

Kylie wouldn't have dared to show her face at the Poetry Olympics at the Royal Albert Hall in July 1996 without Nick's support. He persuaded her that it would be good for her to face her past and confront her demons. She was unbilled, which was a wise precaution as it kept the cameras away from what might have been a humiliating experience. She stood in the wings, waif-like, wearing green tracksuit bottoms and a clashing purple T-shirt on which there was a sticker with her name on it. She was as scruffy as an unmade bed and wore no make-up. On stage a white-haired old man with a long beard was reading poetry in Braille. She was having second, third and fourth thoughts about taking her turn and whispered to Nick, 'God's on stage. How can we follow that?'

Eventually, it was her turn, and Nick literally had to push his poetry protégé on stage. Apprehensively, she stood in front of the microphone and began, 'In my imagination. . .' It was the start of 'I Should Be So Lucky' and Kylie, with no musical accompaniment whatsoever, spoke the complete lyric to her biggest-selling song. It was daring, courageous and took the audience's breath away. The brief recital was also a defining moment in Kylie's career, because it allowed her to embrace her past and gave her the confidence to push herself forward. Confidence has always been Kylie's drug of choice. She told Sharon O'Connell of *The Times*, 'It was really a cathartic moment for me. I felt like I was face to face with the young girl who was once me.'

She admitted that she had done none of her normal preparation for a live performance that night; she didn't put on the 'ego jacket' that Michael Hutchence had told her always to wear. Kylie remained unsure about the whole thing until she was actually out there, saying the words that she had sung a thousand times. Up until this night, she had distanced herself from her days at The Hit Factory, yet here she was, shouting to the world that this was part of her career and part of her. The extra ingredient of reciting the words in this fashion was that, without the bouncing melody, they took on an ironic meaning.

It was a triumph. Afterwards, Kylie told *Cleo* magazine in Australia, 'People love to pigeon-hole you, no matter what you do. They place a box over you and you can't get out of it, but I have been able to stretch it a little, to lift up one side and peep out, to shuffle it here and there. I don't know how I have done it. I was supposed to be a one-hit wonder.'

The constraints imposed by misguided public perception was the common ground between Kylie and Nick Cave. It gave them an unlikely connection. Nick observed, 'I think Kylie is as burdened by her image as I am, and I recognize and sympathize with that.'

They hit it off personally as well as professionally, although there was never any question of romance between the two. Nick and Michael continued to be pals and for a while were business partners in The Portobello Café, which was one of the most fashionable places in West London. Kylie was often there and in other Notting

Hill spots in the mid-nineties, even though she still lived in Chelsea. When Michael had a daughter, Heavenly Hiraani Tiger Lily, with television presenter Paula Yates, in 1996, he asked his mate Nick Cave to be godfather.

Kylie's friendship with Nick has continued over the years. Like Eric Clapton and Keith Richard, he has come through his heroin addiction to achieve almost venerable status. He is still touring and making new albums, enjoying a reputation as one of music's great survivors. Kylie made a guest appearance on stage with Nick and The Bad Seeds at the Koko club in London in November 2013. They sang 'Where The Wild Roses Grow' to much acclaim. The *Independent* observed that 'he's incapable of writing a bad song', and concluded, 'Where maturity has brought about a decline in so many brilliant careers, 56-year-old Cave simply gets better and better.'

The debt that Kylie owes to her alliance with Nick is that he truly made her cool. The coolification of Kylie may or may not have begun with Michael Hutchence, but by the mid-nineties there was an around-the-block queue of credible artists wanting to work with her. One of them was a former Australian rock musician called Kimble Rendall, who had branched out into television and videos and wanted Kylie to star in a short art-house film called *Hayride To Hell*. Rendall had been a punk guitarist under the name of Dag Rattler before finding lasting fame in Australia in the band Hoodoo Gurus.

Kylie jumped at the chance because it was only a week's work in Sydney but meant that she could take an extended break in the Australian sun in early 1995, when she was still going out with Mark Gerber. *Hayride To Hell* was a short, strange, eleven-minute film, in which she played 'The Girl' who begs a salesman called George Weygate to help her. Her co-star was the acclaimed Australian stage actor Richard Roxburgh, then just starting out on an illustrious movie career. He was a significant step up from the wooden Van Damme.

In some ways, *Hayride To Hell* was little more than an extended video. Kylie, darkly brunette for a change, tells Weygate she is diabetic and insists that he give her a lift to her apartment. She goes inside but faints in the elevator, where she is found by Weygate. She wakes up and hits him with a teddy bear, shouting, 'What the f*** have you done with my things? Where are my things, you shit?' It is challengingly arty, which was the attraction for Kylie. The important thing is that it promoted a different Kylie at a time when she was diversifying. This was no starlet fodder. She achieved a much greater sense of professional pride from this eleven-minute short than from both of her Hollywood films combined.

The second of those Hollywood films was far worse than *Street Fighter*. It would be completely wrong to suggest that she had a Midas touch where her career was concerned at this point. She seemed to be employing a scatter-gun technique and some of her decisions missed the target by a long way – *Bio-Dome* was one of those. It was a film that redefined the term 'turkey'. Critic John Lavin, in *Movie Magazine International*, dismissed it as the 'biggest waste of celluloid space I have ever witnessed'.

It was allegedly a comedy, starring Jewish comedian Pauly Shore, whose brand of idiot, banana-skin humour was popular in the US in the early nineties. *Bio-Dome* was very much his film, although it co-starred the actor Stephen Baldwin. Kylie played one of the straight roles, an oceanographer called Dr Petra von Kant, while the two male leads played two 'goofy guys' who mistake a bio-dome – an eco-research facility – for a shopping mall. And the fun starts there.

For once, it wasn't just the newspapers that disliked it. The *Daily Mirror* may have said it was 'a film to be avoided like the plague', but even the normally phlegmatic Ron Minogue declared it was 'diabolical'. Ron always chose his words carefully, so Kylie sat up and took notice whenever he gave something the thumbs down. Moviegoers agreed, and the film took $2 million less at the box office than it cost to make. Shore's Hollywood career never recovered and Kylie decided it was time to call a halt to her attempts to break through there. She was disappointed and disillusioned with the way these American movies shoved women into tight hot pants or short skirts and paraded them from one scene to another with very little point to their existence. This might work successfully in a Kylie video but becomes threadbare when stretched to an hour and a half. She had wanted US exposure and, once again, had been left in the dark room. She had made a mistake twice and she wasn't about to make it three strikes.

Away from the set, she found Pauly Shore diverting, although superficially it's hard to see why. Until he got together with Kylie, his best-known girlfriend had been a porn queen called Savannah, who committed suicide. He and Kylie dated for about four months after filming had finished, in the Bahamas and California. She described it as 'hanging out' and ditched the comic when she fell under the spell of a larger-than-life Frenchman.

13

Impossible to Predict

Stéphane Sednaoui, a Parisian with Egyptian ancestry, was spontaneous and alarming. For the second time in her life, Kylie had met
someone who took her breath away not because of his looks but
through the raw power of his creative personality. Stéphane was certainly not traditionally handsome. But, just as Michael Hutchence
had done, he made an instant impression on her by behaving outra-
geously. They met at a party in an East End warehouse thrown by
the pop culture magazine *The Face*. He didn't make a risqué suggestion, but he did lift Kylie up above his head and whirl her around,
which certainly caught her attention. 'I'm attracted,' she said, 'but to
what I don't know.'

William Baker described him as a 'creative powerhouse'. It was
the middle of 1995 and Kylie was entering her most creative phase,
encouraged by rock poet Nick Cave. Stéphane became the driving
force of that phase and, with Cave, one of the two key mentors of
Kylie's middle period.

Stéphane came from a multimedia background. His mother was
a photographic agent, his aunt a painter and his uncle a jazz musician. He is a creative talent who sees no limits to his artistic world.
He was a photojournalist who covered the Romanian Revolution of
1989, a fashion photographer for *Vogue* and a video director. One

claim to fame was a series of pictures he took of the ill-fated Kurt Cobain, laughing.

When Kylie met Stéphane, his reputation as an experimental videographer was growing, boosted by his alliance with Madonna. Kylie had seen and been impressed with his video for Madonna's 1993 top-ten hit 'Fever'. Sednaoui's company, Clip-Video, was one of the most sought-after in the nineties. He worked with the Red Hot Chili Peppers, The Smashing Pumpkins, Tricky, U2, Tina Turner and Alanis Morissette. He directed Björk, in the video of her classic 'Big Time Sensuality', dancing on the back of a flatbed trailer as it weaves its way through Manhattan. The weird and unpredictable Icelandic singer was his most famous girlfriend before Kylie. She said of him, 'He has an effect on people like a tidal wave.' One newspaper suggested he favoured sexual encounters in public places – something not unfamiliar to Kylie. His impact on her was dramatic. She decided to drop everything and drive with him across America. Amusingly, her plane crossed mid-Atlantic with one carrying Pauly Shore, who was flying to London to see her. He got the message that their relationship was over.

Kylie and Stéphane had been on just two dates, yet here she was emulating Jack Kerouac's *On the Road* journey with a man she barely knew. They hired a Pontiac Trans Am sports car. She loved every minute and told *Cosmopolitan* magazine, 'We were driving from town to town, desert to desert, staying in $20-a-night motel rooms. We had greasy breakfasts in roadside cafes and talked to truckers for hours about their lives. I was truly anonymous and free to be me.'

By the end of the trip, Kylie was enamoured: 'We were stuck in a car together for three weeks and we really bonded. We're in love.' On the tri, Sednaoui took many pictures, but one of Kylie gazing out from their silver convertible during a stop in North Carolina encapsulated the vulnerable, natural look that she favoured during her time with Stéphane. It was a naked look.

They also travelled to the Far East, where he introduced her to Asian culture and, in particular, a new wave of Japanese artists and photographers, including Nobuyoshi Araki, famous for his depictions of women, Stéphane's former lover Björk in particular. Stéphane took a series of photographs during this period of their relationship in which Kylie seemed to be modelling every imaginable design of kimono.

The couple travelled extensively during their time together – to Australia, Hong Kong, Tokyo, Seoul, Los Angeles and between their respective houses in Paris and London. Kylie did take Stéphane home to meet her parents in Melbourne, but we will never know what Ron Minogue made of the avant-garde Frenchman, then sporting an interesting Mohican haircut. They were pictured splashing around in the surf on Bondi Beach in Sydney, and slipped away for a romantic break in Hawaii, where at least one magazine was convinced that Stéphane had popped the question. It was all a great adventure for Kylie. But they were also apart a good deal, and she became addicted to her computer, vainly trying to conduct a relationship using the messaging and chat mechanisms that existed before Facebook.

Stéphane encouraged her to see things differently. He was a tough critic, armed with traditional Gallic bluntness that the oversensitive might mistake for rudeness. Kylie trusted his judgement and looked to him for encouragement and direction, particularly when it came for her next music project. She explained to *NME* what she hoped to achieve: 'I would like to put myself in an experiment. You know you've got the Bosnian compilation [the 1995 War Child charity disc *The Help Album*] where the common denominator is the theme of the album? Well, I'd like to make the common denominator myself and see what a load of different producers and artists can do for me.'

Kylie realized that she had hit upon a good formula with 'Confide In Me' and wanted to develop her working relationship with Brothers In Rhythm. As a result, she found herself sharing a modest terraced house with them, across the road from Peter Gabriel's Real World recording studios in Box, Wiltshire, about five miles from Bath. Dave Seaman recalled how Kylie had developed since their first collaboration: 'She came with a lot of ideas. I mean most of the songs were instigated by her. I think she was growing as a person and was moving more into the Indie Kylie stage as people called it. She very much wanted to get more involved in the writing process.'

Kylie was so consumed with that process that she was living and breathing her music for the three weeks or so she spent in the West Country. She would work in the studio until dinner-time and after eating would disappear up to her room, where she would spend the rest of the evening on her laptop or on the phone to Stéphane, creating lyrics and melodies for the next day. Her new boyfriend had a huge effect on her self-belief. If Nick Cave had given her the means to embrace her past, then Stéphane Sednaoui gave her the confidence to develop her own vision of her future.

It wasn't all work and no play. The residential aspect of studio life made for a relaxed atmosphere. The band Black Grape were also recording there and their larger-than-life singer Shaun Ryder drifted in to chat to Kylie armed with a couple of cans of Boddingtons. She loved meeting people like Shaun, who brought a big personality to the table. 'She was very personable and open to building friendships,' observed Dave. 'She was a pleasure to be around but she was very professional when the job needed to be done.'

Each morning, Kylie would present them with her labours from the night before. Dave remembered, 'It was a song a day really in terms of lyrical ideas. She would write the lyrics down and, as a natural singer, she would sing her ideas of how it might go melodically. We were obviously trying to do the production backing tracks with them and find a suitable style for each one as we were demo-ing them all.'

She wasn't coming downstairs in the mornings with variations on the theme of being lucky or crooning love songs. Hers was a darkly autobiographic song sheet that reveals far more about Kylie than any interview in a glossy magazine or a newspaper. Her standard replies to the same old questions about life, love, marriage and babies seldom rise above the mildly interesting. Here, though, the songs were complex, serious, introspective and challenging – none more so than 'Dreams', which chronicled the dreams of an 'impossible princess' wanting to 'give into pleasure with no boundaries'.

The first song she worked on with Steve Anderson and Dave Seaman at Real World was called 'You're The One', which didn't make it onto the album but stayed on the back burner until Kylie eventually recorded it and performed it on the *Anti Tour 2012*, a collection of B-sides and unreleased tracks. The more famous compositions from the Box sessions, 'Too Far', 'Did It Again', 'Limbo' and 'Cowboy Style', stand the test of the time.

Initially, deConstruction had very much taken a back seat with the new album, and let Kylie develop it as she wanted. Pete Hadfield, the label's creative force as head of A & R, was going through a spell of ill health that lasted nearly a year. When he returned to the fray, he was concerned that there was no obvious single among the songs she had written with Brothers In Rhythm. The original release date had been set for January 1997 but was put back to bring in other collaborators to work with Kylie. Perhaps deConstruction was being influenced by its alliance with the commercially minded BMG group. Or perhaps everybody involved just wanted the album to be too perfect.

Kylie could be quite cautious sometimes, balancing crowd-pleasing with artistic daring. The following month, she appeared in a special Comic Relief episode of *Men Behaving Badly*, which was hugely popular and had just been voted best sitcom in BBC history. It was arguably the most successful of the 'new lad' comedies and this particular episode, entitled 'Men Behaving Very Badly Indeed', featured Kylie playing herself. The two 'heroes', Gary (Martin Clunes) and Tony (Neil Morrissey), shared an all-consuming lust for

Kylie that had been a running joke in the series. In this particular episode, she turns up at their flat and they don't recognize her. Unlike *Bio-Dome*, it was genuinely funny.

Much more in keeping with the new 'multimedia Kylie' was her next film project, a collaboration with the contemporary artist and photographer Sam Taylor-Wood. It was a three-minute film, entitled *Misfit*, commissioned by the BBC, and was more a work of art than a traditional cinematic experience. Taylor-Wood, who coincidentally would be nominated for the Turner Prize in 1998, was inspired by Kylie's beautiful androgyny. She portrayed Kylie as sexually ambiguous, with boyish red hair, posing in front of a dark burgundy drape, and challenged the audience by having her sing, not with her own voice but that of Alessandro Moreschi, the celebrated castrato. 'Incipit Lamentatio' (1904) is a rare surviving recording of Moreschi who, like many other talented boy sopranos, paid a high price to retain that voice as an adult. The media unsurprisingly focused on the fact that Kylie was 'naked', which was a complete exaggeration. She is topless but filmed from the side with her right arm shielding her breasts. Taylor-Wood wanted Kylie to look like something out of a Caravaggio painting.

Taylor-Wood was, and remains, very influential in the London art scene, not least because of her first marriage to art dealer Jay Jopling. He owns the White Cube galleries, and represented a *Who's Who* of the most talked-about modern British artists, including his wife, Tracey Emin and Damien Hirst. It did Kylie no harm at all to be associated with so celebrated a circle.

Taylor-Wood and Jopling divorced in 2008, but she has remained at the forefront of contemporary art, directing the acclaimed movie *Nowhere Boy*, about the early life of John Lennon, as well as being chosen to direct the film adaptation of *Fifty Shades of Grey*. She is a great admirer of Kylie, memorably describing her as a 'multi-faceted chameleon woman'. Indeed, Kylie's secret for attracting the most original artists of a generation to work with her is her ability to change. That doesn't mean that she brings nothing to the party – on the contrary, her creativity is encouraged by those around her.

If the momentum from the Box sessions had been maintained, then the outcome for her second deConstruction offering might have been entirely different. Instead Kylie became sidetracked, pulled in a number of creative directions. She wanted that, but it also led to a disastrous delay in the album's release. She decided on a number of other fashionable alliances in addition to Brothers In Rhythm. She enlisted Rob Dougan, aka Clubbed To Death, Ingo Vauk and ex-Soft Cell instrumentalist Dave Ball. Some of the collaborations were the result of rock-style spontaneity: 'I have a friend called Skinny who was playing Clubbed To Death around the house. I loved it and, out of the blue, he said he knew the guy. . .'

The best-known collaboration on the album was with the revered Welsh band Manic Street Preachers. They had long been admirers of Kylie – bassist Nicky Wire once claimed to have been beaten up for wearing a Kylie T-shirt at school. She met vocalist James Dean Bradfield at an awards ceremony and discovered that a few years earlier, in 1991, he had tried to reach her on several occasions to discuss working together. He had wanted her to sing on the vintage Manics' song 'Little Baby Nothing', about a starlet used by men, but had eventually enlisted porn star Traci Lords when he couldn't get past the 'gates of PWL heaven'.

Kylie and Bradfield decided to meet for tea at his home, and Kylie took along some cherries. She also brought a bunch of lyrics to try to persuade Bradfield to turn them into a song for the new album. In the best traditions of songwriting, Bradfield strummed a bit and suggested she leave the lyrics with him. He played her a track that he felt would suit her, which sounded to her like Tamla-Motown. She thought he was trying to discover what her tastes were. 'It was a pop moment,' she recalled.

As soon as the outside world heard of the collaboration between

Kylie and Bradfield, she was dubbed Indie Kylie, another of those labels she disliked. The result of that first meeting was that Bradfield sent her a demo of 'I Don't Need Anyone', which Kylie loved. She found it refreshing and so different from what she had been working on before. Bradfield asked for some more words and then mixed two sets of her lyrics into one for 'Some Kind Of Bliss', a rocky pop classic. Both tracks were unmistakably Manics – guitars exploding like squibs around an anthemic melody.

The magazine added that the song was a 'bridge to prepare Minogue's vast audience for a smorgasbord of styles and sounds'. The question would be: was it a bridge too far for her fans? Whatever the popularity of the Manics, these two songs weren't recognizable as Kylie tracks. They didn't build on the universal acceptance of 'Confide In Me' as her mid-nineties sound. The stand-out track amid the new material is, by common consent, 'Too Far', which features Kylie speed-whispering over a drum-'n'-bass beat. Certainly, Steve Anderson and Dave Seaman thought it was the best.

The album's release was put back until September 1997. Kylie decided to call it *Impossible Princess*. That wasn't a deliberate piece of self-deprecation, although it might be considered an ironic nod to her reputation as 'the girl on the show pony at the circus'. It actually came from the title of a volume of poetry by Billy Childish, another hugely influential figure of the time, whose work spanned a spectrum of the arts, including music and painting. Nick Cave had given her the book and it was called *Poems to Break the Harts of Impossible Princesses*.

Stéphane, meanwhile, designed and photographed the artwork for the album. The plans were ambitious: a specially shot 3-D cover that would represent the three-dimensional Kylie that was revealed on this album. It was a better idea in theory than in practice because shooting took a week and was a complete pain. She had to pose as still as stone for hours while Stéphane set up and used a series of static cameras. Even the Mona Lisa would have been scowling. At the end of it, Kylie was thoroughly fed up. Perhaps it was a watershed moment in the relationship with Stéphane: he was simply exhausting and she was tired out.

Commentators in the newspapers were worried about the way she was losing weight and looking dreadful, suggesting that past problems with anorexia had resurfaced. One picture prompted the *Daily Mail* to observe: 'It wasn't just the mousey hair – cut short and scrunched on top of her head – or the absence of make-up. What really shocked was how painfully thin, even ill, Kylie looked . . .' In the picture, Sednaoui, wearing a pair of battered combat trousers, had tightened his hoodie close to his face to expose a single, staring eye. He laughed, 'It will be funny. People will think "who is that crazy guy that Kylie's going out with"?' He was right. They did think that, but they also wondered why she was.

Despite teetering on the edge of exhaustion, Kylie was ready to throw herself into promoting the new album. In the end it was decided that 'Some Kind Of Bliss' would be the lead single in September 1997. Kylie had favoured releasing 'Limbo', a more overt dance track with an incessant beat, which sounded a bit like Republica, the alternative dance band that were also on deConstruction, but for once on this project Kylie was overruled. 'Some Kind Of Bliss' was a flop. It was her first release since the 'Wild Roses' collaboration two years earlier, so the outcome was very disappointing – not least for her record company. Bradfield was apologetic, blaming himself: 'I loved her voice, got on with her and I am embarrassed that I failed her.' The track peaked at a lowly twenty-two on the UK charts and fared even worse in Australia, where the heartland of Kylie's fan base seemed to have deserted her – it only managed a pitiful number twenty-seven. This was not what everyone had waited two years for.

Some critics walloped 'Some Kind Of Bliss'. *NME* called it 'supremely irritating' and declared, 'Kylie belts out the lyrics like she's reading from an autocue. Any soul is lost in a slurry of bought-in brass and a ropey guitar solo that'd be more at home on a Shakin' Stevens record.' The difficulty for Kylie was that, despite the credibility she gained by her collaborations, she was still being perceived in the mainstream as the girl who launched a thousand tragic outfits. Or, even worse, as a girl next door, which in some unfair way suggested Indie Kylie was a fraud. It seemed like a return to the bad old days of Stock, Aitken and Waterman, when kicking Kylie was a national pastime.

With hindsight, releasing the Manics' track may have been a mistake, because the publicity generated by this unlikely alliance tended to overshadow the rest of the album. Steve Anderson forthrightly believes that 'Some Kind Of Bliss' was a cop-out release to satisfy the demands of the media, who wanted it to be the single. He thought 'Too Far' and 'Jump' were more representative of the album.

All the grand plans for the *Impossible Princess* album were scuppered, however, when Princess Diana died. Her death in a Paris car crash cast a shadow over the world and meant any single released at this time was likely to fail. Kylie's press campaign had already begun and she had done all sorts of interviews with magazines, as well as performed the song at the Radio 1 Roadshow in Newquay on 21 August 1997.

She had also found the time to travel to Almería in southern Spain to shoot the video for the single. Directed by the well-respected David Mould (Mouldy), it featured Kylie and the actor Dexter Fletcher as a pair of grown-up delinquents, more Bonnie and Clyde than Lola and Brownie. Kylie wore a very short turquoise dress, which she changed in a gas station toilet into tight turquoise hot pants.

Diana died on 31 August, nine days before the single's release and, despite extensive airplay, everyone was much more inclined to buy Elton John's maudlin tribute 'Candle In The Wind 1997', which accounted for 80 per cent of record sales that week. The whole marketing strategy, of a hit single setting up the release of an album, was thrown. Kylie took the bold step of agreeing to pull the plug – not least because an album entitled *Impossible Princess* didn't seem very tactful just then. She gamely said that it would have been insensitive to put the album out, so it was postponed for three months until after Christmas. 'There's no way you can prepare for something like the Princess of the country dying. It's thrown everybody,' she explained.

While it is very true that the death of Diana caused a thoroughly weird few weeks in the record industry – 'Candle In The Wind 1997' sold 1.5 million copies in the UK in its first week – it still doesn't account for why 'Some Kind Of Bliss' failed to make the top twenty. There were still twenty-one better-selling singles in the UK that week, and only one of them was a tribute to the Princess of Wales. The following week, Kylie's single dropped out of the chart altogether, which was hardly a good advertisement for the album.

There was an even worse case of excruciatingly bad timing involving Kylie. Earlier in the year, she had completed a cameo role, playing herself in a film called *Diana & Me*. Actress Toni Collette played the lead, an Australian country girl called Diana Spencer, who wins a competition in which the first prize is a trip to London and the chance to meet her namesake. That was an unfortunate plot in itself, but Kylie's role involved being pursued down the street by an unpleasant pack of paparazzi – too close to the real-life pursuit of the Princess of Wales to make comfortable viewing. *Variety* noted that the movie had an 'exceedingly dark undertow', which wasn't what was required of a romantic comedy.

The film did manage a theatrical release in Australia in December 1997, after some scenes were added, but it could never recover from circumstances beyond its control. In the UK it went straight to satellite and has barely seen the light of day since.

14

Horribilis

For Kylie, it was an autumn *horribilis*. It would be hard to imagine a more wretched series of events, both in her professional and her private life. The nadir came on a late November day in 1997, when she was awoken at 4 a.m. by a telephone ringing persistently. Calls at that time in the morning are never good news. Michael Hutchence was dead at the age of thirty-seven. He was the first person to die whom she had loved and, understandably, she was completely devastated. William Baker, her Creative Director, says in the book *Kylie: La La La*, 'Kylie felt her world had crumbled under her feet.' She was at home in London and spent the day behind locked doors.

That evening, she was scheduled to perform at G-A-Y in Charing Cross Road and everyone assumed she would cancel but she refused. The strength of her show-must-go-on philosophy was never tested more but, as William recalled, 'Kylie was humbled by death. She felt to cancel a show in front of her ever-faithful gay audience was a cop-out.' She was certain that she wanted to perform for a community that itself had experienced so much sadness and loss due to AIDS.

Michael Hutchence had been found naked, kneeling on the floor behind the door of room 524 at the fashionable Ritz-Carlton Hotel in Double Bay, Sydney. His belt was around his neck, the buckle apparently having broken under his weight as he dangled from the hook on the back of the door. There was at the time, and remains to this day, intense speculation as to the reason for his death. The most controversial is that it was an act of autoeroticism that went wrong.

The New South Wales Coroner, Derek Hand, decided a full inquest wasn't necessary. In his report, he stated, 'I am satisfied that the standard required to conclude that this death was a suicide has been reached.' Hutchence's blood contained a cocktail of cocaine, alcohol, Prozac and other prescription drugs. He was involved in a difficult custody wrangle with Bob Geldof over Paula Yates's children. One of the saddest aspects of the tragedy was that he had twice called his first serious love, Michele Bennett, but both times only connected to her answering phone. On hearing the messages and how upset he sounded, Michele rushed round to the hotel but couldn't raise him when she banged on his hotel door. Reluctantly, she left a message at reception and went home.

The untimely deaths of rock heroes seem to make time stand still: John Lennon, Kurt Cobain, Jim Morrison and Jimi Hendrix are part of a list that will forever include Michael Hutchence. If his death was suicide, it is even more distressing, because he had deserted his eighteen-month-old baby with Paula Yates, Tiger Lily. Just a short time before that fateful night, he had told journalist Sharon Klum that he 'would jump in front of a train for his daughter'. Kylie was once asked what she thought of the idea that Hutchence was in search of an orgasm – something that Prozac could sometimes inhibit. She thought it made it more bearable to think that he died for that reason rather than that he had killed himself because he was in so much pain. She didn't think we would ever know for sure.

When you are a celebrity, you are never allowed to erase a relationship – not one. Kylie would never want to forget Michael Hutchence, but for many years she scarcely gave an interview, both before and after his death, in which his name has not been mentioned. The only time they had reportedly got close following their break-up was after an INXS concert in 1994 when, at the subsequent party, they were spotted disappearing into a toilet cubicle for nearly an hour. It may have been a sexual encounter, or Michael may have just wanted to chat to Kylie while he got 'off his face' on one drug or another. She has always politely explained that Michael was a great influence on her life, and helped her to make the change from girl to woman. Many tears have been shed, some in public and many in private, but they are not bitter tears.

The most poignant reminder came on New Year's Eve 1998, when she was celebrating with Stéphane Sednaoui in the town of Whistler in Canada. They were no longer involved but she enjoyed his company. Out of the blue, an INXS record came on the radio and she heard Michael's voice once more. She exclaimed, 'Of course, you turn up now!' She has sensed him with her on several occasions since his death. Hutchence remains a strong presence in her life, a little like a guardian angel but more an intangible reassurance that life will continue to move forward if she takes control of her destiny. She told the journalist Kevin O'Sullivan, 'I don't mind talking about Michael, but please don't say I cried.'

Michael's funeral was held at St Andrew's Cathedral in Sydney. Kylie, pale and dressed in black, was quiet, dignified and did her best to support his grieving family. Nick Cave was there and, at the request of Paula Yates, sang his hauntingly beautiful composition 'Into My Arms', which he had written outside a country church in Surrey. It was a moving rendition, made truly bizarre by a man threatening to hurl himself off the balcony while Nick was singing.

It was a blazing hot day, but with masterful timing, which would have tickled Hutchence, the heavens opened and a loud crack of thunder greeted the arrival of his coffin. Kylie managed a smile at the celestial intervention. Michael Hutchence was most definitely not saintly nor was he the devil. His throwaway line that his hobby was 'corrupting Kylie' was nothing more than a sound bite. She is demonstrably a stronger, more focused individual than he ever was.

In a sad postscript, Paula Yates was found dead from a heroin over-dose at her London home in September 2000.

By the time of Michael's death, Kylie's relationship with Stéphane was finished. It seemed to come quite suddenly, although things hadn't been what they were for months. In public, Kylie had said in September, 'Stéphane is extremely inspiring. I respect his artistry – he has his own style stamped on what he does.' In November, how-ever, *Cleo* magazine declared, 'She doesn't want to talk about it, but suffice to say, there is much muttering about men behaving badly and Kylie isn't disagreeing.'

The official line is that the relationship just fizzled out and the couple have remained close friends – a familiar outcome where Kylie and past amours are concerned. Perhaps men like Hutchence and Sednaoui are too exhausting for Kylie, or perhaps her expectations are too high. Sednaoui remained in demand on the arty music scene, directing pop videos for, among others, Beck and Depeche Mode. He moved into the world of short films in the noughties. His *Walk on the Wild Side* (2005) was a powerful ten-minute film based on the famous Lou Reed song and was made in New York with the singer's cooperation. Reed even makes a cameo appearance.

In 2001, Stéphane became a father when his then model girlfriend, Laetitia Casta, the face of L'Oreal, gave birth to a baby girl, Sahteene. The beautiful Laetitia, who has the sultry looks of a young Helena Christensen, is ten years younger than Kylie and has subse-quently carved out a successful career as an actress in French films.

A couple of years after she split with Stéphane, Kylie posed for a portrait for a 1999 book of photographs. She has a mock tattoo on her arm with the names Jason, Michael and Stéphane crossed out. It was a little joke but did reveal that Kylie sees herself as a one man-at-a-time woman.

The only video Stéphane made of Kylie was for her collaboration with the Japanese-born, New York-based pop artist Towa Tei. He had achieved international fame as a DJ member of Deee-lite, whose

'Groove Is In The Heart' became an instant dance classic in 1990. He had met Kylie in 1996 and together they produced arguably her weirdest song, 'GBI: German Bold Italic'. The lyric was mad: 'My name is German Bold Italic. I am a typeface which you have never heard of before.'

Stéphane's video was even more surreal. It begins with Kylie in the bath, wearing a red bikini and a geisha headdress, asking the audience, 'Do you like my sense of style?' Then she parades around the streets of New York in full geisha regalia and gets attached to a Japanese man by a purple dog lead. This was many years before Lady Gaga raided the dressing-up box and further proof of Kylie's groundbreaking work in the nineties. The song was a minor hit in Japan on its release in 1997 but didn't surface in the UK until the following year, when it made the merest of ripples at sixty-three in the chart in October. By that time, Kylie had moved on artistically.

After the failure of 'Some Kind Of Bliss', the new strategy was to release another single from the album in the hope it would do better and help to promote a revised release date in the new year. Once more, the more obvious credentials of 'Too Far' were ignored in favour of another underrated song she had written with Steve and Dave, 'Did It Again' – another track that didn't really sound like Kylie. The result was an indie classic, a blend of sitar and electric guitar that might have found its way onto The Beatles' famous *Revolver* album.

Kylie's lyric was revealingly autobiographical, about an artist being pulled every which way as she struggles to find the right new identity. She moans that she is messed up despite having it all. The video, which backed up the theory, depicted four different Kylies – Sex Kylie, Cute Kylie, Indie Kylie and Dance Kylie. They proceed to bash each other up hilariously, as they fight for supremacy while singing the song, which closes with one of the best lines in a Kylie lyric, 'Little Miss Genius, you make it hard on yourself.' She had certainly learned to embrace irony.

The first two tracks released were probably the most indie on the album and the least representative. They gave a false impression of the overall feel and the public weren't buying into it. *Music Week* said 'Did It Again' wasn't strong enough to do much better than the modest performance of 'Some Kind Of Bliss'. That prediction proved to be right when it limped to number fourteen in the UK charts in December 1997. The planned New Year release of the album was put back again while everyone wrestled with the problem of what to call it. The author and Kylie expert Simon Sheridan thought they should have knocked off the Princess and just made it Impossible, which would have neatly summed up the whole nightmare. Instead, it was decided to rename it *Kylie Minogue*, which had already been the title of two of her previous albums and seemed a particularly pointless choice. Kylie always thought of it as *Impossible Princess* and it would subsequently return to its original title. The problem was that the album had been ready to go for months and every passing day was losing everyone money. It wouldn't have been sensible to redesign everything and spend even more money.

When *Kylie Minogue* eventually appeared in the UK in March 1998, three and a half years had passed since her last album. The long wait had driven her to distraction. The copyright on the disc still said 1997, a reminder of the length of time it had sat on the shelves of a BMG warehouse. Embarrassingly, Kylie's list of acknowledgements included a final one: 'Stéphane, merci et je t'adore.'

A third lead single, 'Breathe', had been released but did no better than the first two, despite having a more commercial, faster remix than the album version. She wrote it with Dave Ball and Ingo Vauk. It was catchy, more in tune with later Kylie than some of the other tracks. She did her best to drum up interest on TV, including appearances on *Top of the Pops* and the shortlived *Ben Elton Show*, when she performed the classic punk anthem 'Should I Stay Or Should I Go', a number one for The Clash in 1991 on reissue, when it was used in a Levi jeans ad.

There were rumours that finally 'Too Far' would be released as a last boost for *Impossible Princess*. The track enjoyed a huge club following, especially when Brothers In Rhythm produced an unofficial remix. It was unofficial in that deConstruction originally knew nothing about it, although Kylie, always up for something new, took time to redo vocals and include some ad libs. The new version never made it to the stores. There are literally a handful of copies in existence and they would fetch a fortune if they ever came up for sale.

The critics were of different minds about the album. Spencer Bright thought the record struck an attitude and a pose rather than truly reflected where Kylie was going as an individual, and so was doomed to failure. He explained, 'The chemistry was not right. And most of the material was inferior to Stock, Aitken and Waterman.' Larry Flick in *Billboard* magazine was more complimentary of 'intense groove poems like "Limbo" and "Say Hey", which saw intelligent, often self-examining words turned into timely music that darts back and forth between moody electro-funk and richly layered pop'.

Rolling Stone was nice about Kylie and observed that the album ran 'the full gamut of contemporary music: from classic pop/rock to steam train funk rock, dance songs that soar, and borderline hip hop to trip hop.' She told the magazine, revealingly, 'My music like my images is all over the place... I'm all over the place as a person.'

All the media interest would count for nothing if the public failed to respond positively. Her pride and joy tottered to number ten in the charts, her least successful album of all time. The rubbish bins are littered with the careers of successful pop stars who suddenly think they can do it all and inflict their dreadful songs and sentiments on a public that promptly goes off them. Kylie deserved a better fate.

Impossible Princess is, by some measure, the most challenging of Kylie's albums. With hindsight, it is also one of the classic records of the nineties. Dave Seaman observed, 'I may be biased but it's a forgotten gem.'

15

Intimate and Live

Kylie was heading towards thirty in a slump. The last few months of 1997 could scarcely have been worse on so many levels. Splitting with Stéphane was miserable enough without the disappointment of the *Impossible Princess* project. Kylie could usually find consolation in her private or her professional life if one or the other was going badly, but at this moment there was no good news on either front. At least she still had William Baker in her corner. He was furious at the creation of the label Indie Kylie. He agreed with Steve Anderson that far too much emphasis had been put on her collaboration with Manic Street Preachers. William declared forcefully, 'Kylie has never been, and never will be, indie.'

Her image, though, was in need of a kick up her very famous backside. With William, whom she likes to call Willie, she set about turning her fortunes around. They had become great friends and confidants. He is able to tune into her creative wavelength and shares her sense of campness. Kylie is very camp and always has been. She likes nothing better than diamanté and dressing up.

They decided to return to her roots and build on what was left of her loyal fan base. They plotted a comeback in Australia, where *Impossible Princess* had been much better received than in the UK, and they sought to re-engage her enormous gay following. From the very beginnings of her musical career, with 'The Loco-Motion' and 'I Should Be So Lucky', Kylie was adopted by the gay community of Melbourne and Sydney. Special themed evenings, when drag queens would dress up and perform as Kylie, became hugely popular.

She first came across these events on a trip back to Australia, when she was driving past The Albury, then the best-known gay club in Sydney. It was a Sunday and one of her friends mentioned that it was 'Kylie Night'. She had absolutely no idea such a thing existed and was all for going in and amazing everyone: 'I was almost the last to know about it.' She had this fantasy of herself leaping on to the bar and doing a routine from *South Pacific*. Unfortunately, she wasn't allowed in that night, because the club would have needed to put special security measures in place to handle the pandemonium that would certainly have ensued.

She did get to see the 'Kylie Show' at the Three Faces club in Melbourne on her Christmas visit home in 1993. It was the first time she had seen anyone impersonating her. She loved two performers in particular: one who wore ostrich feather pink hot pants, like those she had worn in the video for 'Shocked', and another who donned the noughts-and-crosses dress in which she had caused such a stir at *The Delinquents* premiere.

Kylie wasn't an innocent where gay culture was concerned. She had been an actress since the age of eleven and inevitably came across the usual blend of luvvies and camp thespians in the profession. She once mentioned that on *Neighbours*, for instance, both her make-up artist and hairdresser were gay, so homosexuality was hardly an eye-opener. It might have been a shock to the naive girl next door – but Kylie was never that.

It wasn't just Australian gay men who adopted Kylie: she became a downtrodden heroine for the gay community throughout the world. She has cited 1989 as the crucial year when a gay audience started supporting her and reacting against the accusations that she was both 'popular and uncool'. These attacks made her appear a victim, a key component in becoming a gay icon. In most cases, there must be tragedy in the diva's life. Kylie noted this anomaly in her status when she proclaimed, 'I am not a traditional gay icon. There's been no tragedy in my life, just my tragic outfits.'

Kylie achieved her standing through her battle to find a true identity and her own voice in a male-dominated pop world that was determined not to take her seriously. Paul Watson explored this idea in his 1999 paper about gay icons in pop. He explained, 'Gay men embrace those who represent embodied conflicts similar to their own and whose oppression explodes into a torrent of sensuality that is sublimated through their sound.' As Kylie has said, she changed her image because it was the only thing she had control over. Gay men could identify with her various incarnations and her search for a true self, especially as she presented an appealing mixture of vulnerability and fragility. Watson believed Kylie became such a powerful image for gay men because she, like they, had fled to the city to escape 'blind suburbia'. Her career has been a personal voyage of discovery, from soap star to servile singer of Stock, Aitken and Waterman songs, to a raunchier persona, and on to the unwelcome Indie Kylie and beyond.

Unintentionally, and much to Pete Waterman's surprise, the music he was producing in the late eighties hit exactly the right note with the gay market. He now acknowledges that he was making money out of the 'pink pound' but didn't realize it at the time. From their earliest number one in 1985, 'You Spin Me Round' by Dead or Alive, Stock, Aitken and Waterman employed a formula of incessantly catchy melodies and very good-looking singers, which was a perfect combination for the the gay clubs of the time. Waterman told BBC Radio 1, 'Kylie is a strange amalgam of pop and gay. We wrote songs about normal feelings – "I still love you, I don't know why". Of course she became a gay icon. She was saying things that, if you are emotionally sensitive, you feel every day of your life.'

Paul Watson elaborated on this theory by recognizing that her gay audience could relate to Kylie, as they 'shared and reflected on the betrayal and indignation that they collectively experienced by men'. This couldn't be better illustrated than by the sentiments of 'Better The Devil You Know', arguably the all-time gay favourite among Kylie's songs. Her performances at the Gay and Lesbian Mardi Gras in Sydney cemented her position of favour. In February 1994, she was the only pop star to perform. She bounced on stage wearing a pink tutu, surrounded by about thirty admiring, similarly dressed drag queens, and sang 'What Do I Have To Do', much to the delight of the 20,000-strong crowd. She had wanted to sing 'Better The Devil You Know', but that number had been commandeered by something like forty other Kylies and she had to choose something else.

Her status as a survivor in the pop world has been absolutely vital to Kylie maintaining the loyalty of her gay audience. Not for nothing is Gloria Gaynor's 'I Will Survive' an all-time classic song for both gay men and women. Kylie is slightly bemused by her appeal to a gay audience of both sexes. When she was asked by *Boyz* magazine if she got 'hit on by girls', she replied ambiguously, 'Not really, no.'

She is really chuffed though to be a gay icon. She confessed, 'They are incredibly loyal. I'm flattered that they pretty much adopted me before I even knew about it.' In return, she has always been happy to perform at gay events. At a charity show for Stonewall at the Royal Albert Hall in 1995, she reprised her duet of 'Sisters Are Doin' It For Themselves'. Her partner on this occasion wasn't Dannii but a man dressed up as Donatella Versace – Elton John at his most flamboyant.

One of the more amusing reviews of a Kylie concert pointed out that the majority of men in the audience were more interested in the embroidered stitching on her hot pants than what lay beneath. Theirs is unconditional adoration and anything that upsets this is liable to be labelled sacrilege.

Crucially, Kylie has never shunned or alienated her gay audience. In what would prove to be her revival year of 1998, when, incidentally, she had no new record releases, arguably the most important concert was her appearance at the Sydney Gay and Lesbian Mardi Gras in February. Dannii had already appeared before Kylie took to the stage to perform 'Better The Devil You Know' – 'BTDYK', as it is known at gay events – and she brought the house down, dressed in a scarlet sequinned dress and little red-devil horns, and surrounded by bare-chested male dancers and drag queens. They were all wearing horns as well. The crowd went ballistic as fireworks exploded into the night sky. This reception endorsed the view that Kylie would always be the pre-eminent gay icon of her generation.

Her experience has been completely different from that of Jason Donovan. In the Stock, Aitken and Waterman days, Jason, too, was adopted by a gay audience. He was a good-looking, muscular blond, who sang prettily of his broken heart. He was also the number-one teen idol. It was the spring of 1992, and Jason was appearing in the Andrew Lloyd Webber musical *Joseph and the Amazing Technicolor Dreamcoat*, when posters of him started appearing outside the Palladium Theatre in London with the words 'Queer as F***'. As fast as one could be pulled down, another would be put up. There was absolutely no evidence to support the assertion. Jason was the victim of a whispering campaign that was trying to force gay celebrities to admit their true sexuality.

The Face magazine, which was seriously cool, wrote about the campaign. They acknowledged that Jason wasn't gay but reprinted the poster. Jason decided to sue for defamation and immediately put himself in a no-win situation. He won the case but was ultimately the loser. If he had ignored the magazine, with its small readership relative to national newspapers, he might have sailed on with nothing more to contend with than the sort of whispers that affect a number of artists, but by fighting the case he turned the original poster into headline news. His gay audience ostracized him because he seemed to be disowning them – as if being called gay was the worst thing that could happen to a man – and his heterosexual audience thought there could be no smoke without fire. Those that were left thought he was picking on a heroic magazine. In his auto-biography *Between the Lines*, he acknowledged he had completely misjudged the situation and had made the biggest mistake of his life.

In effect, the case marked the end of his career as a pop star and he hasn't had a top-twenty record since. The newspapers took delight in stories of Jason falling over in clubs and generally behaving badly, as he sunk deep into a drug haze from which he eventually emerged after starting a family in 2000. Now he is firmly re-established as a television and stage favourite, thanks to appearances on *I'm a Celebrity . . . Get Me Out of Here*, *Strictly Come Dancing* and the stage show of *Priscilla, Queen of the Desert*.

Kylie may have needed a career boost from time to time but she has never suffered from the personal demons that so badly affected her former boyfriend. She did, however, need to build on her Gay and Lesbian Mardi Gras success with a strategy to reach a wider audience. She and William felt that camp was the way to go.

She had commitments to *Impossible Princess* in the UK and Europe, but it was decided that she should go back to live shows in her home country, where the album was selling well. It was a case of testing the waters and seeing how it went. The venues selected weren't big – most of them holding little more than 2,000 people. From the first night at the Palais Theatre in Melbourne, five days after her thirtieth birthday, it was clear the smaller shows tactic was a good one. The title of the *Intimate and Live* tour was inspired.

The idea was to present a stage show like a Las Vegas cabaret extravaganza, though admittedly one put together on a shoestring budget. This would be nothing like a normal pop concert. She drafted in Steve Anderson to produce the shows and he jumped at the new challenge. Neither he nor William had been involved in live performances before. Brothers In Rhythm had run its course, with Dave Seaman intent on pursuing a career in the lucrative DJ market at home and abroad. Steve's only condition for getting involved was banning 'The Loco-Motion' from the set list. He wasn't serious, but equally he didn't care for any song that involved moving your arms like a train.

Impossible Princess may have been her most interesting album so far, but it didn't lend itself to visually exciting presentation. It was too brooding and introspective, and not in the least Liza Minnelli. She needed to blend those tracks with the better-known ones that would get the audience out of their seats.

She began with a moody rendition of Steve's pride and joy, 'Too Far'. Dressed in black, with her hair scraped back, Kylie descended a silver staircase in impossibly high heels. She was backed by a rock band, which added to the excitement. Three guitars combined to make the experience seem rougher, more honest and, ultimately, more exciting. 'Too Far' merged into 'What Do I Have To Do' and then on to 'Some Kind Of Bliss', complete with an old-fashioned guitar solo.

William kept everything minimal, although his sense of style kicked in with the first costume change, when Kylie re-emerged underneath a glittery pink 'K' and sang 'I Should Be So Lucky' wearing a tiny, spangly showgirl's dress that revealed her perfectly proportioned legs. But she didn't just belt it out as she had a thousand times before. This was a new jazzy arrangement, a putting-on-a-show Broadway ballad, and it was thrilling. It was fun, kitsch and brilliant.

Next, she moved effortlessly into a new version of Abba's 'Dancing Queen', an honorary Australian anthem since it had featured in the film *Muriel's Wedding* in 1994. Kylie, wearing a showgirl's costume topped by an outrageous pink plumed headdress, was flanked by two male dancers, dressed in a few peacock feathers and vivid pink shorts that left little to the imagination. They were pure Baker who happened, at the time, to be the boyfriend of one of the well-toned, well-muscled men.

The venues were the perfect size to allow Kylie and William to develop their ideas. They wanted to depict the different facets of

Kylie over the years: rock slut, show pony, stripper and even cowgirl for a stand-out rendition of 'Cowboy Style' well before Madonna adopted the same look in 2000. William himself had painstakingly covered all the hats in sequins and silver glitter. He gave some away to fans, who subsequently went to every show and stood at the front, cheering their heroine.

Kylie rediscovered her love for performing live. She had fun – it was as simple as that. Her mother was on the tour to help again with costumes. Carol adores William and the two of them would wait in the wings to offer encouragement or a safety pin if required. During one performance, they enjoyed a drink backstage while Kylie was belting out another song. 'After all,' recalled William, 'it was sponsored by Absolut vodka.' They decided it would be a hoot to dress up in wigs and costumes. Carol was Baby Spice and William was Boy George, one of the heroes he used to follow about when he was younger. Kylie bounced off stage to be greeted by these two 'stars' acting like a pair of old drag queens. She was laughing so much she literally had to be pushed back on for the next number.

On another night, they watched in horror when they realized her cowgirl costume wasn't properly fastened. Ever so slowly it came undone, and the costume started sliding gently to the floor. Underneath, Kylie was stark naked. Suddenly, while Carol and William dithered, her PA Natalie dashed forward and saved her modesty, much to the disappointment of certain sections of the audience.

The encore for *Intimate and Live* perfectly fused old and new Kylie: 'Confide In Me', 'The Loco-Motion', 'Should I Stay Or Should I Go' and, of course, the timeless 'Better The Devil You Know', which sent everyone home happy.

At the conclusion of the Australian tour, Kylie was honoured by a state reception. Jeff Kennett, the Premier of Victoria, praised her as a 'wonderful ambassador for Australia wherever she travels', and added, 'She has done a wonderful job and she is one who has developed, in a sense, through adversity. She is now a much more proficient and professional entertainer than she was.'

Almost as an afterthought, Kylie brought the show to London for three dates at the Shepherd's Bush Empire at the end of July. Even the most jaded of reviewers were impressed. The *Independent on Sunday* couldn't have been more enthusiastic, admiring the new version of 'I Should Be So Lucky' in particular: 'It was fantastic. Not only was it an inspired arrangement, but Kylie even sang it well: the helium she overdosed on in the late 1980s has worn off.' She was overwhelmed at the surge of affection for her at the end of 'Better The Devil You Know' and was teary-eyed as she took her final bow. She had reclaimed the audience that had grown up with her and for the first time fused her image and her music into one. Making them inseparable would be a crucial element in her emergence as a style icon in the late nineties.

The *Intimate and Live* tour had been a triumph, but Kylie couldn't rest there or she would be in danger of becoming part of a nostalgia boom. As an artist, she has always recognized the need to progress and move forward. It came as no surprise when it was officially announced in November that she had parted company with deConstruction. Her alliance with the now defunct record label had been limping towards its conclusion for many months. She had released only two albums in five years with them, so she could hardly have been considered a money-spinner. Her final single from *Impossible Princess*, 'Cowboy Style', was released only in Australia and New Zealand. It deserved a wider audience because the country electric production from Brothers In Rhythm represented another new sound for Kylie. Her lyric was said to be inspired by her relationship with Stéphane when they were still together: she was attracted to him but frightened at the same time.

In the UK, the album had sold just 47,000 copies, which was very poor for an artist of her stature. Kylie was diplomatic about her split with deConstruction, confirming that everything was amicable: 'You become like family with a record company, particularly with deConstruction. They're lovely, genuine, Northern bastards!' The newspapers in the UK didn't see it that way, and enjoyed the opportunity to give Kylie another kicking. The London *Evening Standard* wrote bitchily, 'If you're going to move from the pop world into more credible music, it takes more than a change of wardrobe.'

The media were making the mistake they had often made of underestimating Kylie and choosing to take cheap and easy shots. So often the press are the last to comprehend the extent of a star's popularity. The *Intimate and Live* tour had given Kylie renewed momentum. She wasn't going to sell out Wembley Stadium on the back of its success, but it gave her confidence in the future at a time when she seemed to be lurching from one disaster to another. Kylie would have to be made of stone not to have been downcast after the whole deConstruction experience. Her expectations hadn't been fulfilled. But, encouragingly, the new image of Camp Kylie was taking shape.

16

Santa Kylie

Kylie didn't have any new music in the pipeline, so instead she and William decided to produce a book that would promote her credibility as a woman of substance and style. She said flippantly she chose to do it in a moment of boredom – a throw-away remark that doesn't do the project justice. The book, called simply *Kylie*, would consolidate the good work of the tour, reinforcing that she was a much-loved institution, like Ovaltine and *Coronation Street*. It portrayed a star entirely at ease with all her previous images.

The camera has always been Kylie's greatest ally – a friend who didn't care whether she was short or tall, voluptuous or slim. No one can judge your height if you are the only person in front of the camera. Eventually, Kylie realized that being small actually made her stand out in the crowd.

The camera's love for Kylie was something Jan Russ, the casting director for *Neighbours*, had noticed at her first audition: the plain, mousy girl was totally transformed by the time her image appeared on a television monitor. Kylie has the gift of being able to flirt with the camera. It was the same when she came to London. One stylist recalled, 'Put Kylie in front of a camera and she becomes alive. She makes love to the camera. She is fantastic at posing, as if it is the most natural thing in the world. Not having any inhibitions about your body helps.'

Her lack of self-consciousness is quite clear in the book. *Kylie* – titles have never been her strong point – was a study in reinvention, with images taken throughout her life and career, and featuring close-ups of most parts of her body, many life-sized, including arm, foot, ears and bottom. The final product confirmed that she was reconciled with her past. In many of the previously unseen photographs, quite a few of which were taken by William Baker, Stéphane Sednaoui and Katerina Jebb, Kylie looks absolutely fabulous.

She observed that she had to learn how to have a photograph taken in the early days of her career. She also knows her best angle, such an important consideration for celebrities: 'Years of experience have taught me that angles do exist – everyone has one. Sometimes I'll get photographers trying to do things and I'll be like "I don't want to be rude but take my picture from the front and a little to the side and that's it." People say I do this arched eyebrow thing but they just take over.' Kylie's own favourites among her pictures are the ones in which she is laughing.

One of the photographs in the book, taken in 1994, has Kylie dressed as a schoolgirl five years before Britney Spears adopted the look. In another, she is dressed as a nun on a rocking horse. William's photograph of Kylie from 1997 depicts her naked, kneeling on a velvet sofa, a naughty, yet innocently happy grin on her face and her curvaceous bottom much in evidence.

The project was a little egotistical but did contain some fascinating text – eulogistic vignettes from friends and admirers, like Baz Luhrmann, Nick Cave, Julie Burchill and Katerina Jebb. The violinist Nigel Kennedy revealed that he called his violin Kylie because it was 'small, beautiful and portable'. William was fulsome in his praise of Kylie, asserting that her image changes were not cleverly orchestrated publicity stunts. More pertinently, he recognized that fashion had moved on: what was considered banal in the nineties was now thought to be fabulous – perfect timing for Kylie's renaissance. *Kylie* was all about image and a life lived in the public eye. Her admirers might have welcomed more of an insight into the private woman, but that has never been her style.

The best explanation as to why promoting Kylie as a style icon of a generation succeeded in the late nineties when it had been laughable ten years earlier is provided by Kelly Cooper Barr. Kelly and Kylie used to go to clubs together in the late eighties and it was always the make-up artist who would get chatted up, because the wolves on the dance floor would invariably assume that she was the famous pop star. Nobody recognized Kylie. The difference more than a decade later was age. Kelly explained, 'Most women don't smoulder until they get to their early thirties and reach sexual maturity.' In other words, sex appeal has given Kylie style, and style has given her sex appeal.

Doing the unexpected might be another factor. The same month that she parted company with deConstruction, she could be found in Sydney shooting a small independent film called *Sample People*. The unknown director Clinton Smith had sent Kylie a script two years earlier and had been astonished to receive a call from Terry Blamey, saying that she had chosen to appear in his film. She wasn't the star, because it was an ensemble piece, but she was by far the biggest name. The schedule was very tight, so Kylie did most of her scenes in one take.

The result was a brash, low-budget indie thriller that follows the fortunes of four diverse groups of characters over a 48-hour period. Kylie played the girlfriend of a nightclub gangster or, as the *Daily Telegraph* put it, 'a drug snorting, ex-hooker who is about to betray her psychotic gangster boyfriend'. It was the usual 'realistic' mix of sex, drugs and gratuitous violence set to a noisy soundtrack of club mixes.

Smith accurately observed, 'If you go to *Sample People* expecting a

Kylie Minogue film, then you are going to be disappointed.' Most of the audience were just that when it was eventually released in Australia in March 2000. In the UK, it went straight to video in August 2002.

Kylie said she took the role because she wanted to gain further acting experience when the spotlight wasn't on her, but it was another weird choice. Her movie career was continuing to move backwards in a way that made one nostalgic for the good old days of *The Delinquents*. Perhaps the confidence that enabled Kylie to thrive musically had deserted her on screen.

She wasn't deterred, however. In March 1999, Kylie could be found on the beautiful island of Barbados – not relaxing, as she was fully entitled to do, but acting on stage. It was a long way from Ramsay Street. Once again, Kylie was challenging herself. She had been persuaded by Johnny Kidd, father of model Jodie Kidd, to appear in a production of *The Tempest* at a cultural festival he organized annually in the hibiscus and palm tree-lined gardens of his plantation estate. It was a musical version of the play, loosely called *The Caribbean Tempest*, but it was still Shakespeare and completely different from any of her previous work. The mastermind behind the extravaganza was Kit Hesketh-Harvey, best known for his UK fringe act Kit and The Widow. He adapted the Shakespearean verse to use as lyrics for fifteen new songs. His only disappointment was that Kylie, who played Miranda, refused to sing. She was determined to perform the role completely straight and not turn it into a kitsch classic. Hesketh-Harvey observed that she was a model cast member and even helped carry the props.

In the play, Kylie was surrounded by Shakespearean actors, such as David Calder and Rupert Penry-Jones. After Kylie's, the best-known face belonged to the late Roger Lloyd-Pack, familiar on British television in *Only Fools and Horses* and *The Vicar of Dibley*. Kylie's reward for her dedication to the role was an honourable, if slightly patronizing, mention in a review in *The Times*: 'The casting of Kylie Minogue as Miranda may have raised the odd knowing smile in anticipation, but she conducted herself more than adequately.'

Barbados was the perfect setting for a new romance. Kylie had been out with various men since Stéphane Sednaoui but no one too serious. She had, for instance, dated gallery director Tim Jefferies for a second time. They first got together briefly six years earlier and had kept in touch since. Tim had a reputation as one of the premier playboys of his generation, but it wasn't a label he enjoyed. He complained, 'A playboy is a relic of the 1950s, someone who was unbelievably rich, didn't work and who travelled the world in a private plane and that's not me. I am not a playboy – I am a hard-working art dealer.'

He had earned his reputation thanks to a list of lovers that included, among others, Koo Stark, Elle Macpherson, Claudia Schiffer, Lisa B and, of course, Kylie. He was amusing and congenial company, as well as being traditionally tall (six foot three), dark and handsome. He also had the priceless attribute, as far as his conquests were concerned, of being absolutely discreet. He has never blabbed about the beautiful women with whom he has been involved. As Kylie moved away from the world of rock and pop, Tim, as co-owner of Hamiltons Gallery in Mayfair, was one of the people who could open up a more creative world of fashion and the arts to her. He would eventually burn his little black book in 2008, when he married Swedish model Malin Johansson and they started a family.

The next name in Kylie's own black book was a musical director called Cassius Coleman. He made the effort to fly out to Barbados to visit her but, unfortunately for him, she had already fallen for her leading man, Rupert Penry-Jones. The latter had all the credentials of a heart-throb, as well as a spark of creativity – a good combination for Kylie.

Like another blond in her life, Jason Donovan, Rupert came from a show-business background. His mother, Angela Thorne, was one of the stars of the popular comedy series *To the Manor Born*, along with Penelope Keith, and his father, Peter Penry-Jones, acted in the old television drama *Colditz*, as well as the acclaimed *Longitude*. Rupert was privately educated at Dulwich College in London, and disappointed his parents a little by choosing the acting profession, mainly because they knew only too well the times of financial strife that might result. Rupert, who is over six feet tall and has piercing blue eyes, was fortunate, however, to be spotted by model agency Storm when he was just seventeen and was whisked off to the Milan catwalk. He therefore had experience of the fashion world of which Kylie is so enamoured. He also revealed an impressive physique in the film *Virtual Sexuality*, which contained so many sex scenes that he had to spend an entire week naked to get them all shot.

Rupert had serious acting ambitions. He had been understudy to Ralph Fiennes in a 1995 production of *Hamlet* at the Almeida Theatre in London. His Caribbean odyssey helped pave the way for a lead role with the RSC, as the eponymous hero in Schiller's *Don Carlos*. Kylie did her bit by going up from London to Stratford-upon-Avon to support him. She could be seen perched daintily on the back of his motorbike, something she had a lot of practice doing when she rode pillion on Michael Hutchence's Harley. The only difference was the English weather: on Rupert's bike, Kylie would wear socks on her hands to keep out the cold.

Rupert was smitten with Kylie and found it very difficult to follow the familiar path of secrecy: 'We're very good friends,' he declared, unconvincingly. 'We're not going out with each other. But if I was going out with someone, it would be her.' In reality, they went out for close on ten months, but he never admitted it, although he told journalist Chrissy Iley: 'Part of me wanted to scream it from the rooftops!' He did take Kylie home to meet his parents, and they liked her. They had Sunday lunch and Kylie chatted away in her usual relaxed fashion. Her ability to mix easily, even though she is so famous, is a quality that Michael Hutchence's mother noticed when her son first introduced them.

It was an easygoing relationship that chugged along while Kylie, supported by William, worked out her next career move. By far the best-received numbers at the *Intimate and Live* concerts were 'Better the Devil You Know' and 'Dancing Queen'. A return or, more precisely, an updating of that old disco sound was the most obvious progression for her. Now all she had to do was find a record label that thought the same.

Happily, one of the most famous labels in music had the vision. Parlophone, a subsidiary of EMI and home of The Beatles, decided Kylie still had a future as a significant recording artist. Forward-thinking A & R executive Miles Leonard, who signed Blur and Radiohead among others, knew she had a strong fan base but now needed the right project. He intended to provide the creative team and the blend of songwriters and producers to help her fulfil her potential. He explained to the online site *HitQuarters*, 'I believed that she was still strong vocally, and still definitely a star.'

While Miles set about finding new songs for her, Kylie embarked on yet another odd acting venture. Again, her role in *Cut* wasn't a major one, mainly because she didn't last very long. She played a horror film director called Hilary Jacobs, who has her tongue cut out and is butchered with a pair of gardening shears early in the action. It was really a cross between *Friday the 13th* and *Scream*, but without repeating the success of either of those two movies.

Kylie was doing a favour for *Hayride To Hell* director Kimble Rendall, who was making his first full-length feature, and Mushroom Records boss Michael Gudinski, who was also involved in his first major film project. The leading lady was the former Hollywood Brat Packer Molly Ringwald, star of *The Breakfast Club* and *Pretty in Pink*, who had met Kylie over dinner in LA some six months before. Molly had faced some of the same difficulties as

Kylie had in being perceived professionally as a girl long after she had grown into a beautiful young woman. Although Kylie was only on set in Adelaide for a few days, the two women got on well and Molly gave her advice on how to crack the elusive American market. Coincidentally, Molly had played Miranda in a film called *Tempest*, which was loosely based on the plot of the Shakespeare play. She also shared a love of Paris and France. Molly was briefly married to a French novelist called Valery Lameignère, so the two women could compare their experiences with French men, as well as everything else they had in common.

Cut never made the jump from Australian to British cinemas. But at least its release in her home country would keep the publicity flame burning for Kylie while she finished a new album. She took time out in June 1999 to appear as a guest star at an Australian gala held at the Royal Festival Hall in London, hosted by Barry Humphries in his twin personae of Sir Les Patterson and Dame Edna Everage. After a duet with Kylie of 'Where The Wild Roses Grow', Sir Les reached inside his pants to expose a huge retractable prosthetic penis. He waved it at Kylie, who promptly ran screaming from the stage.

The official announcement that she had signed to Parlophone came the same month. Kylie hadn't released a top-ten single for five years, so Parlophone was determined to get it right. It would be more than a year before her long-awaited seventh studio album made the record shops.

Her relentless work schedule killed off her relationship with Rupert Penry-Jones. It was an all too familiar story: he would be in a play in Stratford and she would be jetting all over the world, trying to keep in touch from Los Angeles or Melbourne, or wherever she happened to touch down. She was in New York to record 'The Reflex' for a Duran Duran tribute album, in Vienna for the Life Ball raising money for AIDS charities, and in Sydney for the opening of the Fox Studios, when she sang 'Diamonds Are A Girl's Best Friend'

dressed as Marilyn Monroe. No relationship could survive such a
schedule. It didn't help that he wasn't that keen on her music. She
was plotting her musical renaissance and he was busy telling her
that she should record a rock, acoustic thing. That didn't go down
well.

To his credit, Rupert is enthusiastically complimentary about his
famous ex-girlfriend: 'I thought I was one of the luckiest men in the
world and, to be honest, I can't believe it lasted more than a week.'
He also revealed Kylie to be a free spirit: 'I don't think she will ever
really belong to anyone.'

For a while, it seemed that Rupert would be just another conquest who would remain most famous for being one of Kylie's
exes. That changed in 2004, when he became the star of the successful BBC series *Spooks*. His acting career had been progressing
with great promise, but he hit the jackpot with his role as intelligence officer Adam Carter. He is now one of the best-known
leading men in television, thanks to subsequent starring roles in the
dark detective thriller *Whitechapel* and the legal drama *Silk*. He is
happily married to the actress Dervla Kirwan and they have two
young children.

The majority of Kylie's relationships seem to end just before the
turn of the year, as if she is putting her house in order before she
returns to Australia for her usual month-long break with her family
and prepares her next career move. After Rupert, for once she didn't
head straight back to Melbourne. Instead, she went to entertain the
Australian troops in East Timor, Indonesia, where they had been
sent to keep the peace after a bloody civil war. She was the forces'
pin-up, but more Marilyn Monroe than Vera Lynn. Kylie, in a tight-
fitting, wet-through white shirt matched with skin-tight olive pants
and boots, handed out Christmas cards that she had specially signed
for the boys.

She flew by helicopter to areas of mud, monsoon rains and mos-
quitoes, to try to cheer up the soldiers who wouldn't be travelling

back home for Christmas, which was five days away. At a special concert, she donned her version of a Santa suit to sing 'Santa Baby', 'Rockin' Robin' and 'Jingle Bells' in front of a wildly cheering audience.

Kylie was profoundly affected by what she witnessed on her visit, especially when those not lucky enough to be singing Christmas carols with her found a mass grave of butchered civilians just a few miles away. She declared simply, 'I am fiercely proud of being Australian and to be part of all this is among the most rewarding things I have done.'

PART THREE

A Free Spirit

17

The Bottom Line

Kylie's bottom was promoted in the cleverest way. It gave her come-back single, 'Spinning Around', an edge. *Neighbours* had been an advantage when she started out, but she needed another for the relaunch of her pop career. Her peachy posterior proved to be an inspired marketing tool – that and the media fixation on a notori-ously skimpy pair of ruched-gold-lamé hot pants that hardly had enough material to cover an oyster shell. As with all the best 'new' ideas, the exposure of Kylie's bottom and her ability to look good in the most minuscule item of clothing was nothing new.

She had worn hot pants many times before. For the video of 'Some Kind Of Bliss', she squeezed into a tiny denim pair, which gave her the germ of the idea that this might be something to exploit in the future. When she asked the producer Johnny Douglas, who was working with her on the new album, why he liked that particu-lar video, he confided that it all came down to those hot pants. Kylie filed the information away for use at the right moment.

Kylie would often joke that her bottom had a life of its own and was entirely separate from the rest of her. William Baker had shrewdly worked out that, from a publicity point of view, Kylie's rear was her best feature. Legend has it that he found the gold hot pants in an Oxfam shop. That became the media myth. They were actually purchased from a market stall for fifty pence by Katerina Jebb, and Kylie had worn them on more than one occasion, as devoted fans already knew. She had been photographed in them by Rankin and also wore them to a fancy-dress party with Stéphane. William can take the credit, however, for discovering them at the bottom of Kylie's lingerie drawer the day before the video shoot and realizing they would make a perfect costume.

She protests that she was self-conscious wearing them and kept wrapping a robe around her between takes. She hadn't realized they were the stars of the video. Arguably, the 'Spinning Around' video was more important than the song itself. It was directed by Dawn Shadforth, who subsequently became one of Kylie's favourites. She provocatively captured the allure of a woman who had reached her sexual peak and wasn't afraid to shout it to the world.

The hot pants featured in the sexual fantasies of the millions of men who couldn't believe they were being worn by the girl with the bubble perm and anaemic eighties hits. More importantly, the video brought her new sexy image to a younger audience, who had no pre-conceptions about the kind of artist Kylie was. It also reinforced the view that she was a pioneer in so many ways – her sexy gyrating grabbing the attention long before stars like Miley Cyrus and Rihanna were shaking their booty all over the place.

The video wasn't particularly memorable as a piece of art, and certainly not a patch on the originality of 'Put Yourself In My Place'. It was little more than a hot pants commercial, but it did showcase the disco feel of 'Spinning Around'. It was set in a remarkably clean-cut club, where everybody danced but nobody seemed to sweat. Kylie spun around nicely, slithered about on top of the bar and tossed her hair back. It was reported to have cost half a million pounds to make, but it was hard to see where the money was spent.

As part of a concerted campaign, Kylie's bottom also featured more controversially on the cover of the June issue of the style magazine *GQ*. Under the banner KYLIE: AT YOUR SERVICE!, she was pictured dressed in white tennis clothing and wearing no knickers. The photographer Terry Richardson had recreated the famous Athena poster 'The Tennis Girl' that had adorned the bedroom walls of many teenagers since it first appeared in 1977.

After the magazine hit the stands, Kylie insisted her G-string had been air-brushed out – which is neither here nor there. Celebrities are always bleating about magazines using technology to change photographs, often protesting that they weren't actually naked. It may or may not be true in this case, but Kylie and her management exercise a stranglehold on photo shoots, careful to protect and project the exact image they want at any given time.

Not everybody was impressed. Charlotte Raven, in the *Guardian*, perceptively wrote, 'This is not a stolen moment but the product of the model's wish to show the world her butt.' In other words, this was Kylie manipulating her public image in a calculating and, ultimately, very successful manner. In her defence, she took a very light-hearted approach to the whole thing. 'I thought it would be fun to show a bit of cheek,' she said. The only truly bogus thing was Kylie pretending to play tennis – as if she would!

All the publicity did a perfect job. 'Spinning Around' went to number one at the beginning of July 2000, giving Kylie the distinction of topping the charts in three decades – a feat matched only by Madonna among female singers. It was also the first time one of her singles had made its debut at number one, although it seemed to have been available for ages before its actual release.

In a complete change from *Impossible Princess*, Kylie had nothing to do with writing the song. It was discovered by Jamie Nelson, one of Miles Leonard's team, on a trip to the US. He brought it back, brimming with enthusiasm that he had found the perfect song to relaunch Kylie. He was right. It might not have been available if the co-writer, Paula Abdul, had recorded it herself as planned. It was the breakthrough hit for another of the co-writers, Kara DioGuardi, who would later join Paula and Simon Cowell as a judge on *American Idol*. She observed, 'I didn't know who Kylie was, and I was heartbroken that Paula Abdul wasn't going to do it. I was thinking, "Kylie Minogue? Who's Kylie Minogue? I've got to make some money or I'm going to have to go back to my real job."

'And then I saw her ass in the video – she had these hot pants on and the video was sick – and I was like, "OK, I like Kylie Minogue. I'm going to make some money here."'

The critics liked it too. Siobhan Grogan wrote in *NME*, '... the pint-sized Princess of Pop has returned to what she knows best. "Spinning Around" is made of the same fizzing, giddy disco-pop that made Kylie famous in the first place and will thrill gay discos everywhere.'

Kylie was at her busiest during the summer of 2000. She performed a set of seven songs at G-A-Y, including 'Step Back In Time' and 'Spinning Around', before closing with 'Better The Devil You Know'. She managed to change costumes four times, ending up in the ever-popular red spangly dress and a pair of devil's horns. Her gay fans have always appreciated Kylie's outfits, and William seldom disappoints them. The designer Patrick Cox observed, 'She's a living Barbie doll. All gay men want to play with her, dress her up and comb her hair.'

She again showcased 'Spinning Around' and the follow-up single 'On A Night Like This' at the London Mardi Gras in Finsbury Park in July. She welcomed Mayor Ken Livingstone to the stage at the end of her set. A week later, some classic English weather ruined her performance at Party in the Park in Hyde Park. A downpour messed up her sound system, so she couldn't hear the music or her own voice. She battled on, splashing around in trainers, but it wasn't a show to remember.

'On A Night Like This' wasn't an original Kylie track but one recorded by a Swedish disco singer called Pandora. Among the list of writers was Brian Rawling, producer of one of the biggest hits of the nineties, 'Believe' by Cher. Kylie flew to Monte Carlo to make the video with director Douglas Avery. It was inspired by the Martin Scorsese film *Casino* and was quite broody and atmospheric. It featured Kylie as the girlfriend of a mob boss, played by the *Blade Runner* actor Rutger Hauer. She reputedly wore diamonds worth £2 million for a scene shot in a limousine. Publicity was helped by rumours that she had filmed one scene naked, but it has never surfaced.

By the time 'On A Night Like This' was released in September, she had already appeared on *Top of the Pops*, promoting a song called 'Kids', a duet with Robbie Williams. It was slightly confusing: the track would be on both artists' new albums, but Robbie's was coming out first, so the promotion couldn't wait.

Despite his fame, Robbie still had a good old-fashioned crush on Kylie. He may have been the biggest solo star in Britain, but this was Kylie Minogue and he had been just an ordinary fourteen-year-old, football-obsessed boy from Stoke-on-Trent when she had topped the charts with 'I Should Be So Lucky'.

Kylie, the older woman, knew exactly how to play it with Robbie. A record company insider observed, 'He would follow her around and she was like, "Robbie, you stink," but I think she ended up quite liking him really.' The man himself admitted he was slightly nervous of Kylie. They made a fantastic-looking couple, but there was never any romance, despite desperate attempts by the media to link them together. Robbie adopted his usual outrageous, naughty-boy persona, asking publicly, 'Do you reckon she'd shag me?'

She got her own back a little when she joined him on stage to sing 'Kids' during his concert at the MEN Arena in Manchester. He had no idea what she would be wearing. It turned out to be a silver slip of a costume that left nothing to the imagination and had Robbie sweating as she wiggled her bottom in his direction. 'For a second, he lost it and I loved it,' said Kylie. It's fair to say she'd always had a soft spot for Robbie, nominating him on more than one occasion as her favourite member of Take That. She isn't a fan of boy bands but thought Robbie stood out: 'I always knew he was going to be a star. He's such a natural.'

Robbie jumped at the chance to write some songs for her new album. He told her she had everything going for her but needed a good song to turn things around – just as 'Angels' had for him a couple of years before. With his songwriting partner, Guy Chambers, he contributed three songs: the mellow lounge track 'Loveboat', the high camp 'Your Disco Needs You' and the anthemic 'Kids'. Kylie shared the songwriting credit on the first two. She had asked Robbie for a song called 'Loveboat' because she liked it as a title. It was Robbie who thought up the phrase 'Your Disco Needs You'. He also wrote the lyrics to 'Kids', which were quite mischievous, to say the least, with their tongue-in-cheek references to anal sex. Only Robbie could rhyme 'sodomy' with 'Billy Connolly'. The rap was dropped for the version on Kylie's album. 'Kids' was a superb dance track, although Robbie seemed to be struggling with a high-pitched falsetto for most of the song. U2's anthem 'Beautiful Day' denied the dream couple a number-one hit.

Robbie and Kylie were perfect musical partners. They made each other appear sexy and naughty at the same time. Putting them together was a smart move by their management teams – Robbie was on Chrysalis, which, like Kylie's new label Parlophone, is a subsidiary of EMI. Although Kylie might prefer to disagree, Robbie made her appear hip at a vital time. 'Spinning Around' went straight to number one on a wave of support from Kylie's gay fan base, but that achievement would have been wasted if her comeback had begun and ended there. An alliance with Robbie was virtually guaranteed to cement her position in the mainstream marketplace.

His flamboyant single 'Rock DJ', which had been a big-selling summer number one, became a great favourite among the transvestite ladyboys of Bangkok when he toured the Far East. They loved it when he bared his bottom and simulated sex with a cardboard cut-out of Kylie. Not only was he acceptable to her gay fans, but he also introduced her to a whole new generation of young girls, who would see her next to Robbie and want to be just like her.

Kylie showcased 'Your Disco Needs You' when she appeared at Privilege in Ibiza, which billed itself as the largest nightclub in the world. The fact that she was chosen as the inaugural live act at the venue was testimony to the fact that it was now officially OK to be a fan. The 'K' from the *Intimate and Live* tour had been replaced by 'Kylie' in neon bulbs – very seventies disco. Her dancers, clad in black, made robotic movements close to the swimming pool at the front of the stage. And then there was Kylie at the top of the stairs – Tinkerbell herself – dressed in a pink vinyl jacket, pink micro skirt with a slit up the back and little pink boots, giving the crowd a big, cheesy 'Lucky' grin.

The last time there had been live music on the Mediterranean DJ Mecca of Ibiza was in 1988, and you can bet nobody would have been seen dead turning up to watch Kylie Minogue perform her Stock, Aitken and Waterman fodder. This island prides itself on a reputation for hedonism and Kylie then was too naff for that – not any more. 'Your Disco Needs You' outcamped Village People. Kylie's dancers removed their tops to reveal oiled pecs (men) and powdered breasts decorated with black tassels (women). She, meanwhile, had changed into a gold bikini top and frilly hot pants. There was the decadent air of *Cabaret*, with none of the threatening undertones. One reviewer noted, 'No one really dances during Kylie's set – they're too busy leering.'

Her much anticipated new album, *Light Years*, made its debut at number two in the charts in October 2000. Any lingering feeling of introspection from her more mature sound of the mid-nineties was swept away in its frothy exuberance. Miles Leonard had succeeded in his goal for this first Parlophone album, one that proclaimed, 'Look, I'm back and I'm making pop records.' Kylie told *Rolling Stone* that she had only one instruction for the various writers: 'I said, "These are my keywords: poolside, beach, cocktails and disco." I wanted to indulge the over-the-top side of my character and I think we did it.' *NME* gave the album six out of ten and said, '*Light Years* is all you need to know about Kylie in less than an hour: fun, perfectly-formed, not too taxing and occasionally annoying.'

If 1997 had been an *annus horribilis* for Kylie, then 2000 was *mirabilis*. The best was still to come: her spectacular performance of a lifetime at the closing ceremony of the Sydney Olympics in October 2000. More than 3.7 billion people in 185 countries watched the event. What an entrance Kylie made! A bevy of muscled Bondi Beach lifeguards carried her on a surfboard to the centre of the main stadium, where a live audience of 100,000 people had gathered, all in exuberant party mood. She was dressed in a costume similar to that worn by Nikki Webster, the child who had starred in the opening ceremony. It was some sort of slightly tortuous symbolism, typical of the Olympics, of a girl becoming a woman – rather ironic, considering it was Kylie, the most famous of all child-women that Nikki had matured into.

The beach boys hoisted Kylie on to the stage, where her dancers, a vision in pink, obscured her while they began their athletic movements to the strains of Abba's 'Dancing Queen'. Suddenly, the announcer's voice rang out above the audience: 'Mesdames et Messieurs ... Miss [the music pauses for a split second and the dancers are frozen in time] Kylie Minogue.' And there she was, miraculously transformed into a Busby Berkeley showgirl, complete with a magnificent headdress. She performed 'Dancing Queen' and her own 'On A Night Like This' and was, by common consent, magnificent.

Her performance, surrounded by an enormous representation of Sydney's drag queens, was the ultimate in camp and, as such, is unlikely to be topped. Many of Australia's most popular figures performed or appeared at either the opening or closing ceremony, but it was Kylie, not Greg Norman, Paul Hogan, Elle Macpherson nor even Olivia Newton-John, Kylie's own childhood heroine, who stole the show. Hers was the performance that stuck in the memory.

The Olympic Games established Kylie as the world's all-Australian heroine. Even though she had deserted her homeland for London a decade earlier, hers would be the first name inked in during a game of 'list five famous Australians'. To use an old cliché, you can take Kylie out of Australia but you can't take Australia out of Kylie. She once admitted, 'In my heart I am so Australian. I am so ridiculously patriotic.' To prove the point, she was back on stage two weeks later, to sing a plaintive and moving version of 'Waltzing Matilda' at the opening ceremony of the Paralympics. She could 'Kyliefy' any song.

There was still time for one more notable first for Kylie in 2000. At the MTV Europe Music Awards in Stockholm, she performed 'Kids' with Robbie and backstage met someone she had never spoken to before. It was the other great female survivor of popular music, Madonna. She was wearing a T-shirt with the word KYLIE written across the front.

18

Bumlash

Kylie Minogue was now in her thirties with no husband and no children. She had only to walk down the street smiling and a frenzy of media speculation would follow. If she was within touching distance of a man, then she was practically engaged. It was getting so ridiculous she decided to keep her new romance entirely secret for as long as possible just to give it the chance to develop naturally. It began well, with no public scrutiny, and ended really badly in the glare of a quite unwelcome spotlight.

Kylie had met James Gooding at a pool party in Los Angeles at the beginning of 2000. She had flown to California to add the finishing touches to *Light Years*. Her relationship with Rupert Penry-Jones was over and she, as usual, was throwing herself into work. Gooding was a six foot one model with dark, brooding looks. When they were introduced, she went weak at the knees. The party was a bit boring, so James, who at the time was living in LA, suggested they go and get something to eat. But they didn't rush into a full-blown passionate affair at once, instead going for a series of getting-to-know-you dates, which was a refreshing change for Kylie. He, endearingly, recalled, 'She was just this little, funny, geeky girl I thought was really cute.' He took her bowling, which she enjoyed. She called him her 'delightful scruff from Essex'.

Kylie managed to keep her new boyfriend hidden for several months, an outstanding length of time considering her fame. She confessed that there was someone special, but didn't name him, although she said she was 'enjoying the romance'. Gooding settled back in London, but didn't move in with Kylie. Her cautious approach may have had something to do with his age, as he was seven years younger. He had been in the world of fashion since he was eighteen, however, with his photogenic looks so much in demand that he had earned the unwanted sobriquet of 'super-model'. There is something of a role reversal with Kylie and certain of her men. Zane, Mark, Rupert, James – they are trophy boyfriends, great-looking adornments to hang off your arm.

One of the qualities Kylie liked in James Gooding was his domesticity. Long-term, Kylie hasn't reacted well to the energy-sapping relationships she experienced with Hutchence and Sednaoui. Gooding was not hard work. One of his favourite pursuits is making little cardboard boxes. He takes a blank piece of card and then makes a little box from it, into which he puts a gift. He recalled making a 'really cool box' for Kylie. Somehow he never seemed exciting enough for Kylie. If they were at her place, they would sip drinks on the balcony or curl up on the sofa together to watch *Pop Idol* with a tub of ice cream.

Gooding painted a picture of their relationship in the *News of the World* that made them resemble Darby and Joan. At his flat in Shoreditch, they would breakfast on coffee and croissants before wandering round Brick Lane market, buying old records and bunches of flowers. Then they would go home, where James, who liked cooking, would prepare a Sunday roast. Kylie's favourite apparently was a 'nice leg of lamb, broccoli and roast spuds'. They would then settle down to watch television or a *Bridget Jones* movie. Cor blimey, Missus, the only detail missing from this scene of domestic bliss was a slice of Battenburg cake and *Last of the Summer Wine*.

Kylie went to stay with Gooding's mother, Jenny Young, who

lived in a modest terraced house in the quaintly named Kirby-le-Soken in Essex, near the seaside resort of Walton-on-the-Naze. James split his time as a child between Essex and Scotland, where his father David lived and where he originally went to a boarding school in Rannoch. Jenny got on well with Kylie, as all mums tend to do, and then had to run the gauntlet of everyone asking her if her son was going to marry the superstar.

Behind the public façade of happiness, however, there were already tensions building that would eventually lead to meltdown – in particular, the difficulty James had in reconciling the public Kylie with the private one. He did not, for example, appreciate the game that Kylie was happy to play, suggesting in the media that she and Robbie fancied each other and might become an item. She was such an experienced tease in these matters, with a deft touch that she had practised with Jason Donovan many years before.

Gooding was angry over the stunt and the way Kylie fuelled the rumours, as if denying his existence. He later told the *News of the World* that he asked her to issue a public statement denying that she and Robbie were an item, but she refused. 'It was the first time I saw how Kylie's ambition was the most important thing in her life.'

Kylie didn't take James with her when she travelled back to Melbourne for her Christmas break. It wasn't all soaking up the sun with turkey and trimmings. She had agreed to film a brief appearance in a new film, *Moulin Rouge!*, directed by her friend Baz Luhrmann. A fellow Australian, he was a great fan of Kylie. In the Oscar-winning musical, starring Nicole Kidman, she played The Green Fairy, a sort of Tinkerbell, complete with a scream provided by Ozzy Osbourne. Kylie is seen twinkling in the night sky and then she is gone.

She was already feeling exhausted and 2001 hadn't even started yet. It was shaping up as one of her busiest years yet, with a full-blown tour, recording a new album and then promoting it. She had to push one more release from *Light Years*, a track called 'Please Stay', which was slightly lost in the Christmas record jamboree but still crept into the UK top ten. She had co-written the track with Biff Stannard, the man behind many of the Spice Girls hits, including 'Wannabe'.

She probably would have had a much bigger hit with either 'Your Disco Needs You' or the Johnny Douglas composition 'Disco Down', but Miles Leonard was worried that these tracks would take Kylie a step too far down the camp road if they were released as singles. He explained, 'We always had a more electronic, programmed and contemporary sound in mind.' 'Please Stay' was a pleasant enough Latin-inspired dance track, but its release left the impression they were squeezing one more single off an album that had more than paid for itself.

Despite its success, *Light Years* hadn't crossed the Atlantic, and US success remained as elusive an ambition for Kylie as it was for Robbie Williams. It could have been completely different for her if the popular Australian film *The Adventures of Priscilla, Queen of the Desert* (1994) had kept its original plot: the drag queens crossing Australia in a battered old bus were originally going to be acts from the 'Kylie Show' in Sydney. This would have meant colossal international exposure for her. Alas, it was decided that Kylie's name wouldn't sell the film to the American public, so the plot was changed to make them Abba impersonators.

The promoters obviously felt that 'The Loco-Motion Girl' wasn't going to sell ten tickets to a barn dance. It was little better for her to be described as the Australian Madonna, which suggested something parochial and imitative. Kylie wasn't an absolute unknown in the US, because her gay fans there still adored her, but she could walk down Rodeo Drive in Los Angeles and be taken for a boutique assistant rather than one of the world's biggest superstars.

Kylie needed a universally acclaimed, big-selling record to take into battle in the US. Her record label had a commercial tie-up in the

States with Capitol Records, so the framework was in place as long as there was a half-decent single to promote. When the demo for 'Can't Get You Out Of My Head' arrived at the offices of Parlophone in West London, it was already almost perfect.

The voice on the demo sounded very familiar. It was former dance-music darling Cathy Dennis, who had five top-ten records in the 1990s and a much-copied bob haircut, but was a bigger name in Europe and the US than in the UK. Her biggest solo hits were 'Touch Me (All Night Long)' and a version of The Kinks' classic 'Waterloo Sunset'. The melody for 'Better The Devil You Know' was actually inspired by D Mob's 'C'mon And Get My Love', on which Cathy sang the vocal in 1989. She has a similar self-deprecatory style to Kylie: 'It never even crossed my mind that I could be a pop star, because I came from Norwich. Pop stars don't come from Norwich.' She has a healthy contempt for many singers, Kylie excepted, of course: 'They're celebrities, not pop artists – if you asked them about music, they wouldn't have a Scooby-Doo.'

Cathy was probably a bigger name Stateside than Kylie, but had tired of performing and had become a full-time writer. Her collaborator on the song with the most infectious hook of 2001 was Rob Davis, guitarist with the seventies' chart act Mud and one of the campest figures of the glam rock age. Davis was also responsible for the catchiest dance record of 2000, Spiller's 'Groovejet (If This Ain't Love)', which featured Sophie Ellis-Bextor on vocals. Cathy wasn't convinced that 'Can't Get You Out Of My Head' was number-one material, but when Kylie first heard the demo, she leaped around excitedly, saying, 'When can I do it?'

The song was an obvious choice for first single from the new album. It had all the ingredients of a Stock, Aitken and Waterman hit but in a more sophisticated package. By the time it was released in September 2001, Kylie fans were already singing it in the shower, because she had showcased it on the *On A Night Like This* tour, which had proved hugely popular on the back of her success at the Sydney

Olympics. As the posters said, it was her 'biggest show ever'. William and Kylie took their inspiration from the Hollywood musicals of Fred Astaire and Ginger Rogers, Gene Kelly and Kylie's favourite fifties' film, *South Pacific*, complete with sailors and dancing girls and a boat called HMS *Kylie*. The show began with the lady herself being lowered from the ceiling on a large silver anchor.

The tour began in Europe with twenty-three dates. The first night was supposed to be in Dublin but had to be cancelled when storms prevented flights leaving London for the Irish capital. The show premiered at the Glasgow Armadillo on 3 March instead. Three nights at the Hammersmith Apollo brought the British leg to a close. Not everyone was impressed. Lisa Verrico, in the *Guardian*, found the show uneven, though never boring, and thought Kylie 'sounded awful' during 'Put Yourself In My Place'.

Kylie barely had time to draw breath before she was back in Australia for a further twenty-three dates. William, in *Kylie: La La La*, reveals that they were both bored by the end of it and that he personally was 'disheartened' by the whole experience – not quite the triumph that it had appeared to be. Michael Bodey of the Sydney *Daily Telegraph* wasn't aware of the behind-the-scenes disquiet when he described the show: 'This first concert was as camp as tinned ham and as derivative as a two-bit cover band. But it was oh-so ace and as refined and as assured a show as Kylie has ever done.'

Nobody knew that Kylie's fragile health issues had surfaced again and she spent most of 2001 battling her familiar problem of exhaustion. The low point came when she caught a bug in Melbourne and a doctor had to stand by in the wings to give her a sharp burst of oxygen between numbers. Eventually, the media realized the price she was paying for her success. *The Face* magazine observed, 'She can't sleep, can't remember what day it is, gets up and cries in the night.' The renowned writer Chris Heath reported that Kylie was running on empty.

The problem was that there was no time to be ill. She had her own brand of lingerie to launch under the banner 'Love Kylie x'. Then she was on the front cover of *Vogue*, modelling a white silk crêpe-de-chine Valentino dress for photographer Vincent Peters. All this time, there were finishing touches that needed to be made to the new album, which was going to be called *Fever*, curiously the name of a famous Madonna song.

To whip up publicity for the release of 'Can't Get You Out Of My Head' and thus increase record sales, there were stories of great rivalry between Kylie and Victoria Beckham. This was a cynical marketing trick to try to persuade more people to buy the record they preferred, thereby increasing sales of both tracks. The media generally colluded with this mock battle. The outcome was complete victory for Kylie, when her record went straight in at number one in the UK charts on 23 September 2001. Kylie sold 306,000 copies in the first week of release, compared with 35,000 of Victoria's 'Not Such An Innocent Girl', which only made number six. As a recording artist, Posh Spice wasn't taken seriously by the media or the public – something Kylie had experienced at times in her own career.

Ironically, it was Kylie who could more fittingly have released a track called 'Not Such An Innocent Girl'. In any comparison between the two famous women, it is Kylie – single, available and sometimes a little dangerous – who deserved that description. The public didn't buy into an edgy image for Victoria at all and she could only envy Kylie's success as her single proceeded to top the charts in twenty countries worldwide.

The futuristic video, another directed by Dawn Shadforth, helped. It's the famous one in which Kylie wears a white hooded jumpsuit that looks like a fashionable scene-of-crime uniform. She discovered the outfit in the North London attic studio of a designer called Fee Doran, whom William knew. It caught Kylie's eye hanging on a rail while she sat with Fee's baby son George in her lap. Fee had actually made it for herself and she is six feet tall, so it wasn't exactly made to measure for Kylie. Nevertheless, she tried it on. Fee recalled, 'Kylie's half my size – a little fragile bird and I'm this big clumsy oaf. It was laughable because it drowned her, but she knew what she wanted. Her granny was a seamstress, and she knew all about sewing, so we decided how to tweak it.'

The adjustments resulted in a neckline so plunging that another half-inch and she would have been arrested. Kylie was surrounded by robotic dancers wearing red and black, with scarlet helmets on their head that looked suspiciously like plastic flowerpots. Whenever the video played – and it was everywhere – it would take the rest of the day to get the 'la la la' tune out of your head.

In the months that followed, scarcely a day went by without Kylie featuring on a newspaper front page, a magazine cover, on television or radio. Overnight it seemed Kylie was in danger of becoming a national treasure, the most clichéd of titles, even though she was a proud Australian. She may have been perceived as a sexy and stylish survivor, making current and relevant music, but she was also a reassuring presence in a world shaken by the 11 September atrocity in New York. As Bryan Appleyard observed in a profile of her six weeks later in *The Sunday Times*, 'God's in his heaven. Kylie's at number one, surely nothing really bad can happen now.'

Not everything Kylie was so positive. A few weeks after the release of the single, a suspect package arrived at the EMI offices. It allegedly contained soil and a note warning the record company that owns Parlophone to drop Kylie or else staff would be infected with anthrax. The perpetrator apparently loathed *Neighbours*.

On a jollier note, Kylie featured in *An Audience with Kylie Minogue* on ITV. Brendan and Dannii were there, and her brother grinned uncomfortably when the spotlight settled on them. Dannii has always basked in the attention but, for the most part, Brendan has managed to keep well away. He has had to suffer some embarrassments over the years, particularly when Kylie revealed he used to borrow his mother's high-heeled boots and paint stars around his eyes in homage to his heroes, the rock group Kiss.

Mostly, however, it has worked out well for him: he has the reflected adulation of having famous sisters with none of the aggravation of being a star. When Kylie became well known, Brendan, a good-looking, dark-haired boy, would accompany her to parties, and generally have the girls swooning in his direction. One admirer from the *Neighbours* days recalled wistfully, 'He was gorgeous, quiet and just a really nice guy.'

Kylie remains protective of Brendan, who is very much part of her private world. Keeping away from public scrutiny allowed him to take time out to backpack around the world before settling in Sydney, where he now earns his living as a respected cameraman and can enjoy a low-profile family life.

Pete Waterman was also on show at *An Audience with . . .*, looking every inch the proud father watching his daughter in a school nativity play. A tremor of expectation filtered through the audience when the band played the opening bars of 'Especially For You'. Kylie and Jason together again? Poor Jason – he had been replaced by Kermit the Frog, who said to Kylie, 'If you kiss me, I might turn into Jason Donovan.' Kylie replied, 'I like you just the way you are.' Everyone had a good laugh at Jason's expense.

When *Fever* was released in October 2001, it debuted at number one in the UK album charts. Job done. The critics took it seriously, appreciating that it was a work full of potential top-ten hits. Michael Hubbard at the online site *musicOMH* thought it 'saccharine pop at its finest'.

Alexis Petridis in the *Guardian* called it 'startlingly slick, a combination of house beats, fashionable electronic effects largely borrowed from Daft Punk, and choruses designed to lodge in the brain after one listen.' The mere fact that serious critics were now bothering with a Kylie record was a sign of her progress, even if Alexis also said, 'It's a mature pop album only in that it's aimed at the boozy girl's night out rather than the school disco.'

Fever was more Europop and less Vegas than *Light Years*. One of the effects of that was Kylie's vocals seemed to lack variety and depth. She is a much better singer than she is allowed to be on this tight production.

At last, in early November, she could have a proper break and she spent a happy weekend in Puerto Banús on Spain's Costa del Sol with James. They were seen looking in the window of a jewellery store, which prompted a frenzy of engagement speculation. They reportedly lingered over a £50,000 engagement ring. Kylie told Dominic Mohan of the *Sun* that she had enjoyed a 'wonderful weekend with the man she loves'. The romantic interlude even made the front cover of *OK!* magazine. Inside, Kylie gushed, 'James treats me like a princess – I think all women should be.' At the end of the day, it was just a weekend away shared with the press, although the signs were encouraging.

The momentum of her revival showed no sign of slowing down. She won a *GQ* Award for Services to Mankind and a German BAMBI for Best Comeback of the Year. Tickets for four UK dates in 2002 sold out within one hour. 'Can't Get You Out Of My Head' was released in the US and Kylie was promoting it everywhere, including on the *Tonight Show with Jay Leno*. She reached number one in the dance charts and climbed into the top twenty of the *Billboard* Hot 100 chart.

Fever was released in the US just after the 2002 Brit Awards at the end of February. The reviews there were good, although the description of Kylie as a pop vixen was cringe-making. *Billboard* said, '*Fever* harks back to a more innocent time when sex and dance floors merged to create one carefree nation under a groove.' The album entered the charts at number three, a wonderful result. The same week the single finally made the top ten.

The Brit Awards were absolute confirmation of Kylie's musical credibility. She won Best International Album for *Fever* and Best International Female. When she got up to be presented with the latter award by Russell Crowe, she remembered to kiss James, who was sitting beside her. This was the professional Kylie, wearing her ego jacket, a totally different person to the one nibbling roast lamb and two veg in Shoreditch. She slipped into a white mini dress that scarcely covered her famous bottom and a pair of knee-high silver boots and sang a mash-up of 'Can't Get You Out Of My Head' and the New Order classic 'Blue Monday'. On the back of her Brits success, her sultry-sounding new single 'In Your Eyes', co-written and produced by Biff Stannard and Julian Gallagher, climbed to number three.

Perhaps inevitably there was a backlash over Kylie's bottom, with newspaper suggestions that all was not as it seemed. After all, she was nearly thirty-four and there was no sign of her spectacularly pert behind heading south. Kylie was mortified by the stories, especially as they undermined her perfectly natural image. The controversy was amusingly described in some papers as a 'bumlash'. A rearguard action in friendly magazines strongly refuted the very idea of cosmetic enhancement.

Irritatingly, 'bumlash' occurred just after her behind had been the runaway winner of a Best Arse competition after the MTV Europe Music Awards, voted for by users of MTV's interactive service. The online site eulogized, 'We believe that, if used properly, it [Kylie's arse] could help worlds come together in peace and harmony, rebuild cities, and probably crack a nut the size of a continent.'

All good fun, but Kylie was getting a little touchy about her bottom. There was nothing wrong with having websites devoted to her rear, but she was fed up with people asking her to turn around so they could get a closer look. When one interviewer asked if he could talk about her arse, she replied firmly, 'I've put it away for a while now.' That was a sensible move. Having used her bottom as a pertinent weapon in her re-emergence, it was time for Kylie to play down this particular feature in case it had a counter-productive effect.

*

In any case, she had more serious matters to worry about. For starters, her father Ron, at sixty, had to have an operation for prostate cancer. He had always been the rock in Kylie's life, so it came as a huge shock to her, stuck 12,000 miles away while he was in hospital. For once, Terry Blamey was positively garrulous. 'Thankfully, the news is good,' he said. 'Kylie was very concerned, but the operation was 100 per cent successful and Ron has been cleared by the doctors. He is fully recovered and is resting at home with his family.'

When Kylie went back to visit, she promptly bought her parents a new home in Canterbury, with a heated swimming pool and tennis court. Although in need of a little refurbishment, the two-storey house is in one of the most prestigious residential streets in the whole of Melbourne. Kylie purchased it at auction for Aus $2.43 million, which then was the equivalent of about £890,000 – a very expensive property by Australian standards.

At the Brits, Kylie had made a point of paying tribute to her father: 'He will be so proud of me. He'll be the first person I call when I come off stage.' Perhaps none of the men in her life have ever measured up to her dad.

The media certainly had hopes for James Gooding. 'Friends' seemed to be quoted everywhere, saying that the couple were planning a wedding very soon. 'Friends' also said Kylie was taking time off in the hope of starting a family. Yet, just as the couple passed the two-year mark together, the cracks were beginning to appear. There were whispers – ones that Kylie would have found all too familiar – that he had a roving eye and pictures appeared of him enjoying the company of other glamorous women, like Sophie Dahl and Beverley Bloom, described in the newspapers as a socialite. He was spotted holding hands with the former and kissing the latter in the back of a taxi.

Kylie was also seen storming out of a restaurant in tears, after apparently having words with him. This may or may not have been the time he told her that he had, indeed, slept with Sophie on a trip to New York, a confession he would later confirm in the papers. The row continued into the street before they stormed off in opposite directions.

By the time they made the split officially known in May, it was common knowledge that the relationship was on the rocks. He hadn't turned up to the first night of her *KylieFever2002* tour at the Cardiff International Arena at the end of April. On the same night, he was seen out with another woman in London. Their official statement read, 'They still love each other and it's an entirely amicable split. Contrary to media reports, there is not and never has been any truth to marriage, pregnancy or infidelity stories. Therefore, they play no part in this decision.'

The *Daily Mirror* commented simply, 'Yeah, right.'

19

Enraptured

The 5,000 fans in Cardiff were the first to glimpse the Ky-Borg, the giant £40,000 robot in which Kylie opened the show to the strains of 'The Hills Are Alive' from *The Sound of Music*. Limb by limb, the armour was peeled away to reveal the butterfly inside – Kylie dressed in a Dolce & Gabbana sparkling silver bra, mini skirt and silver boots. She then launched into 'Come Into My World', another song written by Cathy Dennis and Rob Davies and one of the stand-out tracks on the album. For once, 'Better The Devil You Know' didn't close a show. That honour went to 'Can't Get You Out Of My Head', which became her biggest single of all time, eventually selling close to 1.2 million copies.

Kylie's first words were 'Sut mae, Cardiff?', which, broadly speaking, means 'How are you, Cardiff?' in Welsh. She was suffering from a bad sore throat but reassured the fans, 'Cancel isn't in my vocabulary.' She also told her Welsh audience that many of her relatives were from nearby: 'It's the home of my mother's family. Are there any Joneses out there?' The tour was her most ambitious so far: forty-eight big shows spread over three months in the UK, Europe and Australia, ending with five August nights at the Rod Laver Arena in her home town of Melbourne. The *Daily Mirror* called it a triumph and conducted an exhaustive survey, which apparently proved that Kylie wiggled her bum 251 times each performance.

Publicly, the tour was indeed a huge success, but the demands of more than two hours on stage every night, combined with the emotional fall-out from the split with James, were taking their toll. Dannii revealed that Kylie was 'very upset about splitting up as they had been together a long time'. She added that the split had been 'one of her downs'.

In another story, the *Mirror* quoted a 'friend' as saying that Kylie, in fact, dreaded opening a magazine and seeing another picture of him with a woman who wasn't her. There were rumours that they tried to patch things up during her tour and had even shared a romantic break in Bali, but by the time the *Fever* tour ended, it was clear that wasn't the case, especially after he was reportedly seen spending three nights in a row at the former *Hollyoaks* actress Davinia Taylor's flat in Belsize Park.

Poor Kylie didn't seem to be taking it well and once again needed a spell of recuperation with her family. Her parents remained the only true constant in her life. When, in the mid-nineties, she was feeling down, she asked them out of the blue if they could come and visit her in London. They immediately dropped everything and took the first plane they could to make sure she was well. They stayed for two weeks, cheering her up. Nothing had changed. Once more, she had reached breaking point. This time, Carol took her to a special retreat in the Western Australian outback, where there were no mobiles, televisions or intrusive magazines and newspapers.

Even though they had officially split, it was James who was quoted in the press as saying she was taking a well-deserved six months off and had nothing planned for the future except recording a new album. In the eyes of the world, she still had to settle things with James. Was he in her life or out of it? He made up her mind for her at the Brits in 2003. What a difference twelve months made! The happiness she felt a year earlier contrasted sharply with the ghastly night of 23 February, when they had their final bust-up. The unwitting catalyst for their last row was Justin Timberlake, then heart-throb of the moment, just as Robbie had been a couple of years earlier. It was a publicist's dream. Justin and Kylie appeared on stage together to perform the old Blondie hit 'Rapture' and Justin fondled Kylie's bottom – a master stroke that ensured maximum media coverage. The reports that he 'grabbed' her bum were a little over the top, as the number was thoroughly rehearsed. Kylie looked sensational in a little black mini dress and Justin, in black-and-white-silver hip-hop gear, seemed to linger over his public grope.

Justin, a consummate professional, said all the right things afterwards: 'She's got the hottest ass I've ever seen. On a scale of one to ten it was a fifty-eight.' James was in the audience and, according to his subsequent account in the Sunday papers, enjoyed the show, but was less happy afterwards when he found Kylie sitting with Justin. She apparently frostily refused his offer of a drink and the two proceeded to have a very public and frank exchange of views.

Eventually, Gooding followed Kylie outside to continue their conversation, only to have a bouncer block his way, leaving Kylie to step into her limo without him. He probably didn't realize that she was still on her 'date' with Justin. She and Dannii joined the American for a cosy dinner 'a douze' – the three stars with assorted minders and hangers-on – at the Montpeliano restaurant in Knightsbridge. Then they moved on to an EMI reception at the Sanderson Hotel just off Oxford Street, where they were joined by Janet Jackson. Dannii left the party with Justin and they drove back to the Mandarin Oriental Hotel in Knightsbridge, where the singer had a suite for his stay in London. This was the starting point for speculation that Dannii spent the night in his room – not true. She later confessed that she was just catching a ride in Justin's car and never went to the hotel room at all. 'It was the best one-night stand I never had,' she laughed.

While Dannii returned to her Battersea home, Kylie slipped into the Mandarin Oriental, entirely unnoticed except by a tabloid journalist who gleefully reported a night of passion between her and Justin. Hardly – Kylie clocked in at 3.53am and clocked out of the back entrance at 6am. It was practically a carbon copy of the ruse Robbie Williams had perpetrated with Nicole Kidman – another non-romance. All Justin would say is that he had phoned Kylie and invited her over for a drink, and that was probably all there was to it. Justin categorically does not have a reputation as a 'player'.

After the Brits, it was time for the Grammys and a possible master plan became clearer. Kylie flew to New York to present an award on stage to Justin, who quipped, 'Can I grab your ass again?' She had provided him with publicity gold in the UK and now he was return-ing the favour in the US. It was clearly a case of, 'You scratch my bum and I'll scratch yours.'

This all passed James Gooding by when he was spotted banging on Kylie's front door while she was at the Mandarin Oriental. According to his account, he spent the rest of the evening drinking champagne, taking coke and munching on sleeping pills. Not sur-prisingly, it wasn't long before he was booked into rehab at the Farm Place clinic in Surrey. He stayed ten days and sold his story to the *News of the World* shortly after leaving.

For such a high-profile star, Kylie has been fortunate to have escaped old-fashioned kiss-and-tell stories until Gooding, but it must have been a total shock to see the intensity of his feelings about her. Even by the standards of the now defunct Sunday paper, it was a cracking exclusive, announced under the sensational front-page headline 'Kylie Wrecked My Life'. Inside, he described her as a 'washed-up eighties star' when they'd met. He complained, 'She turned into a self-obsessed, virtually friendless control freak, des-perate to pursue her own ambitions.' And that was only week one!

Week two of his story was more familiar tabloid territory, with Gooding recalling the night 'Kylie was intent on lust in the forest'. It was all good knockabout sex-in-a-tent fun and, to add to the interest, Gooding disclosed that he'd had romances with Davinia Taylor, which we already knew about, and Martine McCutcheon, which we didn't. He also confirmed his affair with Sophie Dahl had happened while Kylie was on tour in 2001. His relationship with Kylie was distinctly on–off after that. Following his newspaper revelations, it was permanently off.

Kylie once described her relationship with James as a 'nice simple romance'. It had proved to be anything but that. She reacted to his revelations in a dignified and surprisingly tolerant way – at least in public. She suggested that James should move on. 'We had a great time,' she said. 'But it's run its course even though I remain fond of him.' It would have been very easy for her to lambaste Gooding for disloyalty, but she quickly put it behind her. Her recovery was made considerably easier by the fact that she had already fallen for France's answer to Brad Pitt.

Gooding turned his life around by giving up drugs and becoming a photographer. An exhibition of his work called 'Game On', in 2002, featured one picture of Kylie naked in the bath. He is still described as Kylie's ex-boyfriend when he pops up in the papers. The last time was in October 2012, when it was reported that his then girlfriend, actress and fashion entrepreneur Sadie Frost, had been cautioned for allegedly assaulting him. The stories brought up his kiss-and-tell again, so it seems he will never be allowed to forget that indiscretion.

There's nothing like a new romance to consign the old one to the bin as yesterday's news. Kylie had kept her affair with James Gooding secret for as long as she could. She did exactly the opposite with Olivier Martinez. He and Kylie bumped into each other in a hotel lobby the same night she had appeared at the Grammys. She liked what she saw.

With an easy charm, he suggested they might dine together the next time she was in Los Angeles, which, it just so happened, would be almost immediately. Their first 'date' was at the very fashionable restaurant The Ivy in Beverly Hills. Being seen at such a well-known celebrity-spotting haunt signified that Kylie had no intention of keeping this new man under wraps.

Shortly afterwards, Olivier and Kylie were photographed, hand in hand, arriving at the renowned Café de Flore in his home town of Paris. It was 5 March 2003, just four days before the notorious Gooding revelations in the *News of the World*. The occasion was the fiftieth birthday party for the fashion house Chloé. Kylie was graceful and smiling. Olivier oozed Gallic charisma in a black leather biker coat and patterned red neckerchief. He looked raffish and handsome. Allowing herself to be photographed by paparazzi and general hoi polloi wasn't something Kylie enjoyed, so it was interesting that she was so outgoing with her new boyfriend. These early pictures, with Olivier leading her by the hand, suggested that here was a confident, self-assured man. Kylie sang four jazz songs: 'Big Spender', 'Peel Me A Grape', 'Fever' – not her track but the moody Peggy Lee classic – and the Nina Simone standard 'My Baby Just Cares For Me'. Observers suggested she seemed to be singing them for Olivier.

Kylie's close friend, the novelist Kathy Lette, was struck by his magnetism the first time she met him for drinks with Kylie: 'Every woman in the bar is immediately swimming in a pool of her own drool. The air around crackles with sexual heat . . .'

Although little known in the UK, Martinez, who is two years older than Kylie, had been acting since 1990. He had only started to reach a large international audience the year before he met Kylie, when he made his Hollywood breakthrough in *Unfaithful*. In the film, he played a handsome stranger with whom Diane Lane has an adulterous affair. She was nominated for an Oscar for her performance and took most of the attention, but nevertheless it represented good progress for Olivier in the US.

For his role as the New York bookseller, he needed to reveal a smouldering, sensual side in order to make it believable that Diane Lane would cheat on Richard Gere. The love scenes were steamy and quite explicit. Vince Passaro in *Interview* magazine noted, 'He plays the books dealer with just the right mix of callousness and caring that a decent but essentially immature man would feel toward an older, married woman who really, really likes to drop by and have sex with him. A lot.'

Rather winningly, Olivier confessed that he had been raised in a very traditional way and wasn't particularly comfortable with such erotic love scenes. He pointed out that it was very rare in French films for actors to appear naked. The director, Adrian Lyne, who also made *Fatal Attraction* and *Basic Instinct*, paid Olivier the compliment: 'He's very beguiling, doing even ordinary things.'

Before his Hollywood breakthrough, Olivier was already very well known in his own country. If he were British, we would be describing him as a working-class hero. He describes himself as a 'real Parisian', although he is, in fact, half Spanish. As a young man, he looked set to go into the family firm, which in his case wasn't a business but a proud tradition of boxing. His father, Robert, a Spanish Moroccan, was a champion welter-weight in his native North Africa. 'He was very good,' explained Olivier, simply but proudly.

Olivier left school early, as Kylie did, and had a number of jobs, like selling jeans and waiting tables, before trying his luck in the boxing ring. He boxed professionally, also as a welter-weight, for three years, although, unlike many of his cousins who also box, he was never particularly serious about it. A near-fatal motorbike accident ended any ambitions he had in the ring. He spent months immobilized and, for a while, it was touch and go if he would survive. After the accident, he observed, 'It puts everything into perspective, the money and fame . . .'

He had a good sense of humour about his former trade: 'If you compare me to an actor, I'm probably one of the best boxers in the profession. But if you compare me as a boxer, I'm probably one of the best actors.' His former prowess, however, would later garner him unwelcome headlines.

Olivier grew up in a community of open-minded people, which

meant he never felt obliged to follow in his father's footsteps as a mechanic. Instead, when he finished his mandatory military service, he was persuaded by friends to train to be an actor. On little more than a whim, he auditioned for the Conservatoire National Supérieur d'Art Dramatique in Paris and, to his surprise, was accepted. He observed, 'It was a kind of miracle. By chance I had this opportunity and I took it and my life changed.'

After a couple of television parts, he was cast opposite the great Yves Montand in *IP5: L'île aux Pachydermes*. Encouragingly, he was nominated as Most Promising Actor for a César, the French equivalent of the Oscars, for his role as a young robber, on his way to the Pyrenees, who picks up an old man (Montand). Essentially, it was an elegiac road movie and, poignantly, proved to be Montand's last. The doyen of French cinema, one of Olivier's idols, died of a heart attack shortly after completing the film.

He may not have won the César at his first attempt, but Olivier made no mistake in his second feature, *Un, Deux, Trois, Soleil*, in which he played alongside another of his heroes, Marcello Mastroianni. Again, he was nominated as Most Promising Newcomer for his role as a thief. This time he had to use his seduction techniques on a young girl from a Marseilles slum. 'I'm going to change your destiny,' he whispered as he unhooked her bra. *FilmCritic.com* thought his performance 'wonderful'. By any standards, Martinez's introduction to the movies was sensational. Here was an actor of substance and promise and by no means just a slice of Gallic beefcake.

Olivier became accustomed to dealing with a voracious media when he starred opposite the beautiful Juliette Binoche in the acclaimed film *The Horseman on the Roof (Le Hussard sur le Toit)*, which at the time was the most expensive French movie ever made. The gossip soon began that the two were dating. The rumours proved to be entirely true, even though the couple threatened to sue a magazine for wrongly suggesting Binoche was pregnant. This time, Binoche won the César, although Olivier received many plaudits for

Kylie's appearance at the 2002 Brits was a triumph. She won two awards and stole the headlines when she performed in this Dolce & Gabbana creation.

Her boyfriend at the time was male model James Gooding, whom she called her 'delightful scruff from Essex'.

The following year's Brits and Kylie again stole the headlines when Justin Timberlake groped her famous bottom during a duet of 'Rapture'.

Kylie dazzled during her 2005 *Showgirl* concerts, but the tour had to be cancelled when she was diagnosed with breast cancer.

A surprise appearance on stage with Dannii at G-A-Y in June 2006. It was her first appearance since the successful treatment of her illness.

Happy to be alive – a radiant Kylie introduces Scissor Sisters at their free concert in support of the charity Red in Trafalgar Square in September 2006.

Her relationship with handsome Frenchman Olivier Martinez lasted four years. He was her rock during her cancer ordeal, but they announced their split in February 2007.

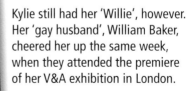

Kylie still had her 'Willie', however. Her 'gay husband', William Baker, cheered her up the same week, when they attended the premiere of her V&A exhibition in London.

Kylie could have a special room in her house just for her honours and awards. She was joined by her mother and father when she was made a Knight in the Order of Arts and Letters in Paris in May 2008.

Two months later, she is proud to show off her OBE for photographers after receiving the award from Prince Charles at Buckingham Palace.

For once a colourful costume was not part of a show. Kylie salutes the audience after being made a Doctor of Health Sciences at the Anglia Ruskin University in Chelmsford in October 2011.

Everyone realized there was an important new man in her life when she cuddled up to male model Andrés Velencoso at a birthday party in a Paris nightclub for burlesque star Dita Von Teese in October 2008.

Kylie only had eyes for her boyfriend when they attended a gala for the American Foundation for AIDS Research at the New York Public Library in June 2010.

Their relationship was still going strong in July 2012, when they enjoyed watching the tennis from the Royal Box at Wimbledon.

Kylie finally made it to Glastonbury in 2010, but just for one song as a guest of Scissor Sisters.

She dressed as a Pearly Queen for her show-stopping performance at The Queen's Diamond Jubilee Concert in June 2012.

Kylie, it seems, will never stop performing. Here she is as the goddess of love during her *Aphrodite* tour in Cape Town in July 2011.

It made a change to dress down for her 2012 *Anti Tour*. There was just the one outfit for her concert at the Manchester Academy.

Her fans were thrilled to see her in Jason Donovan's arms once more. She reunited with him for a performance of 'Especially For You' at the O2, London, in December 2012.

Portofino on the Italian Riviera is one of Kylie's favourite destinations. She was accompanied by William Baker for her holiday there in August 2011.

Time for a selfie. In 2013 she was joined by girlfriends on her July break.

Back to work . . . with will.i.am on *The Voice*.

his romantic portrayal of a young Italian officer helping a woman search for her husband in cholera-ravaged Provence.

It was during the American promotional tour for the film that Martinez was first described as the French Brad Pitt. He hated it and the comparison didn't seem to improve his Hollywood prospects, though he could authentically have starred in the film *Fight Club* instead of Brad.

In the end, he lived with Binoche for three years. They split in 1997 and he saw in the new millennium in Los Angeles, making English-language films in a not very convincing accent. He spoke very little English when he met Juliette Binoche and had to take lessons to prepare for Hollywood.

Martinez is very ambitious – not to be the world's biggest movie star but to be considered a great actor. Although he was respected in France, his native movie business was frustrating him. He admitted that the whole process of film-making there didn't move fast enough for him. The move to the US was a new beginning. 'My goal,' he revealed, 'is to get some interesting parts and make enough money to live free.'

One of the first things Olivier did when he moved to LA was to start dating the actress Mira Sorvino. She is best known to British audiences for her role as the ditzy prostitute in Woody Allen's *Mighty Aphrodite*, for which she won an Oscar for Best Supporting Actress. In real life, Sorvino is renowned as one of the most intelligent and articulate women in Hollywood. She speaks fluent French, which was helpful for Olivier. She is cultured, well read and studied Chinese at Harvard. She spent a year in Beijing researching a prize-winning thesis on racism in China and is fluent in Mandarin Chinese.

Olivier's relationship with Sorvino wouldn't have lasted a minute if he had only brought looks and charm to the table. Martinez is considered and thoughtful, and far from being a trophy companion. Crucially for Kylie, more than any man she had ever been linked with, Martinez was accomplished in dealing with the everyday problems of being a star. He may not have particularly enjoyed the constant attention, but he was able to handle it. Alain Grasset, a well-known columnist for *Le Parisien* newspaper, described the Frenchman as 'well-grounded', and a man who could be Mr Right for Kylie if she craved stability in her life. Olivier told *Interview* magazine, 'I see my friends, my family, my cousins work all day long for very little money, so it's not a big deal if I have this problem of not being able to walk on the streets.'

Three days after being photographed with Kylie in Paris, the couple headed south, turning up at a football match in Marseilles before moving on to St-Tropez. It was a part of France that Kylie had enjoyed so much with Michael Hutchence, and here she was again, looking up old haunts on the back of a motorbike. Olivier has a passion for them and owns two. After the Côte d'Azur, it was on to London, where they were pictured strolling down the Fulham Road, enjoying a coffee, before catching an open-topped tourist bus; they were seen kissing and cuddling in the back.

Their spring idyll continued through to May, when they were photographed sailing in the romantic surroundings of Portofino in Italy. Two weeks later, they had reached Monte Carlo, where they again appeared very relaxed in public, arriving for the Laureus World Sports Awards. They were beginning to look like one of the world's most glamorous couples. Kylie was fabulous in a bright red gown, while Olivier, who obviously had forgotten to pack his razor for their sailing trip, seemed cool and sophisticated in head-to-toe black.

So many public sightings took the mystery out of Kylie's new romance. There was absolutely no point in a paparazzo jumping out of the bushes and exclaiming, 'Aha, caught you!' The world knew that all the rumours were true. Even Dannii enthusiastically endorsed the romance, saying that Martinez was 'gorgeous and really nice' and that Kylie wanted kids soon. Dannii is always delightfully open with the press, but even she would have been more guarded if Kylie had insisted. Clearly, Kylie wanted the world to know she was with an eligible French film star. Olivier may have been brought up amid the sweat of the boxing ring and the grease of the garage, but he was now a mature, urbane man of the world, who loved jazz and French movies. Kylie likes to be challenged by the important men in her life.

She called him Ollie and he called her Honey. Kylie speaks French but doesn't pretend to be fluent. She has many friends based in France and went out with Stéphane Sednaoui for two years, so she was considerably better than the average tourist. She probably spoke French as well as Olivier spoke English. Of course, it didn't take long before the glossy magazines were suggesting that Olivier was famously well endowed – a Kylie essential, it seemed.

After their holiday, it was time to face the reality of their careers once more. Olivier had spent much of the previous year filming the action blockbuster *S.W.A.T.* alongside Colin Farrell and Samuel L. Jackson. He was not yet the star, but it was more than helpful to his career when the movie took over $37 million on its opening weekend. Almost inevitably, because he is handsome and French, Martinez quickly gained a reputation in Hollywood as a ladykiller. It may or may not have been justified, but Kylie was soon plagued by the same old doubts that separation brings. While she remained in London, finishing her next album, Olivier was making a movie, *Taking Lives*, in the Quebec and Montreal areas of Canada with, of all people, Angelina Jolie. Angelina played an FBI agent on the trail of a serial killer and Olivier was a local cop. It took about ten seconds for the tabloid press to suggest that Angelina and Olivier were getting close. Poor Kylie, was the implication, she's picked a bad 'un again.

Infidelity has been such a common thread running through Kylie's troubled dating over the years so, understandably, she is more than a little touchy. The rumours reached her back in London and were followed up by the alleged proof – pictures of Olivier and Angelina at a baseball game with her adopted son, Maddox. He insisted that Angelina was merely a friend, but Kylie acted decisively by hopping on a jet to Canada to find out for herself what was going on. She reportedly left Heathrow with a 'thunderous expression' on her face. The official line put about by 'sources' was that Olivier and Angelina were just friends and there was nothing going on. It didn't help that Mira Sorvino's mother was quoted as saying, 'If it's commitment she's after, she's dating the wrong man.'

The no-smoke-without-fire aficionados were congratulating themselves when pictures appeared of Kylie and Olivier looking glum on set. She arrived when Olivier and Angelina were filming scenes together, which wasn't the best timing. According to eyewitness sources, things were 'tense'. One said, 'Kylie arrived early and went straight to Olivier's trailer. There were no raised voices but they did not look too happy.' Kylie kept her own counsel about whether she believed the rumours, but her trip certainly seemed to be making a drama out of a crisis. A week later, Olivier appeared on American television and said that Kylie was 'cute, nice and interesting', which all seemed very gentlemanly.

For her part, Angelina Jolie said she was 'amazed' at all the gossip: 'Olivier and I were said to be together because we were at a ball game, but everybody else was there also. Basically, I'm single. I worked with a bunch of men on a film recently, so I was tagged to all of them.'

That was pretty much it for the Angelina and Olivier rumours. There's always a great deal of hype to filter whenever a film needs to place itself in the public consciousness. From Kylie's point of view, Angelina Jolie was the worst nightmare for a woman trying to make a relationship work. At that stage of her career, Angelina was depicted as voracious, Amazonian and beautiful. By a curious twist of fate, having been linked to the French Brad Pitt, she was subject to yet more rumours when she started filming *Mr. and Mrs. Smith* with the real one the following year – this time they turned out to be true.

Kylie's adoring public were undecided about Olivier Martinez's commitment to their favourite. Unfortunately for Kylie, he would be linked to other beautiful women in the future.

20

The Kylie Effect

Fever was a hard act to follow. While her fans watched to see if Olivier would be a keeper, Kylie was faced with the problem of what to do next. She decided to go backwards, to the sounds of her young teenage years, when she was growing up and going out in Camberwell. She wasn't looking to copy the music of Donna Summer, Adam Ant and Prince, of course, but to produce a contemporary record using the best elements of that time. What was immediately apparent was that *Body Language* was no *Fever II*. It was neither camp nor disco.

'Slow', the first track on the album, was released at the start of November 2003 and became her seventh number one single. It was her ninth number one in Australia and was also top of the US *Billboard* dance chart. It was a supremely sexy song, written by the acclaimed Icelandic singer-songwriter Emilíana Torrini and her producer, Dan Carey. Emilíana, who was surprised to be noticed by Kylie, had been discovered and brought to London by a record company executive who heard her singing in a restaurant in Reykjavik. She subsequently was best known for singing 'Gollum's Song' for the blockbuster *The Lord of the Rings: The Two Towers*. She joked, 'I still think Kylie's people were trying to call Jamelia, and they just got the wrong number.'

The seductive feel of 'Slow' was greatly enhanced by a suggestive video shot in the sun of a Barcelona lido. Kylie was centre-stage, writhing around in a little blue dress on a beach towel, surrounded by a host of well-toned bodies. The song invited the listener to 'Read my body language', a line that inspired the title of the album. There was no denying the body language of the video. It was unambiguously all about sex and making love, slowly. Kylie would later nominate 'Slow' as her favourite track among the hundreds she had recorded. It's one of those classics that should be filed under 'Bedroom' on your playlist.

When *Body Language* was released a couple of weeks later, Jordan Paramour in *heat* magazine said the album heralded the era of 'electro-pop Kylie' and was 'unashamedly sexy'. For once Kylie had decided against a full tour to promote the album. Instead, there would be just two exclusive gigs: one in London and one in New York.

Perhaps Kylie was finally listening to her father's advice. On one of her trips home to recuperate from overdoing it, he had told her that she didn't have to say yes to everything. As a result, she'd had practically a year off, and even now wasn't hurtling around doing a million things to publicize the album. The new image that accompanied the album was inspired by Olivier and paid homage to her love of France – she'd once gushed, 'I adore Paris.' She was a Brigitte Bardot figure and revealed the same blonde hairstyle, come-hither eyes and pouting lips of the Gallic sex symbol. It was an uncanny likeness.

She revealed the new look at the one-off hour-long concert at the Hammersmith Apollo that was rumoured to have cost £1 million to produce. Paris came to West London that night in November. She called it the Money Can't Buy concert, because none of the 40,000 tickets ever went on sale. Instead, they were made available in competitions and via her website, although, as Simon Sheridan amusingly commented, not many of the celebrities in the audience won their tickets answering questions on BBC Radio Cornwall. Many of her greatest hits featured alongside the new album tracks, but the most memorable number was a mash-up of 'Breathe' with the French love classic 'Je T'Aime . . . Moi Non Plus'. Kylie wore the Bardot uniform of stripy onion-seller top and black leggings for 'On A Night Like This', which had been imaginatively linked to 'Singing In The Rain'.

Surprisingly, *Body Language* was not a number-one album, suggesting that this promotional strategy didn't completely work – a tour round the country might have produced better sales. The album was well received, however, both in the UK and the US, where Kylie was hoping to build on her success.

The *Independent* made the point that Kylie no longer had to prove herself: 'She finds herself in the previously unthinkable position of not needing to chase either popularity or hipness: she now has the luxury of taking both these things for granted. Perhaps as a result, *Body Language* is an incredibly assured record.' *New York* magazine enthused, 'You can't help but get lost in Minogue's music.'

The problem was that the rest of the album failed to match the impact of 'Slow'. It was, in fact, a slow-burner. *Metro Weekly*, the Washington-based magazine, noted, 'With its alluring minimalist rhythms and lyrical eroticism, the album works best when taken as a whole.' That might account for the slightly disappointing performance of the follow-up single 'Red Blooded Woman', a song that sounded like it might have been recorded by Destiny's Child; it peaked at number six. The track was number one in the Hot Dance Club Play Chart for Kylie in the US, where her new popularity reached a peak when she won her first Grammy. 'Come Into My World' was named Best Dance Recording. The only drawback was that the track was from *Fever* and not *Body Language*, an album that is probably more interesting in the long run than either of her previous two. It was certainly much smoother.

Parlophone had big plans for Kylie's next project – a modern, all-guns-blazing greatest-hits package that would precede her biggest world tour so far. That seemed like a good idea when the Johnny Douglas/Karen Poole ballad 'Chocolate', the third single from *Body Language*, also peaked at a disappointing number six in the UK, despite another stylish video from Dawn Shadforth. Kylie danced seductively in a floaty red dress, as if she were taking part in an advertisement for Turkish delight. That was it for *Body Language*.

Kylie was already busy recording new tracks for the greatest-hits album. It's a common marketing ploy to include a couple of unreleased songs to help increase royalties. *Ultimate Kylie*, while not her first hits collection, was noteworthy because it included tracks from Stock, Aitken and Waterman and deConstruction, as well as the more recent Parlophone output. In all, there were thirty-four of her hits and two extra, very catchy dance numbers. They were 'I Believe In You', written by the Scissor Sisters, and 'Giving You Up', with Xenomania, the production team responsible for many of the Girls Aloud hits. One of Kylie's ongoing strategies is to work with names that are the most current and fashionable in the music business. Both of these numbers would eventually be top-ten hits and qualify properly for inclusion on the album.

Soon after the album's release, in October 2004, Kylie announced details of the *Kylie Showgirl: The Greatest Hits* tour, which would begin at the SECC in Glasgow the following March and include dates across Europe and the Far East before ending in Australia. The UK dates sold out in less than two hours.

Kylie and William worked on the show for a year. While she was naturally excited and nervous at the prospect, she hadn't been feeling well in the run-up to opening night. It was her usual complaint of stress and exhaustion. She even said that maybe she was getting too old for the travelling circus that her tours had become. Nobody could have known that this was far more serious than just feeling shattered.

It didn't help that a week before the tour was due to start, the media was aquiver with excitement that Kylie might be pregnant. She was pictured apparently showing the first signs of a little baby bump. The green tunic dress she was wearing when she stepped out of her London home seemed a little too snug. That, of course, is all the evidence required for an orgy of speculation. Male pop stars never have to put up with this sort of nonsense.

Showgirl was, in many ways, a development of the Kylie introduced at the Sydney Olympics. When she took to the stage in Glasgow, there was more talk of designer costumes than music, as now seemed de rigueur for Kylie performances. For the opening number, 'Better The Devil You Know', the lights went up to reveal Kylie in a jewel-encrusted corset by John Galliano that took four months to put together, each jewel painstakingly sewn by hand. The body-hugger turned out to be a minuscule sixteen inches around the waist, which guaranteed maximum press coverage – although she denied it was so small. The ensemble was topped off by a plumed headdress and a tail. Kylie was carried aloft by her customary near-naked male dancers, wearing eight-foot feather wings. Dave Simpson in the *Guardian* sardonically thought that it would be the 'first pop tour to prompt the interest of the Royal Society for the Protection of Birds'. After the thirty-minute interval, she emerged on a glittering moon in a pink ballgown and sang 'Over The Rainbow'.

Kylie was definitely encouraging nostalgia, and she achieved the right response with the enthusiastic singalong to 'Especially For You'. She had now accepted the song for what it was: a pretty melody that her fans love. It was either the high spot or the low spot of the concert, depending on how slushy you were feeling. Less successful was a crooning, smoky version of 'The Loco-Motion'. This was a song that existed solely to dance to. The overwhelming impression at the end of the evening was that Kylie could do a greatest-hits show every year. Alternatively, she could just take the whole set to Vegas.

Simon Price, in the *Independent on Sunday*, observed Kylie's vulnerability was part of her appeal and likened her to Edith Piaf, the great French songbird who so articulated longing: 'Our feelings towards Kylie are protective rather than lustful: we can't believe that all those horrid boyfriends are so mean to her.'

Olivier, one of those horrid boyfriends, if you believed the rumours, flew in from Los Angeles for the opening night. He was still shrugging off persistent gossip about him and other actresses, including the exotic Mexican, Selma Hayek. They were seen out in the evening in LA on four different occasions – once, he was apparently feeding her sushi. He was also photographed kissing his *S.W.A.T.* co-star Michelle Rodriguez, and pictured dining with French beauty Celine Balitran, a former girlfriend of George Clooney.

Everything on the tour seemed to be going well, although there were the inevitable hiccups along the way. At one point, Kylie found a wardrobe girl in floods of tears before the show. Apparently, the distressed young woman had tied the silver boots Kylie wore on stage to a lorry's wing mirror so that they would dry after she had resprayed them. Unfortunately, the driver drove off. Kylie's boots were eventually spotted sailing down the motorway.

All good fun, but behind the scenes all was not going quite so well. Out of the blue, during the Birmingham dates in April 2005, Kylie disclosed that she was splitting from her Creative Director, William Baker. This was a big deal, but the announcement was very low key, with no indication of a tiff. It all seemed very friendly, although everything that happened in Kylie's life always appeared completely amicable, whether it was splitting up with record labels or boyfriends, or, as in this case, her gay husband. It was just the way Kylie liked to do things in the press. She announced on her website, 'This is something we have been talking about for a while and it was always our intention to finish our creative partnership with the greatest-hits album and *Showgirl* tour. Willie and I have worked closely together for eleven years and both feel it is the time to move on.' She added that the timing was perfect, which, of course, it wasn't.

Olivier, however, wasn't bothered about any falling-out with William. He was far more concerned by the cold sweats Kylie was getting. And when she started being sick practically all the time, he decided enough was enough – it couldn't all be put down to the infamously narrow corset. He strongly encouraged her to have a check-up. Her doctors ran some tests and said they would get back to Kylie in due course with any findings.

During the break between the British leg and the Australian segment of the tour, Kylie and Olivier flew to Melbourne to spend some time with her family. On 15 May, just four days before the first date at the Sydney SuperDome, her doctor came to see her at her parents' home. Olivier, Ron, Carol and Brendan were all in the room with her. The physician told her that she had early-stage breast cancer. 'The moment my doctor told me, I went silent. My mum and dad were with me, then we all went to pieces.' Kylie then became insistent that she had to get back to work and her flight to Sydney left in two hours. Eventually, Ron had heard enough and told her firmly to 'just sit down'.

She had a day to prepare herself before millions of fans all over the world needed to be told. How on earth do you prepare yourself? Kylie went for a walk along the beach with Olivier and Brendan. The next day, her private agony would be front-page news.

Kylie's own statement was rather dry, but what could she say in the circumstances? Ever the professional, she said, 'I was so looking forward to bringing the *Showgirl* tour to Australian audiences and am sorry to have to disappoint my fans. Nevertheless, hopefully all will work out and I'll be back with you all soon.'

At this stage, nobody was in the least bit interested in the fate of the tour. The promoter Michael Gudinski, a fixture in Kylie's team from the beginning, said all the right, reassuring things: 'It has come as a shock to her, the world and to her family but she is very fit. She is a fighter and hopes to be back doing what she loves sooner rather than later.'

The Australian Prime Minister, John Howard, wished her well: 'Any young woman of that age to be diagnosed with that condition – it does send a shudder through you. I think all Australians feel for her'. David Wood, who had been her first kiss all those years ago, popped round to her house to deliver a get-well note: 'I was wishing her the best. She is the strongest girl I've ever met and known, and it was just a little note saying "I know you'll come through this".'

Dannii, who would be such a trooper over the coming months, caught the first plane back to Melbourne. She echoed what everybody thought: 'The news is very upsetting,' she said simply. Elton John, when he heard, shouted, 'Oh, my God, the poor girl,' and got straight on the phone.

The good news, if there was any, was that her family were with her, she was home in Melbourne and Olivier was there too. Her father was, by all accounts, a little wary of the actor's reputation as a ladies' man but at least he was at his daughter's side. Olivier was a man who had once faced death himself. He said, 'This is *our* fight. I'm not going anywhere. I'm here for you now and nothing else matters. Just get well.' Olivier would honour that statement.

Three days after the official announcement, Kylie was quietly admitted to the St Francis Xavier Cabrini Hospital in Melbourne, where a tumour was removed from her left breast in a partial mastectomy. That was just the beginning of a painful process of chemotherapy and uncertainty. Ron and Carol, who had been more like close friends to their daughter as she grew older, rallied around as mother and father. Kylie explained, 'It was as if I was a little girl to them again.'

She stayed at home with her parents for the first couple of months, literally under siege from photographers anxious to get a picture of 'brave' Kylie. She was too preoccupied with her own plight to worry about the media, but she felt bad for her family around her.

Kylie had the anxious wait while tests were completed to ascertain the strength and spread of the disease. Then she stunned everyone by deciding that she wanted to go back to Paris for her chemotherapy. 'I wanted a life with my boyfriend in Paris,' she admitted. It wasn't easy breaking the news to Ron and Carol, who, naturally, were so worried but, in the end, a compromise was reached and her mother went with her. Carol stayed during the worst days of her treatment. Kylie said, touchingly, 'I don't know how I would have got through it without her.'

These were the darkest days, when Kylie was sometimes too ill even to get up. She would feel a sense of achievement if she made it as far as the corner shop. She would go into her bedroom for twenty minutes to contemplate her life in quiet and solitude. She confessed, 'I had moments when I didn't want to look in the mirror.'

She voraciously read everything she could find on the Internet about her condition. The stark facts were that breast cancer affects one in nine women. One of her greatest concerns was the effect chemotherapy might have on her future chances of conceiving. Kylie opted for additional treatment aimed at improving her chances of becoming pregnant at a later date.

Surprisingly, she was relatively unfazed by losing her hair, the inevitable consequence of chemotherapy. First of all, she cut it short, and then, with a deep breath, 'buzz-cut' the whole thing. Kylie also became extremely adept at tying her headscarf so that there would never be a picture of her without her head covered. She was so used to changing her look as an actress and performer that she took that part of it in her stride.

In Paris, Kylie rented a huge old apartment in St-Germain surrounded by the fashionable boutiques and quirky shops that make this quarter of the French capital so vibrant and appealing. Dannii, who she says was 'fabulous' during it all, would travel over on

Eurostar from London to cheer her up. Always a ball of energy, she would try and get Kylie off the sofa and moving about, or singing along to some cheesy old favourites, just as they had when they were kids. If Kylie wasn't up to that, they would just sit quietly solving a Sudoku puzzle together or watching *Ready Steady Cook* on TV. Sometimes Kylie's old friend Kat would pop by and take her out to a local café if she was feeling up to it. William was another visitor she was pleased to see.

Kylie kept a chemotherapy diary, because she realized she was forgetting everything and her whole life had to revolve around her medication and calendar of treatment at the Institut Gustave-Roussy, a leading oncology centre in south Paris. She called this dreadful time 'chemo-brain'. She was desperately ill. By October 2005, her weight had dropped to six stone. She was also too poorly to contemplate any visit back to Australia for Christmas, something she always loved to do.

She had her final session of chemo just before Christmas 2005 and then had an anxious wait for the results of more tests. Eventually, she was given the all clear after New Year's and was well enough to travel to Melbourne for the back-up radiation treatment. She needed ten-minute sessions five times a week. Fortunately, Olivier flew back with her and she was able to enjoy her new £400,000 home on French Island, off the Melbourne coast. Her progress was promising. Dannii let slip on her website, 'My best news to start the year is that my sister is in full remission,' although it may have been on purpose to let the world know what was happening. Olivier's mother, Rosemarie, revealed that his family, who got on very well with Kylie, were delighted. 'All we want is for her to be happy,' she said graciously.

Kylie stayed in Australia until after the birth of her first nephew in April. Her brother Brendan's girlfriend, Rebecca, had a baby boy, Charles, a first grandchild for Ron and Carol after forty years of marriage. Aunt Kylie spent her time making plans and writing lyrics about her ordeal. It was cathartic, even if they would never find their way on to an album.

She also made a list of things she wanted to do, simple things that made living worthwhile. They included going back to a favourite restaurant in the beautiful Italian resort of Portofino to eat langoustine with Olivier.

Throughout her ordeal, Olivier was her rock. Kylie called him a very solid and strong character. He surprised a media that had decided he was a shallow film star and a ladies' man. At least now there were no pictures of him with alluring actresses – for the moment. Instead, when Kylie felt well enough, she would cling on to his back and he would whisk her through the streets of Paris on his motorcycle. With their helmets on, they couldn't be recognized.

As she began to feel so much better, Kylie would draw inspiration from the wonderful city of Paris. While it would never be home to her in the way that Melbourne and London are, she loved the city, enjoying brunch in the Café de Flore in St Germain or lunch at her favourite Italian restaurant. And then there was Sheba to take for walks or just have a cuddle with on the sofa. She was Olivier's chocolate-coloured Rhodesian Ridgeback Kylie had first met in Los Angeles. Sheba hadn't taken to Olivier's new girlfriend at first. On one occasion, she had grabbed a particularly expensive shoe out of Kylie's wardrobe and chewed it to bits. Now, however, they were devoted to one another and the dog was a great comfort to her during the dark days.

Kylie tentatively started work on a children's book called *The Showgirl Princess*. It gave her something to think about other than the 'drama', as she called her ordeal. On days when she felt up to it, she would sit at the computer and try to make some progress. She got the idea from all the drawings and paintings sent to her by young girl fans who had seen the *Showgirl* tour. Kylie told the *Mail on Sunday*, 'Some of the pictures were so funny. In some I looked like Marge Simpson because the big blue-feathered headdress I wore looked more like her hair. We all thought I needed to do something with these wonderful images.' The idea would eventually become a book that followed behind-the-scenes events of one day on tour.

At last, Kylie's hair was growing back slowly, including her eyebrows and eyelashes, allaying her fears that she would be the one person for whom this did not happen. The world saw a new, happy Kylie for the first time in April, when pictures of her taken by Olivier were posted on her website and subsequently published throughout the world. Olivier has never taken photographs professionally, but he managed to capture Kylie positively glowing with happiness – and with very short brown hair – when they were visiting Portofino. That was one wish fulfilled.

Her ordeal lasted fourteen months – no performances, no records, no Kylie, except for the dribble of news about how she was doing. And then, in July 2006, she appeared on television in an emotional interview with Cat Deeley, and the world could see how well she looked, full of smiles and sparkle. She told Cat that on one memorable evening she was in a back storeroom at home in Paris and, glancing through a small window, could see the lights of the Eiffel Tower. She said, 'They were twinkling for me.' It made for riveting viewing and gave everybody a rare insight into the true despair of such an awful thing happening two weeks before your thirty-seventh birthday.

One of the most interesting things she talked about was the 'Kylie Effect': women had sat up and taken notice of what had happened to her, and were monitoring their own health more closely. A greater awareness of the risks of breast cancer would inevitably lead to more lives being saved.

Olivier Martinez summed up Kylie's ordeal: 'What doesn't kill you makes you stronger. When life tests you, you have to do your best. I'm there for her.'

Kylie commented, 'Obviously, someone up there likes me. Thank Heavens!'

21

A Second Chance

For once, the old cliché about there not being a dry eye in the house was true. Unannounced, Kylie crept onto the stage at G-A-Y in London with a bunch of flowers for her sister Dannii, who was performing that night in June 2006 to promote her own greatest-hits album. It was a complete surprise, although pictures of their embrace were in all the papers the following day. It was very touching that Kylie decided to make her re-emergence with a lovely gesture to her sister. She even joined her for part of one of her early hits, 'Jump To The Beat'. It was a thank-you for the dark days of chemo in Paris, when Dannii had shone a little light on the day merely by being there and bringing her zest for life with her.

But Kylie was under no illusions as to how lucky she had been. Shortly afterwards, Nigel McCarroll, her chauffeur for more than ten years, succumbed to cancer himself. At his cremation service in London, Kylie, clearly upset, laid a wreath in the shape of an Audi sports car. Her good fortune was brought painfully home to her once more when Dannii's best friend Laura also died from the disease.

It appeared that Kylie was gently moving back into the limelight, but the truth was that she couldn't wait to return to normality. Second chances are special and she didn't want to waste a moment of hers. More public sightings followed: strolling in Paris with Olivier, in the front row of a Chanel fashion show with his Rhodesian Ridgeback Sheba, dancing a conga on stage at the Assembly Rooms in Edinburgh and attending a first night of *Brasil Brasileiro*, a Brazilian review, at Sadler's Wells. Her name was still much in demand and she signed a perfume deal with Coty Inc., who already had the Beckhams and Jennifer Lopez on their books. Her scent was called Darling – her preferred way of addressing close friends – and landed in stores in time for Christmas. Kylie described it as 'sexy, generous, playful and quite surprising', and it became an instant best-seller.

She also announced that she would be resuming her Australian tour in November 2006, followed by a week in London in January 2007. Demand for the dates at Wembley Arena was so high that they sold out in six minutes. She was outraged when ticket touts started to make huge profits from the gigs by reselling tickets on eBay. She wanted those tickets cancelled and resold to genuine fans. She added four more shows in Manchester and they sold out in the blink of an eye as well.

There was a big difference between strolling along the Seine and being in shape for a gruelling concert tour. She joked that instead of six quick changes, there would be six slow ones and she might even use a chair. She moved back to London full time and began rehearsing six hours a day, including in the boxing ring – a suggestion from Olivier, who still liked to spar a little. She was getting some informal coaching from World Cruiserweight Champion David Haye, whom she met at The Third Space gym in Soho. Funnily enough, the PR department at *Neighbours* once put about a story that she was called 'Bruiser' Minogue on set after she punched Jason during her first-ever scene on the show.

One of the more sensitive tasks she undertook was shooting her new 2007 calendar. She had spent many months trying to avoid the camera or even her own reflection, but now, when she was a cancer victim in remission, she had to pose professionally again at the age of thirty-eight. She chose to dress up in outlandish Kylie fashion. In one shot, she is wearing a black and gold leotard, elbow-length black gloves and a metre-long conical hat. In another she is leaping in the air like a ballet dancer in a black leotard, oversized tutu and a gold wig. It was good fun and didn't take itself too seriously.

The best news in the lead-up to her concerts was that William Baker was back by her side after spending the previous year on various projects of his own, including helping to style Victoria Beckham. Kylie's huge affection for him remained.

Kylie didn't want to wear exactly the same costumes that she had squeezed into for the greatest-hits shows. The opening outfit looked surprisingly similar though, except for the obvious fact that it was now all pink instead of blue – a tribute to the pink-ribbon campaign that is the symbol of breast-cancer awareness. The feathered head-dress was just as over the top as it had been before. The corset seemed just as snug, but perhaps not sixteen inches this time around.

When she emerged on stage for the first time at the Sydney Entertainment Centre, she greeted the audience simply, 'Good evening, Sydney. How are you feeling tonight?' She went straight into the first number, which, as before, was 'Better The Devil You Know', to a mixed reaction of sobbing and cheering. She engaged in some banter with her fans: 'Generally, I'm ten minutes late but this is a year and a half, so I'm fashionably late.'

Kylie was clearly moving in a more careful and sedate style around the stage – leaving all the energetic moves to her dancers. She was trying hard to be realistic about the impact of her illness and what she could and could not achieve: 'I am not the same person. I can't do the same things.' A waiter would bring her a glass of water while she chatted to the audience. She did require a chair to sit on when she went backstage, and her mother, 'Quick Change Carol' as she was affectionately nicknamed, was there, as usual, to help with the Formula One pit stop – her struggle into the next costume. She performed for two and a half hours, a Herculean effort under the circumstances. To say she was tired at her final bow would be an understatement.

The universal reaction was one of pleasure and relief that she was back. The *Independent on Sunday* even carried an editorial about her: 'It was not so long ago that a diagnosis of breast cancer was a death sentence. Her comeback tour dramatises the advances in medical science that have transformed survival rates . . . she has helped raise awareness among young women for whom early diagnosis is the key.' It was a timely reminder of how sick Kylie had been just a short time ago. There is no better story than turning adversity into triumph.

On the second night, she was joined on stage by Bono, who sang the Robbie part from 'Kids'. At the Melbourne Rod Laver Centre, his place was taken by Dannii. She wore a corseted black leotard, while big sister had put on a leopard-print catsuit, complete with ears. Needless to say, they brought the house down. For her final show in the city, she wore a leather jacket with Olivier's face on it.

Backstage, she thanked her grandmother Millie, now eighty-five, for braving the crowds to attend. Millie replied, 'I wouldn't miss this because I love you.'

Surprisingly, considering how devoted he had been, Olivier wasn't standing in the wings watching her triumphant return. That gave the media the green light to have another go at him. He was pictured in Paris with a gorgeous Israeli actress and model called Sarai Givati, aged twenty-four, who had been in one or two shows on American television such as *CSI: Crime Scene Investigation*. One problem for Olivier was that he had starred in the film *Unfaithful*, which gave the papers the opportunity to describe him as the '*Unfaithful* actor'.

Sarai had stopped off in Paris en route from her home in Los Angeles to visit her parents in the city of Tiberias on the Sea of Galilee. She stayed in a hotel and joined Olivier during the day to tour the Musée d'Orsay, where he showed her some of the modern art he liked. On a walk along the Left Bank of the Seine near his apartment, he took off his scarf and wrapped it around her to keep her warm. For her part, Sarai confirmed that they had met up, but was insistent that there was nothing romantic going on between them at that point, despite the implications.

The official reason for Olivier staying in Paris was post-production work on a new film called *Blood and Chocolate*. He did, after all, have a career to start up again, just like Kylie, although this particular movie, in which he played the leader of a werewolf pack, didn't seem a good place to resume. He was amusing about it: 'A part of my character is played by an actual wolf and I think he was quite good playing me – smart but with a bad reputation.' The film flopped at the box office.

Everyone seemed to think Olivier's relationship with Kylie was on the rocks – except his mother, of course, who was quoted as saying they were madly in love. Kylie had originally planned to spend a relaxed Christmas in Melbourne with her family and had hoped Olivier would be able to join them. He appeared to have no intention of doing that. The rumours coming out of the French capital changed her plans, and she took a 22-hour flight to Paris to find out what was going on. The official line was that Kylie needed to rehearse for a special extra concert in London on New Year's Eve.

It was the first time they had seen each other for two months. That is one of the things the public don't always realize about celebrity relationships: they can be 'together' but work commitments mean they see each other only occasionally. It's not a formula that had worked for Kylie in the past and it didn't seem to be working now.

They were seen meeting for the first time at a café near Olivier's apartment. An eyewitness said that instead of greeting each other with a kiss, he leaned over the table, stroked her face and said, 'Ça va?', a simple 'How are you?' in French. Kylie replied, 'Fine. Fine.' A customer in the café told the *Sunday Mirror* that they both looked tense and anxious: 'It was obvious from the tone of their voices and body language this was not casual romantic chatter.'

The heart to heart seemed to clear the air, because they then went back to Olivier's flat with Kylie hanging on to his arm. They didn't go out much after that. She was exhausted after her flight and could manage only the occasional short walk with Sheba.

Olivier travelled with her to London for her concert at Wembley Arena. She didn't wear the jacket with his face on it, but she did wear one that proclaimed 'Kylie's Back'. The critics were impressed. Marcus Dunk in the *Daily Express* observed, 'There's something so endearing, lovable and friendly about Kylie that she could have simply stood there and we would have been enraptured.' She hadn't lost her ability to hang her personal life on a peg in the dressing room and emerge as the star everyone was expecting to see.

While the new costumes and dance routines ensured the show was nearly as much of a spectacle as before her illness, there were the signs of an inevitable change in direction. For once, the music seemed almost as important as the razzmatazz. A new song called 'White Diamond' was an unexpected highlight because it was the only one the audience didn't really know. She had written it with Jake Shears during some new recording sessions the previous year. The overall sound was very Scissor Sisters.

She mixed 'Burning Up' from the *Fever* album with the Madonna classic 'Vogue'. It proved an apt mash-up when the lady herself showed up in the audience for one of the Wembley concerts. Dannii, of course, was also there to sing with her sister. Olivier stayed for the London shows, but had left before the Manchester leg began on 12 January. That was his birthday and he celebrated it with friends in Paris.

By the time she was settled into her suite at the trendy Malmaison Hotel in Manchester, there were genuine concerns, both in private and in the media, that Kylie was attempting to do too much too soon. Those misgivings seemed well founded when she had to abandon her second show at the MEN Arena because of a bad bout of flu. It was the first time anything like that had happened to her.

She told the audience right at the start that she was struggling: 'I'm sorry about my voice tonight. I've got a cold. Do you mind if I just stand here and pose all night?' She battled through the first half, but after she and Dannii sang 'Kids' it was clear she couldn't continue, and she told the fans, 'I can't sing on.' Nobody seemed to mind, appreciating how amazing it was for her to be there in the first place.

Doctors insisted that she rest thoroughly until the infection had cleared. While this setback had nothing directly to do with her cancer, Dr Emma Pennery, a clinical expert at Breast Cancer Care, explained, 'When your body has been through that amount of trauma, your ability to fight off illness can be compromised, so straightforward flu might knock you off your feet.'

Kylie postponed concerts for a couple of days and rescheduled the abandoned one for later in the month. By this time, Olivier had left Paris for Los Angeles and begun dating Sarai Givati, who had now split from her boyfriend. According to an exclusive that Sarai gave to the *Daily Mail*, there was no overlap between her affair with Olivier and his break-up with Kylie: 'When we first met up again after Christmas I told him I was single and he replied, "Me too." I think that when we both realized we were single, there was an immediate sense that something was going to happen.' He refused to speak to her about Kylie. All he would say when she asked him about it was 'it was time to break up and that the relationship had run its course' – which it probably had. They met up at the Chateau Marmont Hotel, where he was staying. The following night he was seen dining with Michelle Rodriguez, the actress he had been linked with two years before.

A week later, on 2 February, his split with Kylie was officially announced, nearly four years after they had first met. A joint statement said, 'Kylie and Olivier have made it clear that the decision to go their separate ways was amicable. The media's false accusations of disloyalty have saddened them both.' 'Amicable' – that word again.

Unfortunately, the statement didn't seem to stop the accusations, and Olivier was described as 'love rat' and 'heartless' amid reports of him driving around LA in his Aston Martin with an attractive woman in the passenger seat. Twenty-four hours after the announcement, he was seen embracing the exotic actress Penelope Cruz at the Chateau Marmont, prompting one observer to comment, 'Why doesn't this guy get a house?' Penelope was actually having lunch with three girlfriends, so it wasn't the cosy date that was implied.

The general backlash against Olivier was so strong that Kylie took the unusual step of defending him on her website: 'As for the treatment Olivier has received of late, I can only reiterate that he simply does not deserve the kind of harassment or vitriol to which he has been subject. For someone for whom I have enormous love and respect, and communicate with, it is so grossly unfair to demonize an honest man. I would ask of you, my fans, to show your support for both Ollie and myself, as a separation is never easy.'

Kylie was again left distraught by a break-up, although the suspicion remains that it was inevitable following her recovery. Olivier, according to friends, is very much his own man and unlikely to be happy as part of an entourage. Whether they would have stayed together as long as they did without the intervention of her cancer is something for amateur psychiatrists to speculate about. But the fact remains that he did stick around throughout her ordeal, pretty much abandoned his own career and took her for langoustine in Portofino.

Their relationship then was full-time; after she resumed her career, it went back to being part time. Her description of him as 'honourable' suggests that he did the right thing by her during her ordeal. She needed him both privately and publicly and he was equal to the task. She was once asked the place she considered to be the best in the world and she responded sweetly, 'In Ollie's arms.' He may have broken her heart like Michael Hutchence had done, but the relationship with Olivier was certainly challenging and that kind were always the most important ones for Kylie. Charisma remained for her the most attractive quality in a man and Olivier certainly had more than his fair share of that. As she did with Michael and Stéphane, she established a platonic friendship with him after the dust had settled.

Olivier stayed in Hollywood, although his career never really picked up its former momentum. He has appeared in three films and one television part since *Taking Lives* in 2004, although his latest, an adventure movie called *The Physician*, was more promising. He is no longer best known as a former boyfriend of Kylie Minogue, however. Instead, he is the husband of the Oscar-winning actress Halle Berry. They married at a chateau in Burgundy in July 2013 and she gave birth to their son, Maceo, three months later.

He received some unwelcome headlines in 2012 when he was involved in a fight with Halle's former partner, the model Gabriel Aubry. By the look of the latter's face after the altercation, Olivier had lost none of his boxing skills.

22

The Disco Mouse

The private and the public Kylie were a million miles apart once more. Personal disappointment made a stark contrast to a professional life that could scarcely have been going better. Everyone was so pleased she was well that she was liable to receive a standing ovation just for walking into a room.

The papers were sympathetic after her break-up with Olivier, although they seemed to have given up on her chances of having children. There were unhelpful and unconfirmed reports that she had endured two failed attempts at IVF, as well as concerned murmurings about her biological clock. Kylie sensibly kept her mouth shut on the subject.

She was a loving aunt and comfortable in the company of friends' children. And, without much fanfare, she had been closely involved with children's charities, in particular Childline and the National Society for the Prevention of Cruelty to Children. She had been the NSPCC's first-ever ambassador when she was appointed to the role in 2003 and, since then, has continued to donate tickets and lend support to fundraising. It is a cause she feels very strongly about: 'All children should have the right to grow up loved, safe and happy . . . Children are so precious, we need to do all we can to look after them.'

Those values were in evidence when she presented a Child of Courage Award to a six-year-old cancer victim called Katy Miles, from Argyll in Scotland, who was in remission from the disease after more than six months of painful treatment. As part of the Pride of Britain Awards, Kylie had surprised the little girl with a bunch of flowers and the words, 'How about a little cuddle?' When Katy obliged by throwing her arms around her, Kylie shouted, 'Hug me harder!' It was one of those moving occasions when you didn't know whether to laugh or cry. Kylie sang 'Can't Get You Out Of My Head' just for her and blew kisses at the delighted child. Kylie's name alone gave a boost to many charity initiatives following her recovery.

The appreciation of all things Kylie was evident from the number of awards and accolades that poured in. She began 2007 by being named Gay Icon of All Time in a special poll that placed Dolly Parton, Abba and Judy Garland immediately behind her. She was voted Britain's favourite Australian and Madame Tussauds unveiled a new waxwork. It was her fourth – a number only bettered by the Queen. The new 'Kylie', wearing a long red dress, smelled nice because it was sprayed with Darling twice a day as part of a strategy to make the figures multisensory. The waxwork, perched on a sparkly crescent moon, replaced the better-known one of Kylie on all fours. The real woman had never cared for that because visitors could walk around her and inspect her bottom. They would ignore the DO NOT TOUCH sign.

A new stylish, more Parisian Kylie was being appreciated. Julien Macdonald, the designer probably most closely associated with her fashion over the years, said, 'I believe you are either born with style or not. The most stylish and sexy person in the world to me is Kylie Minogue. It doesn't get any better than working with her.' As if to prove his point, she topped *Glamour* magazine's annual Best Dressed list, a vast improvement on her lowly twenty-sixth place the previous year. The editor, Jo Elvin, observed, 'We've seen a newer, softer-looking Kylie emerge this year – she's still sexy but she's not flaunting that side of herself in gold hot pants any more.'

The notorious shorts were by now a genuine museum piece. They were one of the star attractions at an exhibition chronicling her changing image over the years, which opened at the V&A in South Kensington in February 2007. *GMTV* carried a report on the show that made one viewer pay special attention. A former dancer recognized the gold hot pants that were featured. Michele Renee, aged sixty, recalled she'd had them specially made twenty-five years earlier when glam rock was at its peak. They had cost her £15. She said, 'I couldn't believe my eyes. I recognized them immediately – right down to the stitching.'

Kylie barely had time to draw breath after the split from Olivier before she was thrust into the spotlight once more. She was accompanied to the opening by William, who planted an affectionate kiss on her cheek for the photographers. The fact that Kylie showed up at all was revealing. She wasn't going to hide away but instead smiled winningly whenever a camera was near.

This type of exhibition isn't unusual these days – a David Bowie retrospective was hugely successful in 2013 – but Kylie's was the first, ground-breaking one. The costumes also included the white hooded jumpsuit, and there were a large number of outlandish stage costumes, as well as the dungarees she had first worn as Charlene Mitchell. One of the more famous outfits was the Julien Macdonald black mini dress she had been wearing when Justin Timberlake groped her bottom. It was far-sighted of someone to have kept all the costumes and not put them on eBay.

The hoarder turned out to be Carol, who had carefully pressed, folded, catalogued and put away everything Kylie had worn from the start of *Neighbours* to the *Showgirl: Homecoming* tour – twenty years of memories. The idea for *Kylie: The Exhibition* had originated in Melbourne four years before, when Ron Minogue had contacted the city's Arts Centre. He told them that Kylie had six hundred costumes she wanted to donate. Fifty of the best were chosen for the exhibition that came to London.

Kylie found it funny that outfits, which literally had been thrown on the floor, were now being handled as if they were great works of art by specialists wearing white gloves. Special small-sized mannequins were purpose-built to wear the clothes. Liz Jones in the *Daily Mail* described how the exhibition portrayed Kylie's journey to enduring stardom. She wrote, 'It is an intimate portrait of how a girl became a woman, how she shed the bubble perm and the snow-washed, high-waisted denim, made her own decisions, became beautiful and sexy by sheer force of will, and emerged stronger and wiser and lovelier than ever.'

Not all the response was as positive as that, with some traditionalists believing there was no place for a pop artist in such a venerable institution. The museum wasn't the least bothered by such negativity, because 4,000 tickets were sold in advance and it promised to be their most successful temporary show ever. The curator Vicky Broakes said, 'You can see through the clothes that she's taken lots of risks and she doesn't take herself too seriously.'

As well as the costumes, there were gold and platinum discs, and photographs depicting all the images of the 'chameleon woman'. A selection of her best-known videos was projected onto the walls. One of the most-visited sections was devoted to what seemed like a thousand Manolo Blahnik shoes, all in a dainty size four.

Critical opinion was mixed. Joan Bakewell was unimpressed, not by Kylie but by the downmarket tone of the presentation: 'She [Kylie] is dazzlingly pretty, hugely popular, unaffected in her personality and recently fought bravely against cancer. All this commends her. She also works extremely hard to make her shows the very best. The V&A should do the same.' Suzy Menkes in the *International Herald Tribune* was dismayed that there had been no attempt to put the clothes in any sort of context. She thought it lively, but added, 'The curators have just died in the face of stardom.' The lasting impression was that it was homage rather than a meaningful retrospective.

*

Quietly, Kylie arranged for her possessions from the Paris flat she had rented to be sent over to London – it was the division of some treasured things that all couples face when they separate. She only wanted to keep a few items from that period of her life, like a lamp and a rug. She packaged up some belongings for Olivier and shipped them to Los Angeles for him. It was sad but a sign that she was moving on. She seemed to be reacting to the break-up in very much the same way she had when it all went horribly wrong with James Gooding: by appearing happy and smiling in the company of a handsome man.

She needed to be careful, however, because there was a suspicion that her new friendship might tarnish her reputation. The man she was linked to, a minor Chilean-born film director called Alexander Dahm, was married, with one child and another on the way. Being labelled a husband-stealer by the media wouldn't be good for any of her images.

She had met silver-haired Alex, who at thirty-nine was the same age, when she flew to Acapulco to model bikinis for her H&M swimwear range. Taking on that assignment was a further indication of her defiant attitude to her cancer surgery. She was confident enough after her body's ordeal to launch the 'H&M Loves Kylie' range of swimwear and kaftans. She called the outfits a 'summer indulgence'.

She struck up a friendship with Alex then that nobody knew about until May, when, out of the blue, she was seen with him in Chile, of all places. It took everyone by surprise to see a smiling Kylie in South America. His wife, Laura, meanwhile, at home in Mexico City, was quoted as saying it was a coincidence that they were in Chile at the same time, although reports suggested they were sharing a week's holiday near the fashionable beaches of Viña del Mar. Laura very firmly said any romance was not happening.

Kylie and Alex were photographed together and were seen having lunch, but there was no evidence they were anything more than just friends enjoying each other's company. It may not have been the most tactful alliance, but Kylie had no track record whatsoever of chasing after another woman's husband. She was quite categorical on the subject: 'I've never been unfaithful to a partner and would find it completely immoral to be involved with a married man.'

It was a firm denial. She was photographed with him once more a year later, when he visited London. She was in the back while he was in the front seat of a car. At the time, he claimed that he and Laura weren't actually married and their relationship was over. It was all a bit confusing. She was on much safer ground being linked to Calvin Harris, an up-and-coming 23-year-old DJ and record producer. His real name is Adam Wiles and he hails from Dumfries in Scotland. He was best known in his pretty home town as the boy who worked on the bread counter in Safeway until he put some of his music up on Myspace. That led to a breakthrough when he was noticed by a record-company executive.

Calvin had a publishing deal with EMI, and was an obvious choice to work with Kylie. His first album, *I Created Disco*, came out in the summer of 2007, so he wasn't then the superstar DJ he is today. He was perfect for her new album because he was fresh and getting talked about, as well as being influenced by the electronic sounds of the eighties that would continue the dance themes of her previous album, *Body Language*.

His alliance with Kylie was at the start of an irresistible rise. His studio album *18 Months* produced a record eight top-ten hits – nine if you count the Rihanna blockbuster 'We Found Love' that went to number one in the US. *Forbes* magazine named him as the world's highest paid DJ in 2012, with estimated earnings of £27.5 million.

He admitted to needing a drink to calm his nerves before he met Kylie for the first time: 'That wasn't a very good idea. It was early in the morning and I ended up a bit drunk, but just as nervous. But Kylie was amazing.' He found the whole experience of recording with her slightly surreal though fun and was surprised by how much she contributed musically.

His relationship with Kylie was strictly a working one, although a little tittle-tattle in the papers did neither of them any harm. The stories threatened to get out of hand when his visit to Melbourne was front-page news, but Calvin laughed them off, pointing out that he did, in fact, have a steady girlfriend, a student in Glasgow. He said the rumours involving Kylie were 'so far from the truth, it's a joke'.

From Kylie's point of view, they deflected some attention away from Dahm and her ongoing friendship with Olivier. Kylie might have preferred it to be something more, but she settled for them becoming real friends. Sometimes, if she needed to get away, she would pop over to Paris for a day or two and stay in his flat even if he wasn't there. Her love of the city hasn't diminished. By mid-summer, she was at a café on the Left Bank with Olivier, the first time she had been seen with him that year, but there was nothing more to it than a meeting of friends, however much the media might have wished it otherwise. Kylie was making trips back to Paris for regular check-ups at the Institut Gustave-Roussy, to ensure she continued to do well. Her friends and family were fighting a losing battle trying to get her to slow down, however. She appeared to have no intention of cutting back her commitments. In fact, the opposite seemed to be true.

One morning she was with William in the street outside her home. He was clutching a large white envelope on which was scribbled a things-to-do list. An enterprising photographer, one of those who were continually stationed there, took a picture of it. In this technological day and age, it was slightly reassuring that Kylie would have such a casual reminder.

The first item was 'Mugs', which may have been written there because they had broken one in the kitchen or, more likely, they needed to sort out something regarding official merchandise. The mugs from the *Showgirl: Homecoming* tour were proving extremely popular. They were the ones with the logo KYLIE SAYS RELAX on the back.

Next were the words 'tour next year' – a reference to her plans to tour her new album in 2008. The *Showgirl* tours had been hugely demanding but here she was already sorting out her next one. Then it was 'Coty Perfume', probably a reminder to check something with her perfume company or discuss future plans.

Underneath was the cryptic 'Songs (from WD) to Parkinson'. The WD became clearer on the next line, which said, 'White Diamond promo (film stills / release / downloads)'. The list concluded with references to an exciting television plan. First it mentioned 'acting coach number' and finally 'when Dr Who script arriving – Russell's number'. She had apparently agreed to appear in *Doctor Who* and was awaiting the script from its showrunner, writer Russell T Davies.

It wasn't clear from the hurried handwriting if Kylie or William wrote the list. Clearly, though, it was going to be a chaotic day for her. No wonder those close to her were concerned by her reluctance to take it easy. It was literally all work and no play.

White Diamond: A Personal Portrait of Kylie Minogue turned out to be a highly personal documentary that William had directed. It was loosely based around her cancer battle and the *Showgirl: Homecoming* tour. Most of the footage was shot between August 2006 and March 2007. It also revealed the relentless treadmill of her life as she moved from London to Milan, on to Paris and Sydney before a concert in Brisbane and then to Acapulco for the H&M photo shoot.

The film didn't go on general release. Instead, it was shown for one night only at Vue cinemas throughout the country. Kylie attended the Leicester Square premiere in a fabulous diamond-studded white and sheer Dolce & Gabbana dress. The jewellery she wore was said to be worth £1 million.

Kylie hadn't been entirely happy with a project that threatened to be more intrusive than she might like, but was persuaded by her

Creative Director's enthusiasm. In the end, there was nothing controversial about it, although Olivier featured fleetingly from time to time. Caitlin Moran, in *The Times*, described it as a documentary made by a very discreet friend that lasted for 'an arse-fatiguing two hours', which wasn't much of a recommendation. She added that the film left you in no doubt that 'Kylie is a charming, merry, adorable disco mouse with a fabulous collection of shoes'.

Caitlin wasn't the only one unmoved by the bland and superficial fare on view. Paul English in the *Daily Record* bemoaned a lost opportunity to say something significant about cancer and the effect it had. He wrote, 'Will followed her into her dressing room, into the back of limos, onto the stage, back off of the stage, back into her dressing room, back into the limos without asking a single question anyone really wanted to know the answer to.' Kevin O'Sullivan was to the point: '"I'm bored to death," said Kylie Minogue on *White Diamond*. Know the feeling.'

Oh, dear, it seemed that Kylie's movie career wasn't faring any better even when she was the star, the subject and didn't have to act. William's next venture as a director was better received. *The Kylie Show* was a television special celebrating Kylie's twenty years in the music business. Quite simply, it was a feel-good hour, a combination of music and light-hearted sketches. Kylie poked fun at her image, at one point pretending that a prosthetic arse in her dressing room was actually a hat.

In one very funny sketch, Jason Donovan appears and fails to recognize her. They pass in the corridor at London Studios and he thinks she wants an autograph. He signs it 'Especially For You, Love Jason'. They were no longer close in real life and this was the first time they had worked together for many years.

In another scene, Dannii and Kylie, dressed in identical leopard-print frocks, trade insults and have a hair-pulling, rough-and-tumble catfight in the latter's dressing room. Simon Cowell walks in and says to Kylie, 'You must be Dannii's mum,' whereupon, Kylie punches him in the face – 'Bruiser' Minogue again. Some viewers labouring under the misapprehension that the sisters truly loathed each other probably thought it was all genuine.

The special gave Kylie the opportunity to showcase material from her first studio album in four years. It was called *X* because it was her tenth. By coincidence, this was also the title of a 1990 album by INXS that featured Michael Hutchence, though nobody thought to mention that. Kylie began the new songs with '2 Hearts', which would be the lead single. Previously, her most successful albums had been preceded by classics like 'Spinning Around' and 'Can't Get You Out Of My Head', so everybody expected something more from '2 Hearts'.

It was by no means a bad song, but perhaps Kylie fans, starved of original material, wanted something more substantial than this fluffy and glam-style dance track. The song was written and produced by the electronic duo Kish Mauve. Victoria Newton in the *Sun* described it as a sure-fire number one. It made number four even though most critics liked it. It just wasn't the best song on the album.

On *The Kylie Show*, she also sang 'Wow', which became the second single, and another called 'The One', which sounded as if it would have been a much more memorable choice. By the time it was given a limited release, seven months had passed and nobody much cared about an old song. Kylie couldn't have done more promotion for *X*. In *The X Factor* final she sang 'Wow', but the track only reached number five in the charts. It sounded like it had travelled forward in a Tardis from the days of Stock, Aitken and Waterman, which was no bad thing.

Despite all her efforts, however, the performance of *X* was a disappointment. It, too, had been expected to reach the top but stuck at number four. It was probably a combination of bad luck and bad timing because, like *Body Language*, it was a slow burner that improved every time you listened. Today, anything involving Calvin Harris is almost guaranteed to reach number one. 'In My Arms', in particular, is one of his classic tracks, with Kylie asking in a seductive whisper, 'How does it feel . . .' and was another that would have performed well as the album's debut single.

It wasn't all bad news. The Christmas Day episode of *Doctor Who* attracted an audience of more than 13 million, the highest viewing figure in the history of the revived series. Kylie's television work always seemed to be better received than her films.

The special, entitled 'Voyage of the Damned', featured Kylie as the Doctor's companion, a maid called Astrid Peth. In one scene outside a hotel in Swansea, Kylie had to wear an old-fashioned waitress uniform. During filming, this confused an elderly lady, who approached her and enquired if it was too late to get a cup of tea. Kylie dissolved in a fit of giggles. Off-set, Kylie and David Tennant, who played the Doctor, became good friends when she offered a sympathetic ear following his mother's death from cancer. He was enthusiastic about working with her: 'She's as big a legend as *Doctor Who* itself, if not bigger.' He had no problem with doing extra takes of the scene in which Kylie kissed him.

23

A Model Relationship

If there had been a song 'I Left My Heart In Saint-Germain', then Kylie would have sung it. London prides itself on being her adopted home, but the French capital could legitimately challenge that claim. She had enjoyed the sunniest of times there and endured the darkest, but her affection for the city was unaffected. She was gracious and sincere about her feelings when she accepted an honour from the French Minister for Culture and Communication, Christine Albanel.

Mme Albanel presided over a ceremony in May 2008 at which Kylie was made a Knight in the Order of Arts and Letters (Chevalier dans l'Ordre des Arts et des Lettres) for her contribution to French culture. She described Kylie as the 'queen of the dance floor', but also saluted 'the courage you have shown in publicly revealing, three years ago, that you had been stricken with breast cancer'.

Kylie responded modestly in French, 'C'est un moment exceptionnel pour moi,' before adding enchantingly in English, 'I fell in love, and it's a love affair that continues to blossom like an eternal spring.' In Britain, she had to make do with a more prosaic-sounding OBE for services to music, although it was a proud moment later in the year when she received her honour from Prince Charles at Buckingham Palace with her family watching. Dannii had rushed over from *The X Factor* auditions in Wembley to join everyone. Then they went to the Admiral Codrington pub in Chelsea to celebrate.

Fittingly, considering her feelings for Paris, Kylie marked her fortieth birthday with a low-key dinner with her family at the city's world-renowned George V Hotel. She had celebrated in the same way the previous year.

She also chose the Bercy arena as the venue for the first concert of the *KylieX2008* tour in May. Yet again, Kylie was beginning a taxing series of dates with a bad throat, which almost forced the cancellation of the concert. On this occasion, Olivier was there to lend his support, as were Carol and Ron. They were joined by the actor Mathew Horne, best known for his role in the hit sitcom *Gavin & Stacey*. He had become a friend since he'd appeared with her in the sketches for *The Kylie Show*. He played her over-the-top gay dresser – a very funny performance possibly modelled, very loosely, on William Baker.

David Tennant had also flown in to cheer her on. His relationship with Kylie had been the subject of intense speculation since their friendship began on the *Doctor Who* set. He had taken her to see *Cinderella* at the Old Vic, interviewed her about her life for BBC Radio 2 and sat in the audience as she sang with Paul McCartney on *Jools' Annual Hootenanny*. He also presented her with the Brit Award for Best International Female Solo Artist, literally sweeping her off her feet when she came on stage to collect it.

Kylie was single, so she couldn't be seen with any man without ludicrous claims that he meant more to her than he really did. Both the former Beatle and Mathew Horne were talked about. There were even suggestions that she was engaged to Tennant. Kylie didn't help matters when she described him as 'adorable and lovely'. The rumours only died down when he unveiled his new girlfriend as the actress Georgia Moffett, whom he subsequently married and who is the mother of his three children. Kylie, meanwhile, mischievously admitted that she googled celebrity men she fancied to check if they were single. Apparently, it was something Dannii did, so she was just following suit.

When there was a lull, there was always Olivier gossip to fall back on. She dined with him at Ginger, a popular Vietnamese restaurant off the Champs-Élysées. Ron, Carol and William were also seated at the table, but little mention was made of that. She was seen out in a loose, floaty dress and immediately the headlines were IS KYLIE COVERING A BUMP?

When the full extent of Kylie's marathon tour was revealed, it was hard to imagine how she would ever find the time to start, let alone sustain, a relationship. It was for all intents and purposes a world tour, with eighty dates spread over fifteen months. The 2008 concerts alone grossed $90 million, according to her official website. She had wanted to broaden her interests, but anything new would have to wait until the European leg finished after seven nights at the O2 in London in August.

For this tour, William was again Creative Director, while Steve Anderson resumed his role as Music Producer. The majority of the outfits for the seven costume changes were designed by Jean Paul Gaultier – each one representing what Kylie called 'a show within a show'. She wanted it to be over the top, observing, 'I'm releasing my inner Freddie Mercury.' The cost of staging the two and three-quarter-hour extravaganza, during which she performed twenty-eight songs, was reportedly £10 million.

In one act, for instance, she was a cheerleader and sang 'Wow', 'Shocked' and the Calvin Harris track 'Heart Beat Rock'. In another, she was dressed as a nineteenth-century coachman and launched into 'On A Night Like This'. Kylie has such an extensive back catalogue these days that she could pick and choose which songs she added to the set list on any given night. She didn't, for instance, perform 'Better The Devil You Know' every night, but she made sure she included it for all the concerts in Sydney, because her fans there wouldn't have forgiven her if she had omitted their favourite track. David Pollock in the *Independent* thought the show veered between 'sexy, sophisticated futurist pop and the cheesy Saturday-night talent-show aesthetic which captures an array of mums, dads and grandparents.'

Her encore on this tour featured a rousing performance of 'I Should Be So Lucky', which one reviewer described as an anthem – an indication of how far this particular song had come in twenty years. Kylie's musical journey, and the way attitudes had changed during that time, was encapsulated by Simon Price in the *Independent on Sunday:* 'There was a time when the dominant attitude towards Kylie Minogue was that she was a puppet. As the years have passed, the supposed puppetmasters have changed, the only common element from era to era being the alleged puppet herself, surely forcing all but the most stubborn rockist to acknowledge that Kylie is actually a pop genius.'

Other sections of the media were more interested in the fact that Alex Dahm was in the audience at the O2 for the fiftieth gig of the tour. He was spending the evening filming her with a video camera. All was revealed a few months later, when *12 Hours* was released as part of the DVD package of *KylieX2008*.

Alex had filmed Kylie continuously for half a day, from the moment she got out of bed until the backstage congratulations at the end of the concert. There was no commentary or conversation. Instead, there were plenty of close-ups of Kylie's face, especially her eyes, as well as glimpses of her smiling towards the camera as if Alex had just said something amusing. While not exactly intimate, the film, which lasted less than twenty minutes, was nevertheless engrossing, perhaps because it didn't dwell on anything much before it was on to the next task of the day.

It began with Kylie waking at home, before drinking a first cuppa of the day while gazing thoughtfully out of the window at the Thames. Her car arrived to take her to the O2, so that her day could begin properly at noon with yawning, exercises to warm up her voice (la, la, la) and signings of a new book called *K*, which was a series of photographs taken by William. It was a limited edition of 1,000 copies and Kylie had to sign them all to justify the £250 asking price.

We saw Kylie with a huge plate of food for lunch, although she seemed to eat only a morsel before it was time for the sound check. At 5 p.m. she was sitting in front of a mirror while doing her make-up. It became less interesting during the concert itself, when the footage seemed to consist of shots of her facial expressions.

The film was pleasant enough but, like the more ambitious *White Diamond*, didn't reveal much about the real woman. It was twelve hours with Kylie Minogue the star, not the person. One good thing was that in spite of it being the fiftieth concert, she didn't appear at all tired or irritable.

Perhaps the few occasions when Kylie had been seen in Alex's company were more to do with this project than anything else, despite what the media implied. He certainly was no longer of interest once she'd met her next serious boyfriend.

Bearing in mind her love of all things Parisian, it was fitting that a party in that city was the setting for revealing the new man in Kylie's life – a very handsome six-foot-four supermodel. Andrés Velencoso was the real deal. He met Kylie when he was chosen to appear with her in an advertisement for her new fragrance for men called Inverse. He was the High Street face of H&M, so he was already on the fringes of Kylie's world. She was impressed when he took off his shirt to spray himself with the scent, and they embarked on a fling that became so much more.

The world discovered his identity when they attended a birthday celebration in October 2008 for the burlesque dancer Dita Von Teese at Le Milliardaire club. She nuzzled his chest in an obvious display of affection, while he placed a protective arm around her shoulders. Aged thirty, he is ten years younger than Kylie, and some perceived him as a trophy boyfriend, following in the footsteps of the male models she had previously dated. Harriet Walker in the *Independent* called Kylie a 'modeliser'. For centuries, powerful men have had a beautiful woman on their arm but now it was acceptable for famous women to follow suit.

There was no escaping the dark eyes and chiselled jaw of Andrés, however, because his face was everywhere. He is one of the best-known male models in the world. He was brought up in the unfortunately named but very quaint fishing village of Tossa de Mar on the Costa Brava, about sixty miles north of Barcelona. His full name is Andrés Velencoso Segura. His father, also called Andrés, runs a local restaurant and bar in a castle overlooking the town, while his mother, whose name he has tattooed on his chest, died in 2002.

Even though he signed a modelling contract with a Spanish agency after leaving school, initially he didn't impress the fashion houses of Milan. They apparently thought he was too tall and a bit goofy. Despite his good looks, he didn't stand out among the best-looking men in the world. An agent from New York, Natalie Kates, took a chance and signed him for Q Model Management and, in 2001, he moved to the United States, where his career began to take off. He could speak only a few words of English.

The leading fashion photographers started to use him, and his profile was greatly increased in 2002 by a campaign for Banana Republic that saw his face on a billboard in Times Square, the ultimate in street advertising. He featured in prestigious magazines, like French *Vogue*, but his status was confirmed when he was chosen by the designer Marc Jacobs for the Louis Vuitton autumn campaign in 2003. It did his prestige no harm at all to feature alongside Jennifer Lopez. He seemed to be in almost as many underwear ads as David Beckham. Campaigns for Chanel, Armani, Lacoste and Jean Paul Gaultier followed, so that by the time he met Kylie he was well established.

It was difficult for them to be more than ships passing in the night while Kylie was on tour, but she was able to squeeze in a week's holiday at a chalet in the fashionable Alpine resort of Chamonix. Andrés injured his arm showing off on a snowboard and needed to see a local doctor, which was a little embarrassing. They met up with the actress Penelope Cruz at a private party, but most of the time they kept their own company, enjoying the snow by day and the excellent restaurants at night. Eyewitnesses noticed how attentive and gentlemanly Andrés was towards her. They moved on from there to stay in Barcelona, where he had a flat. They spent some time shopping in the many designer stores before driving up the coast to visit his family. She impressed them by volunteering to do the washing up after dinner.

Kylie took him to Melbourne to meet her parents and Ron apparently liked him. Andrés didn't have a womanizing reputation. During their time together, he was never the subject of gossip involving other women. One of his two sisters, Sonia, observed, 'My brother has had few relationships because he is so dedicated to his work. He travels around the world, which makes it difficult to be with someone.' The last sentiment could equally be said of Kylie.

Andrés was looking for his own place in London, but for the moment stayed with her when they were both in the capital at the same time. He would occasionally take Kylie to the gym, but more often they would stay in and practise yoga and pilates. She embraced his routine of starting the day with some deep-breathing exercises. Kylie did take him bowling, but mostly they would eat out at discreet restaurants where she wouldn't be bothered.

Fortunately, Kylie didn't have so many commitments after the main segment of the *KylieX2008* tour ended in Australia in December. There were a handful of extra dates in Europe in the summer of 2009 and, more importantly, a short tour of the US to prepare for later in the year, but it was a quieter year overall.

One venture she did take on was playing herself in a Bollywood movie called *Blue*, which involved spending a week in Mumbai. The movie was an underwater adventure involving lost treasure. It was one of her quirky cameo roles and she had little to do other than sing during one of the big production numbers, 'Chiggy Wiggy'. These sorts of interludes in Bollywood movies are very much an acquired taste. This one consisted of Kylie dancing, wiggling her bottom and saying that she wanted 'chiggy wiggy with you, boy'. The film was a flop, with one Indian critic unkindly saying that Kylie was 'as sexy as a fat housewife in a kaftan'. The director Anthony D'Souza countered,

'I think Kylie is looking very beautiful in the film.' *Blue* had a sizeable budget of $12 million, so presumably she was well paid for her trouble. It is another film role that is best forgotten.

Kylie was clearly taking her relationship with Andrés seriously now, because she had started to learn Spanish and to support Barcelona, his beloved football team. She also took up golf. Unusually where sport is concerned, she became quite keen on the game and bought herself top-of-the-range equipment and designer sportswear – even a cap to keep out the sun. She said, 'Golf can be sexy. It's great to be with Andrés in the fresh air.' The only indication that there was fire in the relationship came on a night out at the B Bar & Grill in New York's East Village. She was said to have whacked him in the face with a fan she was using to combat the heat of a humid July night in the city. An eyewitness said she shouted at him after being made to wait outside while he finished his drink inside.

Kylie is known to have a quick temper – something she keeps hidden from the public most of the time. It comes and goes in a flash. William Baker, in *Kylie: La La La*, tells the story of how, following a falling-out, Kylie, dressed in nothing but a G-string, cornered him with a coat hanger in the changing room of a Sloane Street store. On another occasion, on a night out in Sydney, she was playing pool when a drag queen became a little too free with the bitchy comments. He kept his mouth shut after Kylie thrust her cue tip up his nose.

A solution to the perennial problem of separation was found when Kylie asked Andrés to travel with her during her American tour. This was a completely new situation for her. Here was a man who, partly at least, was more interested in spending time with her than pursuing his own ambitions. She performed nine concerts, beginning in Oakland, California, on 30 September 2009, and ending at the Hammerstein Ballroom in New York City two weeks later. The tour had been renamed *For You, For Me*, but much of the material was the same. She included the torch-song version of 'I Should Be So Lucky' as the encore at her final show. Fans in Manhattan had waited for so many years to see her that they started queuing at 2 a.m. to obtain a place near the front. Kylie gave them a stadium show in a ballroom.

The venues were packed, the audiences enthusiastic and the critics positive. They were impressed by her genuine demeanour and her ability to sing live. There was a technical hitch at the Chicago show, and Kylie, instead of being thrown, calmly broke into an a cappella version of 'Your Disco Needs You'. Barry Walters in *Rolling Stone* said that she radiated a 'bliss that can't be bought'.

Many wondered why Kylie wasn't a big star in the US, when she had sold so many records all over the world. The consensus was that she had missed out because she was overshadowed first by Madonna and more recently by Lady Gaga. The perfect setting for Kylie, it was generally agreed, was a season in Las Vegas.

The album *X* had performed badly in the US, so the short tour was more of a thank you to loyal fans than a reflection of its success. After Christmas with her family in Melbourne, she flew to Spain to see in the New Year with Andrés and his family, before another holiday in Chamonix, because they had enjoyed their first visit there so much.

Andrés revealed how their relationship had become serious, in an interview with Spanish *Vanity Fair*: 'I always thought love was something crazy, an out-of-control passion. But now I realize it's about wanting to share everything. To call the woman you love to tell her about a plate of food, a photograph that came out well, or just to hear her laugh. I love that. We love that . . . I've found a woman who loves me, and I love her.'

It was refreshingly open. Kylie was equally forthcoming for once, telling *Elle* magazine that she thought she had missed out on finding love again but was now in a happy, romantic place with Andrés. She paid him a compliment, 'Everybody tries to make you believe that you can't be beautiful and intelligent at the same time, when, like Andrés, it's possible to be both at once.' She also confided that a wedding was not on the cards.

24

Aphrodite

When things happen to Dannii, it brings the state of Kylie's life into sharp relief. It's always been that way. When Dannii married for the first time, it brought it home that her elder sister had not. The same was emphatically true when *The X Factor* judge announced on Twitter that she was pregnant after spending New Year in Melbourne with her boyfriend, Kris Smith, a former Rugby League international who is seven years her junior and took up modelling after retiring from sport. Kylie also took to Twitter to respond, 'OMG OMG OMG!!!! Perfect!!!! So Happy!!! A new Minogue!' It was surprising that she didn't know already.

Having led the way throughout their adult life, Kylie was now, in some ways, falling behind her younger sister. Dannii had met Kris eighteen months earlier, while she was on holiday in Ibiza and he was there celebrating his thirtieth birthday. He had been another positive in her life, at a time when everything was going well for her. Her stint as a judge on *The X Factor* had greatly increased her popularity, as well as being very good for the bank balance. For the first time, Kylie presented her with an award rather than the other way round, when Dannii was named TV Star of the Year at the *Elle* Style Awards in February 2010.

Dannii and Kris had been a couple for about the same length of time as Andrés and Kylie, but now they were adding a new dimension to their relationship. Dannii's private life had been equally disappointing until then. Not only was she divorced, but she had also been engaged briefly to the Formula One World Champion racing driver Jacques Villeneuve. She even moved to Monaco to be with him, only to return to London when it ended tearfully.

Her happiness and excitement at the prospect of a first child for her sister meant that Kylie, who was about to turn forty-two, would face even more questions about her own plans to start a family. She hated such personal enquiries, but did reveal, 'It's one thing your brother having children, and I'm madly in love with my nephews, but then when it's your little sister it's different. Because it's your sister and she's carrying a child, it really hits home.'

In public, she would deflect any gossip about her intentions by claiming she had a new album coming out and she had to get that out of the way before she could contemplate anything more. In private, however, she and Andrés were facing up to the reality that she might not be able to conceive. She would later admit that she had looked into various alternative options and had thought about egg donation.

Kylie didn't want to appear to be in competition with her sister. She never took seriously the idea that she should deputize on *The X Factor* while Dannii was in Australia giving birth. She said she declined to do it because the programme was Dannii's territory. She was also seriously considered as a judge for *Strictly Come Dancing*, but decided to pass because she didn't want sibling rivalry to become the story.

At least Kylie was happy and in love with Andrés, which was lucky, because the new album was going to be called *Aphrodite*, the name of the Greek goddess of love. It wouldn't have been a good time to split up. Andrés seemed to have a calming influence on her, especially when she was working, and she wasn't at all embarrassed about revealing her feelings.

She did take her relationship with Andrés to another level in one way by buying a £5 million house in the same street as the flat she had lived in for fifteen years. Her new home was altogether grander, with five bedrooms. It had one of those interiors that was completely modern while retaining a period feel. The key estate-agent feature was a vast open-plan drawing room with a large fireplace and an impressive chandelier. Kylie has an extensive worldwide property portfolio and this would be a shrewd investment for the future, but the immediate impression was that it was rather a big place for two.

She could afford to pay cash. The commercial side of Kylie's empire was thriving. She had merchandising, cosmetics, a 'Love Kylie x' fashion range and a tie-up with Lexus cars. She could open a perfume shop with the number of Kylie scents that were now available. Darling was old news next to Pink Sparkle, Music Box and Dazzling Darling – and those were just the ones for women. Her home-furnishings collection, 'Kylie Minogue at Home', had been a spectacular success, with everything from candles to bathroom towels available with the Kylie label on it. She was recognized as the queen of luxurious bed linen. Your bedroom and en suite could be a temple to Kylie if you so chose. Record sales and tour receipts improved the bank balance even more, so she regularly drew a salary of more than £1.5 million from the business. She was a money-making machine.

Kylie was being truthful when she said she had a new album to worry about. She had been very disappointed by the performance of *X*. The tour may have been a success, but she had expected more from the record. By common consent, the album lacked cohesion. Every songwriter or producer in London seemed to have knocked on her door. Many were disappointed that they were not on the final cut. The Pet Shop Boys, for instance, were miffed that the song they recorded with Kylie wasn't included.

Kylie was aware that she needed to change things. She was tactful about it, because she was proud of many of the songs, but she didn't want to do another album in that haphazard way. By coincidence, Jake Shears of Scissor Sisters, who had become a dear friend, helped her at the right time. She visited him in Berlin at a point when she felt she lacked musical direction. He could see that she was going down the same path of working with a large number of producers on all sorts of songs and then cobbling together the best ones. He persuaded her that she needed to find just one person to pull the whole thing together. That had been the original intention for *Impossible Princess*, but that plan never came to fruition. This time it was different.

Jake suggested Stuart Price as executive producer – a role he had assumed on *Night Work*, the new Scissor Sisters album. He was originally from Yorkshire but had grown up in Reading, where he became an accomplished musician listening to the synth-heavy sounds of the eighties, produced by groups like The Human League and Pet Shop Boys. He met Madonna when he was hired as a keyboard player on her 2001 *Drowned World* tour. She was impressed and he became the musical director for the *Re-Invention World Tour 2004*. He went on to produce her Grammy Award-winning 2005 dance album *Confessions On A Dance Floor*, which they mainly recorded in the loft studio of his London home. The album was a phenomenal success, with estimated worldwide sales of 12 million, and it secured Stuart's reputation. After Madonna, he went on to work with, among others, The Killers and Seal. He was considered a master of a modern electronic sound that acknowledged the great days of the eighties and nineties – perfect for a Kylie Minogue record.

Kylie was impressed when she went to visit Stuart at the studio in London where he and Jake were recording. Stuart told her that he would be banning all ballads. He was determined to make a 'house-party record' – a continuous and very precise groove.

They decided to work in a small studio Stuart kept in New York. She was energized by the bustling environment outside and enjoyed recording with him. She thought he was a wizard and an 'absolute delight' to be around. She said simply, 'I love coming to work.'

Stuart devised what he called the 'Dolly Parton Litmus Test', designed to check whether a song was strong enough before production began. He would get out his acoustic guitar and Kylie would run through the song in the style of the great country star. She could do a mean Dolly Parton impersonation that would have everybody laughing. If they both could imagine Dolly singing it for real, then the track would get the thumbs up. On the last day of recording, Kylie arrived in a cowgirl outfit and treated Stuart to a rendition of 'All The Lovers'.

The song was a far stronger lead single than '2 Hearts' had been. Coincidentally, both tracks were composed by Kish Mauve, but the former better reflected the overall joyousness of the new album. 'All The Lovers' had a spring in its step that gave Kylie 'goose bumps' when she heard it. She didn't say if the lyrics, that all the lovers that have gone before don't compare to you, were written with Andrés in mind. Stuart described the song as 'magical'.

She was expecting to wear something classy in the video, but when she arrived in Los Angeles for the shoot, the director, Joseph Kahn, changed his mind and she was asked to wear a pair of tiny black briefs. She told the *Daily Record*, 'I just thought, "Oh, my God, I'm in pants again. How does this keep happening?"' Kahn had recently finished videos for Lady Gaga and Katy Perry, as well as one for the charity record 'Everybody Hurts' by Helping Haiti, which featured Kylie among the performers.

His video for 'All The Lovers' is one of Kylie's most striking – a sort of flash-mob striptease in downtown LA. It was inspired by the work of Spencer Tunick, who specializes in photographic scenes involving large numbers of nude volunteers. It demonstrated again that Kylie was aware of key elements of popular culture. She ends up at the top of a pyramid of men and women in their underwear. It was sensual, sexy and uplifting: the casting off of clothes representing the removal of inhibitions. More than 10 million people have watched it on YouTube.

The album *Aphrodite* came out just as 'All The Lovers' was climbing the charts to number four. Kylie summed up the appeal of the album: 'It makes me think of girls getting ready to go out, putting their make-up on. About driving. About sunshine. It has some ravey elements.' The CD was contained in a glossy and glamorous booklet that included a series of photographs William Baker had taken of Kylie looking fabulous. She included Andrés in her acknowledgements, along with Mum, Dad, Brendan and Danielle.

The huge number of credited songwriters included Calvin Harris, Jake Shears, Tim Rice-Oxley from Keane and the underrated Nerina Pallot, who composed the album's title track and another, 'Better Than Today'. She couldn't believe it when Kylie, the global superstar, arrived alone to record her vocals at the tiny North London studio she used with her husband and co-writer Andy Chatterley. They were used to big American stars walking in with a huge entourage of burly minders and hangers-on. Kylie had just taken a taxi by herself. Nerina was impressed with her energy in the studio: 'She's got a very discerning ear and she's a very good singer.'

'All The Lovers' was such a strong song that it propelled the album straight to number one – twenty-two years to the very week since her debut, *Kylie*, achieved the same feat. The critics mostly liked it. Adam Woods in the *Mail on Sunday* said, 'She has made an exceptionally strong pop record, with a particularly positive buzz.' Dave Seaman thought *Aphrodite* her best offering since the nineties, when he had worked with her. It was certainly good for parties in Ibiza. Coincidentally, she launched the album on the Mediterranean island.

In the US, the *Boston Globe* described the tracks as 'euphoric bum shakers'. There was a suspicion, however, that overall it was a bit bland and samey. Kylie's previous albums *X* and *Body Language* had more staying power if not such instant appeal. *Aphrodite* lacked depth. Subsequent singles 'Get Outta My Way' and 'Better Than Today' performed poorly, suggesting the public quickly tired of the material.

Kylie repaid Jake for his friendship and help by taking to the stage at Glastonbury to sing with Scissor Sisters on their new single 'Any Which Way'. It was her first appearance at the midsummer music festival. She had been due to play a whole set there in 2005, before her illness struck. This time she arrived by helicopter, spent four minutes on stage in thigh-high boots and a see-through lace leotard, gave the band's girl singer Ana Matronic a big kiss and then flew back to London. Job done.

She did have to fly to New York almost immediately for another film role, a minor part in a romantic horror called *Jack & Diane*. She had to look rough and scruffy and show off a lot of tattoos, which were supplied by the make-up department. Her character also has a lesbian love scene which gathered a few headlines. It was as if Kylie did some acting from time to time to make sure she didn't forget how – just in case something good came along.

She didn't want to hang around in the US too long, because Dannii had given birth to a baby boy, Ethan Edward Minogue Smith, at the beginning of July, and she was desperate to go back to Australia to see him. Her sister had wanted to have the baby at home, but he was in a bad position, so she had to go to the Royal Women's Hospital in Melbourne and have an epidural after all. Kylie was genuinely delighted for Dannii, who had decided to make her main home in the city and bought a million-pound mansion a few miles away from the proud grandparents.

Ron was relieved that the new parents had chosen a good old-fashioned name for the new arrival. One of Dannii's favourite stories is of the time Kylie had taken her father out for a coffee with Chris Martin, the lead singer of Coldplay, who had just had a daughter with Gwyneth Paltrow. 'What's her name?' asked Ron. When Chris said, 'Apple,' Ron responded, 'And what's her middle name, "Strudel"?' He had honestly thought it was a joke.

Kylie brought the new baby an exquisite hand-embroidered throw, with animals in the style of Beatrix Potter, for his cot. After cuddling her nephew for the first time, she tweeted, 'Yes . . . yes . . . YYYYEESSS Baby Ethan is adorable, perfect and scrumptious!!!'

According to Kylie, Ron and Carol were the two people in her life who had never asked her about children – not once. Everybody else seemed to be in her face about it, although she did tell reporters at her album's launch that raising a family would 'be a dream for me'. Maybe so, but she could hardly rubbish the idea when she was trying to obtain favourable publicity. The album was the story, not her home life.

Privately, she understood that her treatment for breast cancer might mean she couldn't have children. Andrés, she noticed, was a natural with children, so who could say how that might affect their relationship in the future? She told Alice Bedford in the *Mail on Sunday* that she had to be honest and accept that after everything she'd been through she might not be able to conceive: 'I would absolutely love to, but I just don't think it's going to happen.'

Her consolation was the love for the children around her, especially her three nephews, Charlie, James and now Ethan: 'When I'm with my nephews, I turn into this woman who rolls around on the floor, changes nappies and gets covered in poop.'

The saga of Kylie's cancer battle kept the disease in the public eye. She was happy to lend her name to campaigns like Fashion Targets Breast Cancer, which raises money for the charity Breakthrough Breast Cancer. She particularly wanted to show people that they could get through it and return to an energetic life as she had done. On 28 February 2011, she celebrated an important anniversary: five years in remission.

Unsurprisingly, Kylie didn't have time to mark the occasion with a holiday in the sun. She was already in the middle of the *Aphrodite: Les Folies* tour. It had just opened at the Jyske Bank Boxen arena in the city of Herning, Denmark, and would eventually encompass seventy-seven concerts in Europe, Asia, North America, Africa and

Australia, of course. The tour grossed an estimated $60 million, making it Kylie's most successful venture to date.

She launched each show by emerging from beneath the stage in a golden shell like the central figure in Botticelli's *The Birth of Venus*. She was all in white, like a mythological winged goddess. She began with 'Aphrodite', which was strangely unexciting, although 'The One' and 'Wow' immediately improved things. The show didn't have the over-the-top campness of the *Showgirl* tours, but it did highlight Kylie's gift for the theatrical. Each song had its own vignette. If you stopped it at any time, it was like a scene stitched into a tapestry.

It was an ambitious, mammoth production with eight changes of Dolce & Gabanna costumes, a jet fountain and three swimming pools set into the tilting stage. At one point, Kylie is swept high above the audience by a dancer wearing wings. William and Kylie took their inspiration from *Ziegfield Follies*, a 1946 Hollywood movie that featured all the great MGM musical stars of the time, including Fred Astaire and Judy Garland. They had watched it many times together and loved its tongue-in-cheek extravagance. There were no old crowd-pleasers like 'The Loco-Motion' or 'I Should Be So Lucky', although she did find a spot for 'Better The Devil You Know'. The audiences loved it though.

Andrés travelled with her. During the concert in Barcelona, she searched for him in the crowd and then ran off-stage briefly to give him a kiss. Fittingly, it was during 'Cupid Boy', which featured projections of her boyfriend on the huge screen behind the stage. Her former partner Olivier Martinez was in the audience for her Hollywood Bowl concert in Los Angeles with the new woman his life, Halle Berry.

Kylie and Olivier had both moved on.

25

A New Broom

Kylie was not amused. When she arrived on the arm of Jake Shears, for the George Michael charity dinner and concert at the Royal Opera House in Covent Garden, a photographer took a picture of her with what appeared to be a frozen or immovable face. To be honest, she didn't much look like the Kylie everyone knows, because her hair was newly died black and she was wearing a very unrevealing black velvet frock.

The female commentators who have been quick to bitch about Kylie throughout her career seized upon her flawless complexion to make all manner of innuendo about what work she may or may not have had done. Was it simply another round of Botox or something more uplifting?

Kylie hadn't hidden the fact that she had used Botox in the past to stem the irresistible march of wrinkles. She always denied more serious cosmetic treatments. The previous year, she had even invited the journalist Dean Piper to check behind her ears for any telltale scars. He couldn't find any. She told him that she wasn't on a quest for eternal youth and pointed out that her forehead moved: 'I know people are always saying I've had this, that and the other done but I honestly haven't.'

Her assertion that she no longer used Botox was what was seized upon after the gala, which was raising money for Elton John's AIDS Foundation – that, and the suggestion her cancer treatment may have something to do with her perfect complexion. The unkindest comments came from the *Daily Mail*'s Amanda Platell, who wrote, 'Isn't it strange that most women who survive such an ordeal end up looking ten years older, not twenty years younger.' Her comments were not appreciated by women who had undergone the same treatment as Kylie and felt they, too, were looking good for their age.

The real reason why her face was set in stone was that she was angry at Jake, because they were the last to arrive and everyone was already waiting in the auditorium. The organizers delayed the start of George's show just for them. Jake had been due to pick Kylie up at her home in plenty of time for the start of proceedings at 7.30 p.m. Unfortunately, that was the time he rang the bell. They arrived thirty-five minutes late. Jake explained, 'I really pissed her off. She was fuming. When Kylie is angry, she just doesn't say anything.' She obviously didn't feel like smiling for the cameras.

While that solved the mystery of Kylie's stern countenance, it didn't alter the fact that every article about her these days mentions her age. It drives her mad. It is the cross that all women in show business have to bear when they pass forty and gravity takes hold. Some mornings Kylie woke up thinking she ought to bring the hot pants out of retirement. But on other, less good days, she looked in the mirror and saw a woman in her nineties, not her forties.

She also had to deal with the first rumours that all was not well in her relationship with Andrés, after he was seen enjoying the company of an attractive local woman in his home town. His father was quoted in early November 2011 as saying his son and Kylie were doing better than ever but, strangely, since that time, there were far fewer stories about how much Kylie was in love. The couple were keeping a lower profile.

She was at a crossroads now that she was approaching her midforties. She wasn't concerned about growing old gracefully and retiring to sip cocktails on her own deserted beach. She was a performer who needed to perform, but how could she top the *Aphrodite* tour? She decided to celebrate twenty-five years in pop not with a firework display at Wembley Stadium, but by undertaking something much less ostentatious, or stripped back, as she called it.

She devised the *Anti Tour*, playing just four dates in Australia and three in the UK in April. The venues were the smallest for a Kylie concert in years. In London, for instance, she performed just one date at the Hammersmith Apollo instead of a string of concerts at the O2. She had a four-piece band and three backing singers, and ran through a set list of twenty-two B-sides and rarities with no special lights or frills. It was part of what she was calling the K25 project, although it could well have been a taste of the sort of concerts Kylie might perform when she finally hangs up the pink feather boas. She wore denim shorts and a T-shirt, while the only dancing on view was impromptu moves from the bar staff.

Kylie wanted to do the unexpected during K25. She couldn't match some of the grand projects of the past, so she decided to explore other possibilities. *The Abbey Road Sessions* was one of those. She started working in a studio with her long-term collaborator Steve Anderson and the respected arranger and producer Colin Elliot. They decided to rework a number of her most famous songs so that they would sound completely different.

The idea came from the slow versions of 'The Loco-Motion' and 'I Should Be So Lucky' that she used to perform on tour. Sixteen of her most famous tracks were given an orchestral treatment, although, for some reason, 'Spinning Around' didn't make the final cut. 'Better The Devil You Know' and 'Confide In Me' were among the songs newly recorded at the legendary Abbey Road, the studios in St John's Wood forever associated with The Beatles. Kylie persuaded Nick Cave to come over to North London to record a new vocal for 'Where The Wild Roses Grow'. The two friends had remained close and Kylie joined him on stage at the Koko, to perform the song when Nick and The Bad Seeds played there in November 2013.

The only new song, 'Flower', was an atmospheric ballad, one that she had written originally with Steve Anderson for the *X* album but had discarded. The single was released in September 2012 as a taster for the album the following month. *The Abbey Road Sessions* were kept out of the number-one slot by Calvin Harris with *18 Months*.

Kylie performed eight of the songs in a Hollywood-style red satin ballgown at the annual Proms in the Park. She was accompanied on stage in Hyde Park by the BBC Concert Orchestra. After her performance, she changed into some denim shorts for a celebratory dinner at a Mayfair restaurant with Andrés and, among others, Ronan Keating and Emma Bunton.

The Abbey Road Sessions were a risk that turned out well, but they were a much safer bet than a third K25 venture – yet another slightly weird film. For once, however, it proved to be an inspired choice. *Holy Motors* was a surreal film by the acclaimed French director Leos Carax, best known in the UK for *Les Amants du Pont-Neuf*, which starred Juliette Binoche. All Carax had seen of Kylie before asking her to act in his movie was the video of her duet with Nick Cave. Some critics had even described the poetic Carax as the 'Nick Cave of the film world'. He was introduced to Kylie by a mutual friend and they met in Paris to discuss the possibility of her involvement. She told him he was either very brave or crazy to give her a role, so he hired her on the spot.

The plot concerned a man called 'The Sleeper', who travels between multiple parallel lives in the back of a white limousine. The lead role was played by the French actor Denis Levant and required him to play nine different characters, both men and women. In her scene, Kylie, barely recognizable with short brown hair, sings a song called 'Who Were We?', best described as a melancholic show tune, before jumping to her death from the top of a tall building.

Holy Motors renewed Kylie's love of acting. The film was well received at the Cannes Film Festival in the spring, but was probably too arty to be popular when it premiered in the UK in September.

Peter Bradshaw of the *Guardian* wrote: '*Holy Motors* is weird and wonderful, rich and strange – barking mad, in fact.'

Not everything Kylie was involved in was part of her K25 anniversary. She performed at one of the biggest events of the year – The Queen's Diamond Jubilee Concert outside Buckingham Palace. The concert, organized by Gary Barlow, featured some of the biggest names in popular music, including Sir Paul McCartney, Sir Elton John and Sir Tom Jones. Kylie didn't seem out of place in such an illustrious line-up.

She brightened up a pretty pedestrian evening by bouncing on stage in a Pearly Queen outfit, complete with black diamanté ankle boots, and proceeded to sing a medley of 'Spinning Around', 'Can't Get You Out Of My Head' – officially the most played track of the noughties – 'Step Back In Time' and a glorious version of 'All The Lovers'. It was fantastic. She was an artist in her prime, not one who should be worrying about her age. Playing for just nine minutes meant that she could put more energy into dancing than she normally does, but goodness knows how she managed it in heels that high. She finished with one of the broadest toothy smiles.

Kylie stood on the left-hand side of Prince Charles when he gave a short speech on stage to mark the occasion. The Queen looked on approvingly as he made a joke or two. Kylie, who had changed into an elegant, long white gown, laughed and clapped enthusiastically. Afterwards, she joined Gary Barlow backstage to present the artists to The Queen. Among the stars she introduced was will.i.am, whom she would meet up with more significantly in the future. You couldn't help but think it wouldn't be long before it would be Sir Gary and Dame Kylie. Surely, Kylie will receive this honour within the next few years.

When you have been a star for as many years as Kylie has, the anniversaries seem to come around more regularly. She made a surprise appearance at the Artist and Manager Awards in November 2012, to present her own manager of twenty-five years, Terry Blamey, with the Peter Grant Award, named after the notoriously ruthless manager of Led Zeppelin. Michael Gudinski, of Mushroom Records, who had given Terry his first break as a booker of his acts, flew in specially from Australia to support his long-standing friend.

Jon Webster, on behalf of the Music Managers Forum (MMF), who organized the evening at the Troxy theatre in Stepney, said Terry was being recognized for his skill in guiding pop icon Kylie Minogue's career. The lady herself gave a gracious speech: 'We started off in 1987 when I had what resembled a poodle perm. Who didn't? And as you might not know, Terry sported a very fetching mullet. I didn't drink coffee, now I don't turn up for work without my coffee, and Terry didn't drink alcohol. It was that long ago. He would order a cappuccino and I would scoop the foam off the top.'

She observed that he had always been fiercely protective of her, before ending with a very personal tribute: 'I'm just going to ignore the rest of you, if you don't mind, for a second and say, Terry, thank you so much for everything; for helping a nineteen year old girl take on the world and become a woman and an artist. Here's to the future.'

That future, together at least, would last less than two months longer. On New Year's Eve, they officially parted company. Apparently, it had been decided in September, before Kylie made her speech, but it was a bombshell to a music business that didn't see it coming. There were unsubstantiated reports that he had fallen out with her father about the direction Kylie's career should take. She later revealed this was a time when she was feeling a bit lost.

Terry said, 'Kylie has decided to pull back slightly from the pressures of her career and devote more time to herself and her acting career. This is not to say she will be retiring from music, just taking a bit of a break.' He added that the break was amicable. Terry was a very rich man thanks to his association with Kylie, so he would not be joining the dole queue any time soon.

While it was true that Kylie's acting ambitions had received a welcome boost from *Holy Motors*, her spokesman was quick to reinforce the point that she was definitely not retiring from music. Part of the speculation about her intentions had been caused by the uncertainty over Parlophone's future. Eventually, in July 2013, Kylie's record label became part of the Warner Music Group.

Kylie never showed the slightest inclination to stop singing and performing. Before she left for her annual break in Melbourne, she fulfilled one of the biggest wishes of her loyal fans by taking part in the Hit Factory Live – Christmas Cracker concert, a celebration of Stock, Aitken and Waterman. She sang once more with Jason. It was their first duet since 1989, and the audience at the O2 shouted every word of 'Especially For You' with them.

The former lovers had been estranged for many years, but that was no longer the case. It was a happy occasion and Jason literally swept Kylie off her feet. At the end, as the crowd applauded, they embraced warmly and she bounced around with genuine delight. The song has strangely stood the test of time, and could justifiably be called a pop classic.

A much more serious collaboration was being put in place. Kylie had signed a new management deal with Roc Nation, the burgeoning entertainment company founded by Jay-Z in 2008. They already managed two of the biggest female stars in the world, Rihanna and Shakira. Successful UK chart acts such as Rita Ora and Calvin Harris were also signed to the label.

A Roc Nation spokesman explained that Kylie had released eleven studio albums, two live CDs, eight live-concert DVDs, a greatest-hits double album and multiple video packages: 'She has released fifty singles worldwide, including the Grammy-winning "Come Into My World", and has sold more than 68 million albums worldwide. Needless to say, we're excited to have Kylie join the Roc family.'

While Jay-Z is the well-known public face of the company, the power behind the scenes is Jay Brown, the co-founder and president. The days of Terry Blamey were quickly forgotten as Brown posed with his arm around their new signing at Roc Nation's pre-Grammy celebrity-laden brunch party at the BOA Steakhouse in West Hollywood. Kylie was no longer a relatively isolated figure in world music but part of arguably the most successful team in the record business today – and one that was expanding all the time into other areas of entertainment. Interestingly, they referred to Kylie as a recording artist, songwriter, actress and designer, suggesting they intended to promote her brand across all areas, although maybe not in Roc Nation Sports.

Kylie's status in the US has been underestimated recently. She may not be a superstar there, but she is certainly a star, and, since 'Can't Get You Out Of My Head', she is one of the best-known names in American dance music.

While she was working hard on the new album, Kylie was away from the spotlight, on the surface confirming Terry Blamey's assertion that she was going to 'pull back slightly'. Her desire to do more acting was also apparent when she accepted a television role in the *Playhouse Presents* series on Sky Arts. *Hey Diddly Dee* was a black comedy about a group of actors rehearsing to put on a musical about the life of Andy Warhol. She was persuaded to take the part by Mathew Horne, who was also in the cast.

A more accurate indication of the direction her career might be taking came when rumours surfaced yet again that she might become a judge on *The Voice*. Speculation had been rife in 2011, before the first series of the BBC talent show aired. The rumours came to nothing, amid suggestions that she was asking for too much money. They made the papers the following year, but again came to nothing. Third time, they were true.

The producers had decided to bring the third series forward by two months, so they were under a lot of time pressure to find two new coaches after Jessie J and Danny O'Donoghue decided to leave. *The Voice*'s executive producer, Moira Ross, was convinced that Kylie was the big name the programme needed to go forward, even though not everyone at the BBC agreed. There were concerns that Kylie was too quiet.

Moira, however, went ahead and phoned Jay Brown, who told her, 'It's definitely not her thing.' Undaunted, she decided to give it one more shot and flew to LA to meet with him. He proved to be more receptive when she showed him a highlights reel and some of the show's stats. He arranged a meeting with Kylie the following morning, which was a Saturday, when she was having a day off from the studio.

Moira had another pressing job in LA: trying to persuade will.i.am to stay for another season. She spent most of Friday afternoon in the studio with him and felt she was making progress. She told him that she was seeing Kylie the next day and he offered to turn up for the meeting as well. He is not known for being an early riser. 'It's 10 a.m.,' said Moira. 'You'll never make it.' But he replied, 'Let's go get this girl,' so she hoped for the best.

At 10.00 a.m. the next morning, Moira had just started her conversation with Kylie. At 10.02, a very sleepy will.i.am walked in. They were very surprised because he is always late. He told them he had got up two hours early just so he could make it. Moira recalled, 'We spoke honestly about the show and the impact it had on him and the difference it had made to his life; and she listened and the two of them chatted – superstar to superstar. His genuine love of the programme really resonated with her. She was nervous about it but she said she would give it some thought. When she took the DVD of the highlights from me, I thought, "I've got her," and that's how it happened and she agreed.'

It would prove a fantastic coup for the programme, made doubly satisfying because will.i.am agreed to stay on when he realized Kylie was confirmed for the show. Her participation made good business sense to Roc Nation, because she had a new album due in the spring of 2014. The lead single from it, 'Into The Blue', was set for release in March, just as the series was building to a climax. After being quiet for most of 2013, she would be making her comeback in front of a television audience of 8 million every week. It was publicity gold.

After her first day of auditions, filmed at MediaCityUK Studios in Salford, Kylie rang Dannii in Melbourne to chat about how it went. She told her, 'Now I get it.' She understood why Dannii had always been so tired after a day's duty at *The X Factor*. It was because you 'live and breathe' the show.

Dannii was no longer on *The X Factor* in Britain, perhaps as a result of the revelations in Simon Cowell's biography that they'd had a fling – a revelation that hadn't impressed Kylie. Dannii was on the panel of the show in Australia, however, and was happy to give her sister the benefit of her experience. Sadly, she had split from Kris, Ethan's father, in April 2012, once again turning to Twitter to announce their separation.

Less than two weeks after Kylie began filming the blind auditions in October 2013, it was announced that she and Andrés had also separated. They had spent the previous New Year's in Melbourne and were pictured together in August at the J. Sheekey fish restaurant in the West End. However, the suspicion was that things had been cool between them for a long time. There had been few sightings of them together in the past year, while Kylie recorded in Los Angeles. And he was nowhere to be seen when she holidayed in Portofino in July. Her companion then was her loyal friend Katerina Jebb. A spokesman for Kylie described the split, unsurprisingly, as 'amicable', as all her separations appeared to be whatever the actual circumstances. Andrés, who was hoping to become an actor, lost no time moving on. A week later, he was rumoured to be seeing a young Spanish soap actress called Úrsula Corberó, eleven years his junior and twenty-one years younger than Kylie. Once more, Kylie had to face the barrage of cliché-ridden articles that she was putting on a 'brave face' and that she was 'devastated' and 'heartbroken'.

She didn't look downcast three days after the official announcement, when she attended a cancer research benefit in Paris. But then there are two Kylies: the one who wears no make-up, slobs around in joggers and is liable to bite your head off if you cross her, and Kylie the superstar. The world sees the latter but they are both real. Rupert Penry-Jones explained the two sides to Kylie when they were dating: 'When she is in her work mode, I stay out of her way. She becomes a superstar instead of the girl I know.'

Kylie spent a family Christmas in Melbourne as usual, but it was a subdued occasion, following the recent death of her beloved grandmother, Millie Jones, at the age of ninety-three. At least she was able to play the role of Aunt Kylie, which she so much enjoys.

In January 2014, Andrés and Úrsula were pictured together on holiday in a remote village in Spain, where they had seen in the New Year. Kylie was alone again when her first appearance on *The Voice* was broadcast.

Moira Ross was one of many who were impressed by her natural performance: 'Kylie had made a huge difference. She's brought great warmth and a new reinvigorated femininity. Nobody really knew what she was like; we're just used to her in hot pants and music videos. No one's ever seen her as a personality. But her fan base is massive so she has brought big interest with her.' It couldn't have gone any better. She gelled really well with the other judges and seemed to fit in straight away.

There's something about television that brings out the best in Kylie. Perhaps it's the closeness of the camera, which has always loved her. She will never have to return to *Neighbours*, a future that might have been predicted when she was starting out uncertainly as a pop singer. Now, twenty-seven years later, she is one the biggest icons in popular culture.

She hasn't achieved that status through luck or some sort of conjuring trick. She is consumed by a desire to perform and a huge capacity for working hard. She has been ahead of her time for decades now, using her fame to embrace the most modern and experimental thinking in performance, poetry, film, the visual arts, fashion and design . . . and music, of course. It's not all been plain sailing but she is becoming more popular as the years go by.

They are holding auditions in Melbourne for the role of Daniel Robinson, the son of Scott and Charlene, who will be pitching up to Ramsay Street soon. Blimey, where did the time go?

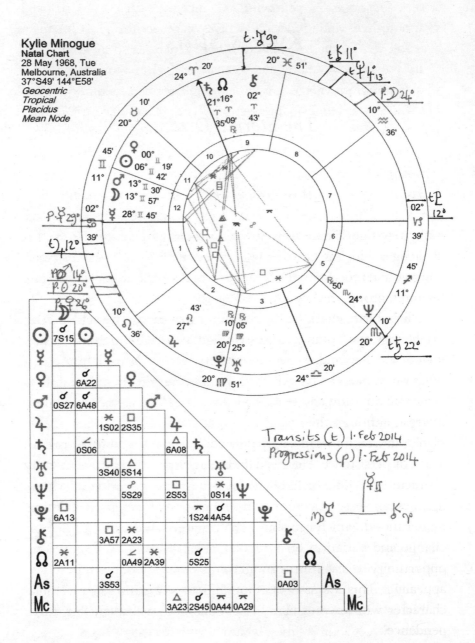

Kylie Minogue
Natal Chart
28 May 1968, Tue
Melbourne, Australia
37°S49' 144°E58'
Geocentric
Tropical
Placidus
Mean Node

Transits (t) 1. Feb 2014
Progressions (p) 1. Feb 2014

Kylie's Stars

The Eternal Dream

Many fine fighters are made by circumstances. Life throws up the challenges and, forced to engage, we ordinary souls develop our courage and muscles in the struggle. Then there is that other, possibly rarer, group: the born fighters – people like Kylie.

Kylie's birth chart has a stellium (wealth) of planets in the bright, airy, not notably aggressive sign of sociable Gemini. These include the Sun and the Moon, planets that respectively represent what we want and what we need. With her agile and curious mind, Kylie will question and seek quick answers to whatever catches her interest, although the restlessness that is associated with so many planets in Gemini would, in many people, show a tendency towards a lack of persistence. Her need for mental connection is a dominant characteristic. Kylie is likely to be a sparkling companion, with a lightness and ease of communication, made all the more interesting by her mood, which can shift in an instant. She needs a degree of change and variation on a regular basis to avoid boredom. The opportunity to learn something from a new situation is inherently appealing. This assessment, though, just skims the surface of a character with extraordinary strength, vision, courage and independence.

The planet that sits at the heart of the Gemini stellium is Mars –

initiator, warrior, aggressor. It is this planet that has provided the daring and stamina needed for her to follow her dreams, they would have remained fantasies if she had not had the nerve and energy to attempt to reach her goals. Mars links beautifully in this chart to the harsh taskmaster, Saturn, planet of discipline and ambition. Kylie will have that perseverance that is so important to any successful career. She will never have counted simply on luck to achieve her vision but worked long and hard, accepting the setbacks and unwritten rules without being daunted. Fear is always part of the Saturn package. Here, it is the fear of not being seen, of not having her individuality acknowledged, of being trapped, but importantly, too, it is the fear of challenging others and of loss and sadness if one doesn't. These worries, coupled with that Martian courage, provide a great incentive for taking a leap into the stratosphere. This important link also confers practicality and common sense, not least in terms of business and finance; here is someone who, despite having so many planets in Gemini, a sign usually fatigued by the mundane everyday issues of existence, will manage resources effectively.

Kylie has the great gift of charm and an ability to win the opposition over simply by being friendly. With a close link between her Sun and Venus, planet of emotional warmth and generosity, she is a genuinely affectionate person who is quite tolerant of faults simply because these are part of the variety in others that she seeks. While she will always bring great positivity and joy to her friendships, she will err instinctively towards keeping some distance, wary of the responsibilities that ensue from closeness, and at times uncomfortable with those who let their feelings override their common sense.

Few dispute the importance of family in establishing a sense of belonging and worth. The planets that signify Kylie's parents and siblings, the Sun, the Moon and Mercury, all reside in this birth chart in the restless, activity-loving sign of Gemini. Within her family, at best, individual differences would have been appreciated, mistakes toler-ated, rules sensibly flexible and, perhaps most important of all, communication generally open. In other words, these people held common values, capable of working as an effective unit. What may have been given little time within the prevalent mode of family func-tioning, however, would be inner emotional conflict. The family would have come together, facing out to worldly challenges, not giving unattractive and subsequently hidden tensions much air space. The impression is of a spontaneous, sometimes verbally sparky family, busy energetic people, supportive of Kylie's creative goals.

The Sun in this chart, which tells much about the paternal her-itage, sits between the relationship planets, Venus and Mars. Kylie's father is likely to have a healthy competitive streak and an ability to accomplish tasks. He will not be scared to stick up for his interests and can be quickly decisive. Happy to reason and talk, her father appears as a sociable and popular figure.

The Moon speaks of the maternal influence, and here a link with the planet Pluto suggests someone who has developed many insights into others and carries few illusions about human nature. Her strengths are such that Kylie will always be able to confide in her. Early on, Mother, as is common when raising a family, may have sup-pressed her own needs in order to nurture and consequently put much energy into supporting the fortunes of her children, encour-aging them to shine. Being generous, and a little proud, she may have found it difficult to ask for help, being happier to give rather than to receive. Verbally dextrous and sensitive, her attempts to accommodate others may have led to frequently changed decisions and annoyance with restraints. Negative energy would have been ploughed into activity within the family.

Kylie's sibling relationships are likely to remain some of the most important in her life. Gemini is the sign of the twin: that is, siblings who, in the hierarchy of the family, are equal – the same, but different, two halves of one whole. Yet in birth order, she is first and, with the placement of Mars, planet of leadership, initiation and competition, so dominant in her chart, there will have been a strong drive towards reaching the top spot, a position conferring inequality. An awkward link between Mercury and Uranus in her chart hints such victory can be gained through courageously developing and communicating her creative originality. However, as an act of rebellion against the Gemini ideal of parity or sameness and her very great desire to be loved, this would not have been achieved without much inner nervous stress.

These early relationships will shape her future partnerships too, and in certain respects a similar conflict between the ideal, where there is a level of equality, and a relationship that is unbalanced in status will exist. Often, Kylie will seek someone who can be peer and friend: someone gregarious, easy to talk to, mentally stimulating and full of ideas – someone in fact, like a brother or a sister, available when a shoulder is needed, understanding when something else appears on the radar. Moreover, with so many planets in fire and air signs, Kylie really does need the room to breathe and space to explore that this type of relationship would allow. However, this desire for light, adaptable and accommodating bonding is at variance with a contrary demand revealed by a link between Venus, planet of affection, and refined, unbounded Neptune, placed in possessive Scorpio. Kylie will be hooked by those who seem able to lift her creatively and spiritually beyond all the ugliness of the world and is likely initially to place her lover on a pedestal. Of course, her idealism will make it hard to maintain commitment to and interest in an ordinary person, not least if they exhibit any sign of a controlling temperament. Conversely, if the partner is not someone to worship, then he is likely to be a victim who needs saving. Neptune seeks enmeshment and closeness at soul and emotional levels; this is achievable when she is acting as saviour but is at variance with her more mercurial traits. There is wonderful strength in this planetary connection because it reveals the extraordinarily selfless and big-hearted love that Kylie can give, but the planets also suggest difficulty in establishing a relationship of equality or duration. Neptune demands sacrifices, and perhaps, for Kylie, art must come before satisfying the hopes of her heart.

This combination of Venus, Neptune and Scorpio suggests a glamorous, rarefied sexuality that will play out both in her choice of partners and in her image – she seeks the unreal and embodies it for everyone. Her ability to fascinate and seduce through seeming elusive, alluring and poignant, is unlimited. Not only will Kylie be energized and lifted by love, but beauty too and her musical talent and creativity will inspire the adoration of others. Most of us have an idealized vision of romance and perfect beauty, and few embody this fantasy more brilliantly than Kylie.

A further strength of the Venus–Neptune pattern is the ease with which Kylie can embrace humanitarian causes. Her compassion may not function well in her own relationships – at least, not until she first values herself as she really is – but channelled into something greater and transpersonal, it will move mountains.

Kylie's chart has a fascinating pattern of planets called a Yod, or 'the finger of God', which speaks much about her ability to read the future and instigate planned creative change. Towards the end of January 2014, a link between Mars, opposite the dominant planet in this pattern, Saturn, suggests she will be involved in an important project that once more will reveal her brilliance in initiating ambitious enterprises. While she can draw upon her usual energy, verve and originality, this is likely to be a time when others find it easy to reach her psychological weak spots and at some level she may feel cut off from people. With her inherent ability to adapt and adjust, this period will confirm her as an outstanding authority in her field, but it won't happen without some initial strain. Success will follow in late May or early June 2014, when Kylie will find it easy to prioritize, get to the core of what she wants to deliver and come to an understanding of any blocks that have previously seemed immovable. She will have a sense of much achievement and inner joy.

Prior to this, in March 2014, Kylie may feel a general lack of emotional satisfaction. Possibly, once more, enterprises may be challenging a deep-seated fear of failure or success, and concerns may involve a male friend or family member. In April, too, there is an awkward link between Neptune in the sky, planet of confusion, deception and escape, and Kylie's Sun, the significator of her vitality, direction and male figures in her life. She may well seek to escape responsibilities, as problems seem overwhelming and her confidence is lowered. This link shifts within two weeks or so, but returns in August and once more in February 2015 – a time that should see the end to a matter. She will feel more balanced with respect to her ambitions and compassionate, spiritual needs.

While the end of November 2014 will be a time when Kylie can make the most of opportunities to expand her world, able to tap into her wisdom and make decisions easily that add to her long-term success, the beginning of the month may be a time of loneliness, with the odd occasion when attempts to reach out to others seem to fail. This is due to a link between Saturn in the sky, the harsh God of Reality, and Neptune, planet of the ideal. Here, Kylie may struggle to keep her mood buoyant and she will also need to watch her health. In December, that restrictive Saturn moves opposite Kylie's Venus, planet of love – a time when affections will be tested. Her need to be a distinct and separate individual may conflict with her emotional desires, or maybe she will feel a wall between her and someone else. It is possible, too, that Kylie will be drawn towards the type of relationship that may in the future be onerous – one in which her responsibilities will restrict her and feel heavy. Saturn moves on to form a delightful link in January to Chiron, suggesting a reprieve of spirits, as she finds she has just the right combination of refection, ability to act and wisdom to find solutions.

Finally, looking a little further ahead, towards the end of April

2016, the unpredictable and exciting planet of change, Uranus, joins up to Kylie's Saturn, planet of ambition and, in the sign of Aries, courage and daring. This is a powerful combination, as it signifies a joining of very disparate energies, which will work rapidly to alter circumstances, ultimately relieving tensions that may have been building over a lifetime. Saturn in Kylie's chart is positively linked to Jupiter, God of Fortune, and is also part of the Yod formation previously mentioned. Ultimately, the changes that occur will be clearly beneficial, although they may well shock at the time. As Kylie's Saturn links also to her Sun, which can represent Father or father figures in a chart, unexpected events may be part of a family situation.

What shines through this nativity is the radiance of a personality that can endlessly reinvent itself to communicate something of relevance and joy to her audience. But it is important not to underestimate the courage, generosity and will required to gift this to us.

Madeleine Moore
January 2014

Life and Times

28 May 1968 Kylie Ann Minogue is born at the Bethlehem Hospital in Melbourne. Her brother Brendan arrives two years later and younger sister Danielle in 1971.

1979 Attends her first TV audition, aged eleven, and lands role of Dutch girl Carla in the Australian drama series *The Sullivans*. Dannii makes her debut on *Young Talent Time*.

1980 Flies to Britain with her family to see relatives in Wales and go sightseeing in London. Starts at Camberwell High School, Melbourne. Appears as Robin in an episode of the Australian TV series *Skyways*; on set, meets Jason Donovan.

June 1982 Dannii becomes a permanent team member of *Young Talent Time* and is temporarily the more famous of the two sisters.

Oct 1984 Wins the role of Charlotte (Char) Kernow in TV miniseries *The Henderson Kids*. Goes on location for the first time, filming outdoor scenes north of Melbourne.

May 1985 Aged nearly seventeen, plays a twelve year old, 'Yvonne the Terrible', in an episode of the children's TV programme *The Zoo Family*. Beats fifty other hopefuls to win female lead, Samantha Collins, in a six-part TV miniseries *Fame and Misfortune*. First episode of *The Henderson Kids* is shown on Australian TV.

Dec 1985 Leaves Camberwell High School, having passed her Higher School Certificate exams in art and graphics.

Jan 1986 Auditions for *Neighbours* and is cast as tomboy car mechanic Charlene Mitchell. Initial contract for thirteen weeks is quickly extended to twenty-six when bosses sense on-screen chemistry between Charlene and Scott Robinson (Jason Donovan).

April 1986 First episode of *Neighbours* featuring Kylie is shown on Australian TV. She has begun a relationship with Jason, which is kept secret from the public.

Aug 1986 Sings in public for the first time at a benefit for an Australian rules football team. Backed by a band of *Neighbours* actors, she sings 'I Got You Babe' and 'The Loco-Motion'.

Oct 1986 *Neighbours* is broadcast on British TV. Sings 'Sisters Are Doin' It For Themselves' with Dannii on *Young Talent Time*.

Dec 1986 Jason and Kylie slip away for a private holiday on Bali. Topless pictures of Kylie sunbathing would eventually reach the pages of the *Sun*.

April 1987 Becomes youngest-ever artist to be crowned Most Popular Actress in Australia at the Logies; Jason is named Best New Talent at the annual television awards.

July 1987 Releases first single in Australia, 'Locomotion', which reaches number one and stays there for seven weeks. The wedding of Charlene and Scott is the TV event of the year. Meets Michael Hutchence at a party after a music-awards ceremony in Sydney. Appoints Terry Blamey as her manager.

Oct 1987 During a break in filming *Neighbours*, arrives in London to record with Stock, Aitken and Waterman. They write 'I Should Be So Lucky' while she waits in reception at their London studios.

Dec 1987 Sings 'I Should Be So Lucky' on Noel Edmonds' BBC TV Christmas special.

Jan 1988 BBC decides to screen *Neighbours* twice a day and viewing figures top 15 million per episode. 'I Should Be So Lucky' is her first single in the UK, where it reaches number one. Meets the Prince and Princess of Wales in Sydney during Australia's bicentennial celebrations, and later admits to being tongue-tied in front of Diana.

March 1988 Wins a record four Logie Awards, including the Gold Logie as Most Popular Personality on Australian TV.

April 1988 Savaged in print by columnist Jean Rook for arriving at Heathrow looking like a 'slept-in Qantas blanket'.

May 1988 'Got To Be Certain', her second single in Britain, reaches number two, where it stays for six weeks. In Australia, it is the first-ever single to debut at number one.

June 1988 Films her last scenes for *Neighbours*. Cries at a leaving party at a Melbourne restaurant, where she is presented with an antique mahogany mirror and a framed montage of her magazine covers.

July 1988 Her first album, *Kylie*, is released in the UK and Australia. Its success will make her the youngest-ever female to top the UK album charts. 'The Loco-Motion' is released for the first time in the UK but just misses the number-one spot.

Sept 1988 Becomes known as 'The Loco-Motion Girl' after the single becomes her first hit in the USA. It will remain her biggest success there until 'Can't Get You Out Of My Head' in 2002.

Dec 1988 *Kylie* is the biggest-selling album of the year in the UK. The accompanying *Kylie – The Videos* also reaches number one. 'Especially For You', her duet with Jason, is denied Christmas number one by Cliff Richard's 'Mistletoe And Wine'. She becomes the first artist to have four consecutive number ones in Finland.

Jan 1989 'Especially For You' finally reaches number one in the UK. It will be her biggest-selling record until 'Can't Get You Out Of My Head'. She has three simultaneous worldwide number ones when 'Turn It Into Love' reaches the top in Japan and 'The Loco-Motion' matches it in Canada.

April 1989 'Hand On Your Heart', the lead single from her second album, *Enjoy Yourself*, becomes her third UK number one. Begins work on *The Delinquents*, her first movie, playing rebellious Lola Lovell.

May 1989 Celebrates her twenty-first birthday with a champagne party for 150 at the trendy Red Eagle Hotel in Sydney. An over-eager bouncer slams the door in Jason's face.

Sept 1989 While in Hong Kong, preparing for her first international tour, has dinner with Michael Hutchence, who has a home in the colony.

Oct 1989 *Enjoy Yourself* is released in the UK and reaches number one. Performs live concerts for the first time – the *Disco In Dream* tour in Japan, followed by *The Coca-Cola Hitman Roadshow* in the UK.

Dec 1989 Switches on the Christmas lights in London's Regent Street. Joins Bob Geldof and other Stock, Aitken and Waterman stars to record Band Aid II's version of 'Do They Know It's Christmas?', which becomes the Christmas number one. At the Australian premiere of *The Delinquents*, Kylie, on the arm of Hutchence, is barely recognizable in 'suicide' blonde wig and micro dress.

Jan 1990 'Tears On My Pillow', from *The Delinquents* soundtrack, is Kylie's fourth British number one from her first nine singles.

March 1990 First signs of a break from Stock, Aitken and Waterman, when she records four songs in Los Angeles with different producers.

She dedicates one, 'Count The Days', to her now boyfriend Michael Hutchence.

April 1990 Takes control of her image with the video for her next single, 'Better The Devil You Know'; she is seen to writhe provocatively in the arms of a naked black man almost twice her size.

May 1990 Sings a disco version of 'Help!' at a tribute concert for John Lennon in Liverpool. 'Better The Devil You Know' reaches number two in the UK, and becomes an anthem for a generation of gay fans. It is widely assumed that the song is about her relationship with Hutchence.

June 1990 Moves to London with Hutchence, who also buys a farmhouse in the south of France that she helps to furnish.

Nov 1990 Third album, *Rhythm Of Love*, is her least successful so far, peaking at number nine in the UK and ten in Australia. A single from it, 'Step Back In Time', reaches number four in Britain.

Dec 1990 Features in an eight-page spread in *Vogue*, shot in the Raymond Revuebar in Soho. For the first time, she spends Christmas away from her family in Melbourne, preferring to celebrate with Hutchence at the farmhouse in Roquefort-les-Pins.

Feb 1991 Splits with Hutchence amid rumours of his philandering on tour. 'What Do I Have To Do', a Waterman favourite, reaches number six in the UK (Dannii appears in the video) and becomes one of the most popular of all Kylie songs live.

May 1991 Wins Best Selling Australian Artist at the World Music Awards in Monte Carlo.

June 1991 'Shocked', which boasts a raunchy video, becomes her thirteenth consecutive top-ten hit, a record. It places her ahead of Elvis Presley, The Beatles and Madonna.

Aug 1991 'Word Is Out' is her first flop, only reaching a lowly number sixteen.

Oct 1991 Releases her fourth album, *Let's Get To It*. The second single, 'If You Were With Me Now', with Keith Washington, is better received and reaches number four in the UK.

Jan 1992 Releases her first cover since 'The Loco-Motion': 'Give Me Just A Little More Time', a 1970 hit for Chairmen of the Board, takes her back to her most common chart position, number two.

June 1992 Takes part in the Rhythm of Life charity fashion gala in London, joining models and other celebrities at the Grosvenor House Hotel, recruited by Sting to support his Rainforest Foundation.

July 1992 Her name is linked in the British press with superstar Prince after they are seen leaving a London nightclub together.

Aug 1992 Her final Stock, Aitken and Waterman release is a compilation of twenty numbers entitled *Greatest Hits*. It is a runaway success, reaching number one in both the album and video charts. Not so her final Pete Waterman single, 'Celebration', which only reaches number twenty in the UK chart.

Feb 1993 Signs to independent British dance label deConstruction, responsible for pop-soul favourites M People. The year marks key restyling, especially after she meets William Baker, who becomes her Creative Director.

Oct 1993 Invited by Baz Luhrmann to pose at Universal Studios for world-famous photographer Bert Stern. The sixties-style spread fills twenty-one pages of Australian *Vogue*.

Jan 1994 Bridesmaid to Dannii at her wedding to Julian McMahon, soap actor and son of a former Prime Minister of Australia. The sisters sing 'We Are Family'. The marriage lasts less than fifteen months.

March 1994 Performs 'What Do I Have To Do' at the Gay and Lesbian Mardi Gras in Sydney.

June 1994 In Thailand for the start of filming *Street Fighter*, in which she takes the female lead, Cammy, alongside Jean-Claude Van Damme.

Aug 1994 Releases her first deConstruction single, 'Confide In Me', a radical departure from Stock, Aitken and Waterman, which receives a thumbs-up from fans, reaching number two in Britain, kept off the top spot by Whigfield's 'Saturday Night'.

Sept 1994 Her first deConstruction album, *Kylie Minogue*, is released to critical acclaim. It features arrangements and mixes by producers Brothers In Rhythm – one half of that team, Steve Anderson, becomes a long-term friend and collaborator.

Nov 1994 One of her most famous videos accompanies the single 'Put Yourself In My Place'. She is seen floating in a spacecraft, slowly undressing until completely naked. Plays herself in a guest appearance on *The Vicar of Dibley*.

Dec 1994 Wins Best Female Solo Singer at the *Smash Hits* Awards. *Street Fighter* proves to be a Christmas box-office hit, but does nothing for her movie career.

Jan 1995 Records 'Where The Wild Roses Grow', a dark and brooding duet with Nick Cave, in Melbourne.

Feb 1995 Films short art-house film *Hayride To Hell* in Sydney. Plays a psychotic girl who terrorizes a man who gives her a lift home.

April 1995 Spends three months in Los Angeles making *Bio-Dome*, playing Petra von Kant, and has a fling with co-star Pauly Shore. The film is a turkey, however.

June 1995 Features on the front cover of *Loaded*, the definitive British lads' magazine.

July 1995 Meets photographer Stéphane Sednaoui at a party. Shortly afterwards, they spend three weeks driving across the USA. The final single from the *Kylie Minogue* album, 'Where Is The Feeling?', only reaches number sixteen in the UK.

Oct 1995 'Where The Wild Roses Grow' reaches number eleven in the UK but does better in Australia, climbing to number two. The video features an apparently dead Kylie floating face up in a stream. She appears on stage for an AIDS benefit at the Royal Albert Hall, to perform a duet with Elton John (in drag) of 'Sisters Are Doin' It For Themselves'.

Jan 1996 Has no record releases in 1996, but performs live throughout the year, beginning with the Big Day Out concerts in Australia with Nick Cave and The Bad Seeds.

July 1996 Reads lyrics to 'I Should Be So Lucky' at the Poetry Olympics at the Royal Albert Hall.

Aug 1996 Hard at work on her next album, writing all the lyrics and playing her most creative role to date. Performs 'Where The Wild Roses Grow' with Nick Cave at the Brixton Academy.

Sept 1996 'Where The Wild Roses Grow' wins Single of the Year, Best Pop Release and Song of the Year at the Australian Record Industry Awards (ARIAS).

Oct 1996 Makes a short film, *Misfit*, directed by acclaimed artist and friend Sam Taylor-Wood. Kylie mimes to a performance by the famed castrato Alessandro Moreschi.

Dec 1996 Appears on stage in London with Manic Street Preachers, performing their song 'Little Baby Nothing'.

Jan 1997 Her second deConstruction album was due for release this month, but is put back. The original plan for exclusive collaboration with Brothers In Rhythm is scrapped in favour of working with a number of producers, including Manic Street Preachers.

Feb 1997 Appears on British TV as herself in a special episode of *Men Behaving Badly* in aid of Comic Relief.

May 1997 Makes a special appearance with Ray Charles and Australian rock legend John Farnham at the opening of the world's largest casino in Melbourne. Elton John is among 1,500 guests.

Aug 1997 Performs 'Some Kind of Bliss', written by Manic Street Preachers, at the Radio 1 Roadshow in Newquay, Cornwall. The song will be the first single released from her new album, *Impossible Princess*. The death of Diana, Princess of Wales, in Paris prompts a radical rethink of the album title and marketing.

Sept 1997 'Some Kind of Bliss' flops, only reaching number twenty-two in the UK chart. James Dean Bradfield of Manic Street Preachers later says he failed Kylie. Wins award for Most Stylish Female Pop Star at the *Elle* Style Awards in London. Release of the new album is put back until after Christmas.

Oct 1997 Films video for 'Did It Again', the second single from the new album. It features four Kylie personas in battle with each other – Cute Kylie, Sex Kylie, Dance Kylie and Indie Kylie.

Nov 1997 Relationship with Stéphane ends. Michael Hutchence found dead in a Sydney hotel room. Kylie attends his funeral at St Andrew's Cathedral, Sydney.

Feb 1998 Performs 'Better The Devil You Know' at the Sydney Gay and Lesbian Mardi Gras.

March 1998 'Breathe', the third single from the new album, reaches number fourteen. Album finally released in the UK under the temporary title *Kylie Minogue*. It just scrapes into the chart at number ten.

May 1998 Kylie turns thirty.

June 1998 The *Intimate and Live* tour begins in Australia. Its camp, Las Vegas atmosphere is rapturously received.

Nov 1998 Begins filming low-budget thriller *Sample People* in Sydney. Announces that she is leaving deConstruction by 'very amicable agreement'.

Dec 1998 Honoured at the annual Australian Export Awards in Sydney for selling more than 30 million records.

March 1999 Plays Miranda in a version of Shakespeare's *The Tempest* in Barbados. Begins a relationship with actor Rupert Penry-Jones.

May 1999 In Adelaide, shoots cameo role in teen horror movie *Cut*, in which she suffers a grisly death.

June 1999 Signs for The Beatles' old record label, Parlophone – the start of a carefully planned musical comeback. At an Australian gala at the Royal Festival Hall in London, she is chased off stage by Sir Les Patterson brandishing an enormous prosthetic penis.

Oct 1999 Publication of acclaimed book *Kylie*, a photographic journey through her life.

Nov 1999 Sings Marilyn Monroe song 'Diamonds Are A Girl's Best Friend' at the opening of the Fox Studios in Sydney.

Dec 1999 Wearing a revealing Santa outfit, entertains 10,000 Australian troops, part of a peacekeeping force in East Timor, who will not be home for Christmas.

Jan 2000 Meets British model James Gooding at a pool party in Los Angeles.

June 2000 Photo of her bottom appears on the front page of the *Sun*.

July 2000 'Spinning Around' becomes the first of her singles to debut at number one on the UK chart. Kylie is unamused when torrential rain spoils her performance at Capital FM's Party in the Park.

Oct 2000 Performs 'Dancing Queen' and 'On A Night Like This' at the closing ceremony of the Olympics in Sydney. The global TV audience is estimated at 3.7 billion. Less than three weeks later, she sings at the opening ceremony of the Paralympics. The album *Light Years* reaches number two in the UK album chart, but fills the top spot in Australia.

Dec 2000 Films her cameo role as The Green Fairy in *Moulin Rouge!*.

Feb 2001 Makes Pepsi commercial in Australia. Appears as a guest on *An Audience with Ricky Martin*, sharing a duet of his biggest hit, 'Livin' La Vida Loca'.

March 2001 The *On A Night Like This* world tour opens in Glasgow. She performs nineteen songs, opening with 'Loveboat' and closing with 'Spinning Around'.

April 2001 Performs a record nine sell-out nights at the Sydney Entertainment Centre. Ticket sales in Australia alone net $8 million.

Aug 2001 Stars at the V2001 Festival in Weston Park, Staffordshire and Chelmsford, Essex. At the latter, she performs twelve numbers to an audience drenched in the rain.

Sept 2001 'Can't Get You Out Of My Head' becomes her sixth UK number one, selling 77,000 copies on its first day of sale. Makes her first British TV advertisement as the face of Eurostar. She is seen catching a train from London to Paris. Wins *GQ*'s Services to Mankind Award.

Oct 2001 *An Audience with Kylie Minogue* is broadcast in the UK. Kermit the Frog and Adam Garcia appear as guest stars, while Brendan, Dannii and Pete Waterman are in the audience. Tickets for her 2002 British tour sell out in one hour. *Fever*, Kylie's second Parlophone album, reaches number one in the UK album charts.

Nov 2001 Wins a BAMBI, Germany's top pop award, for Best Comeback of the Year. A pair of her knickers raises £4,000 as part of a fashion package auctioned in aid of BBC Children in Need. Kylie tops the list of 100 greatest Welsh women.

Dec 2001 Wins two of the inaugural *Top of the Pops* Awards for Best Single and Best Tour. Her advertisement for underwear firm Agent Provocateur is considered too sexy for a TV audience.

Feb 2002 'Can't Get You Out Of My Head' tops the US dance charts and enters the *Billboard* Top 100. Appears on the *Tonight Show with Jay Leno* as part of US publicity campaign. *Fever* is released in the US and sells 107,000 copies in its first week. Wins two Brit Awards, for Best International Album and Best International Female, and says the first person she'll call will be her dad, who is recovering from a prostate-cancer scare.

March 2002 Crowned Best Selling Australian Artist at the World Music Awards in Monaco. She performs at the ceremony wearing a short red dress by Dolce & Gabbana and thigh-high black boots. Allegedly, Prince Albert of Monaco gropes her bottom.

April 2002 Kylie begins *KylieFever2002*, her most ambitious world tour to date, at the Cardiff Arena. William Baker and Kylie devise a show borrowing styles from *Doctor Who*, *Star Trek* and David Bowie's *Diamond Dogs*.

May 2002 Kylie's break-up with James Gooding becomes public.

July 2002 Madame Tussauds unveils Kylie waxwork, which forms centre point of a new interactive exhibition. Kylie is on all fours and breathes seductively 'I Can't Get You Out Of My Head' at passers-by. Her DVD/video *Live In Sydney* is banned in Malaysia, where authorities consider it too hot. She cancels US tour, claiming she wants to devote more time to her private life.

Oct 2002 Kylie is named Woman of the Year at *Elle* Style Awards. Travels with Carol to a remote retreat in Western Australia for complete rest following a reported breakdown. Attends Paris Motor Show as the face of Ford Streetka and is paid £350,000 for a five-minute appearance.

Feb 2003 Steals the headlines at the Brit Awards when Justin Timberlake grabs the Minogue bottom during their duet of the Blondie classic 'Rapture'. Launches her 'Love Kylie x' lingerie range at Selfridges in London. Meets actor Olivier Martinez in a hotel lobby after the Grammy Awards.

March 2003 James Gooding claims in the Sunday newspapers that Kylie had ruined his life, complaining that the public never saw the 'real' Kylie. He admits cheating on her and also reveals they enjoyed wild sex in a tent.

May 2003 The rumours are true. Kylie holds the hand of her new boyfriend Olivier Martinez as they arrive at the Laureus World Sports Awards in Monaco.

Aug 2003 Appointed the first-ever ambassador for the NSPCC.

Nov 2003 Achieves her seventh number one in the UK singles chart with the very sensual 'Slow', accompanied by a sexy video of her writhing on a towel. Album *Body Language* peaks at number six.

Jan 2004 At the age of thirty-five, Kylie is placed first in *Heat* magazine's Sexiest Bodies list. She beats Beyoncé into second.

Feb 2004 Wins first Grammy when 'Come Into My World' is named Best Dance Recording.

July 2004 Earns £200,000 for a half-hour set at the pre-wedding banquet in Paris of billionaire's daughter Vanisha Mittal and Amit Bhatia. Serenades couple with 'Slow' and 'Spinning Around'.

Oct 2004 Tickets for *Showgirl: The Greatest Hits Tour* sell out in two hours. Takes to the floor at a charity ball in London with Jake Shears of Scissor Sisters. Jake wears gold pants; Kylie is in jeans.

Nov 2004 Guest stars in an episode of the cult Australian comedy *Kath & Kim* as a character called Epponnee Rae. She wears a bridal outfit as part of a spoof of her famous *Neighbours* wedding.

Feb 2005 Is the voice of Florence in a film version of *The Magic Roundabout*. Robbie Williams is Dougal.

March 2005 £5 million *Showgirl* world tour begins in Glasgow with six costume changes. Most of the attention is focused on her handmade corset, reducing her waist to an eye-watering sixteen inches.

April 2005 Temporarily splits with Creative Director William Baker, but maintains they are still the best of friends. All three experts in *Heat* magazine's 'Surgery Spy' column conclude that she has had cosmetic surgery.

May 2005 Cancels the rest of her *Showgirl* tour after being diagnosed with breast cancer while staying at her parents' home in Melbourne. Undergoes surgery, in which a tumour is removed from her left breast in a partial mastectomy.

July 2005 Begins chemotherapy in Paris because she 'wants a life' with Olivier. Carol accompanies her. Her weight will drop to six stone during the treatment.

Dec 2005 Final chemotherapy session in Paris is followed by anxious wait to see if the cancer has gone into remission. Faces six months of further radiation treatment and decides to receive that back in Australia when she is well enough to travel.

March 2006 Wearing a floor-length bright blue silk dress and a garland of white flowers, Kylie visits a Sri Lankan theatre troupe formed in the aftermath of the tsunami that devastated the region. She is photographed waving and smiling on top of an elephant.

April 2006 The first pictures of Kylie after the cancer all clear appear on her website. They were taken by Olivier in Portofino and reveal that her hair is growing back and she looks relaxed and happy.

June 2006 Presents flowers to Dannii on stage at G-A-Y, where her sister is performing her greatest hits. They sing 'Jump To The Beat' together. Attends Elton John's White Tie and Tiara Ball, her official 'coming-out' after her illness.

July 2006 Sits in front row at Karl Lagerfeld's Chanel show in Paris. Describes her cancer ordeal to Cat Deeley, revealing there were times when she couldn't bear to look in the mirror, and says, 'It's no picnic.'

Nov 2006 Presents six-year-old Katy Miles with Pride of Britain Child of Courage Award. Resumes the *Showgirl* tour at the Sydney Opera House. Has a chair backstage to rest on between scene changes. On the second night, Bono joins her on-stage to sing 'Kids'. Her first perfume, Darling, is launched by Coty.

Dec 2006 Performs a special New Year's Eve concert at Wembley Arena. At midnight, she sings 'Celebration'.

Jan 2007 *Glamour* magazine names her World's Best Dressed Woman. Fourth waxwork is unveiled at Madame Tussauds. Tells the audience at the Manchester MEN Arena halfway through the show that she can't continue. Fears for her health are eased when she announces that it was just a bad bout of flu.

Feb 2007 Officially announces that she and Olivier have split amicably. Attends the premiere of *Kylie: The Exhibition* at the Victoria & Albert Museum in London.

May 2007 The 'H&M Loves Kylie' summer collection is launched. At an AIDS charity auction in Cannes, she sings a duet of 'Can't Get You Out Of My Head' with film star Sharon Stone.

Oct 2007 Attends premiere of *White Diamond*, William Baker's documentary of her recovery, at the Vue in London's Leicester Square. She wears Dolce & Gabbana and diamond jewellery worth £1 million. Becomes the first woman to win the prestigious Music Industry Trusts Award. At the event, sings a jazz version of 'I Should Be So Lucky' accompanied on the piano by Jamie Cullum.

Nov 2007 *The Kylie Show*, a TV special, is broadcast with comedy sketches featuring Dannii, Simon Cowell, Mathew Horne and Jason Donovan. New album *X* is released but only makes number four in the UK charts.

Dec 2007 Performs 'Wow' and a duet of 'Better The Devil You Know' with Leon Jackson during final of *The X Factor. Doctor Who's* Christmas Special featuring Kylie is the most watched episode of the long-running series. Sings with Sir Paul McCartney on *Jools' Annual Hootenanny*.

Jan 2008 Awarded the OBE for services to music in The Queen's New Years Honours list.

Feb 2008 Launches a range of bed linen called 'Kylie Minogue at Home'. Wins Best International Female Solo Artist at the Brits and is presented with the award by *Doctor Who*, David Tennant.

May 2008, Made a Knight in the Order of Arts and Letters in Paris. The *KylieX2008* tour opens in that city. Celebrates her fortieth birthday.

Sept 2008 Makes Middle East debut when she is paid a reported £2 million for a one-hour concert at the opening of the Atlantis Hotel on the man-made Palm Jumeriah island in Dubai.

Oct 2008 Pictured for the first time with her new boyfriend, leading male model Andrés Velencoso. They attend a birthday party for Dita Von Teese at a Paris nightclub.

Jan 2009 *Boombox*, an album of remixes, is released to critical acclaim. Goes snowboarding with Andrés in Chamonix. Travels to the seaside town of Tossa de Mar near Barcelona to meet his family.

Feb 2009 Manages five costume changes while presenting the Brits with James Corden and Mathew Horne.

June 2009 Named Woman of the Year and Entrepreneur of the Year at the 2009 *Glamour* Awards in London. Performs at the Gdansk shipyard for the twentieth anniversary of the first free elections in Poland.

Sept 2009 Her first-ever tour of the US, called *For You, For Me*, begins in Oakland, California.

Oct 2009 Sings 'Chiggy Wiggy' during a cameo role in her first Bollywood film, *Blue*.

Feb 2010 Five years in remission. Great-Uncle Dennis Riddiford dies at home in Wales, aged eighty. Takes part in the Helping Haiti charity record 'Everybody Hurts' for victims of the Haiti earthquake. Poses for photographer Mario Testino as part of the Fashion Targets Breast Cancer appeal.

June 2010 Makes a surprise first appearance at Glastonbury to sing 'Any Which Way' with Scissor Sisters. Films role in New York as a tattoo-parlour owner in cult film *Jack & Diane*.

July 2010 *Aphrodite*, her eleventh studio album, is launched in Ibiza and goes straight to number one. Becomes an aunt for the third time when Dannii gives birth to a son, Ethan.

Aug 2010 Performs a series of duets with Rufus Wainwright at The Last Song of Summer concert in The Watermill Center in The Hamptons, New York, to support emerging artists. They sing 'The Loco-Motion', 'Hallelujah' and 'Over The Rainbow'.

Nov 2010 Films video for 'Higher', a duet with Taio Cruz. It becomes her most-watched on YouTube, with 40 million views. Mimes 'Get Outta My Way' at the Macy's Thanksgiving Day Parade in New York. Sings 'Santa Baby' and 'Let It Snow' at the annual turning-on of the Christmas tree lights outside Rockefeller Center.

Feb 2011 Performs opening night of the *Aphrodite: Les Folies* tour in Herning, Denmark. By the end of the year, it will have made more than $32 million, the twenty-fifth highest grossing of 2011.

Oct 2011 Made an honorary Doctor of Health Sciences by the Anglia Ruskin University in Chelmsford for her work in increasing breast-cancer awareness. Buys a mansion in the same street in Chelsea where she had lived for fifteen years; Andrés moves in.

Nov 2011 Inducted into the ARIA Hall of Fame by Australian Premier Julia Gillard at a ceremony in Sydney. To date, she has won sixteen ARIAS and been nominated for thirty-nine.

Dec 2011 BBC Radio 2 broadcast *Kylie on Blossom*, an hour-long tribute to Blossom Dearie, who died in 2009. Kylie acknowledges how influential the great New York jazz singer was on her own vocal style.

March 2012 Performs the first date in Melbourne of her *Anti Tour*, a collection of B-sides and unreleased material. It's the first of a year-long celebration of twenty-five years in music, entitled K25.

May 2012 Attends the Cannes Film Festival for the premiere of *Holy Motors*, an acclaimed avant-garde French film by director Leos Carax. In the film, Kylie has a small role and sings 'Who Were We?' before jumping off the top of a tall building.

June 2012 Performs at the Queen's Diamond Jubilee Concert on a stage in front of the Victoria Memorial outside Buckingham Palace. Dressed as a Pearly Queen, she sings a medley of four songs. Backstage, she helps Gary Barlow introduce the Queen to the performers.

Oct 2012 *The Abbey Road Sessions*, a collection of new arrangements of her classic songs, enters the chart at number two. She is named the third biggest-selling female artist in the UK of all time, behind Madonna and Rihanna.

Dec 2012 Reunites with Jason Donovan to sing 'Especially For You' at the Hit Factory Live – Christmas Cracker party at the O2, celebrating the twenty-fifth anniversary of the PWL label. Sings for the Queen at the 100th *Royal Variety Performance*. Launches *Kylie/Fashion* book at Harrods.

Jan 2013 Announces split from her manager, Terry Blamey, after more than twenty-five years together. He says she wants to take a break from singing and concentrate on acting.

March 2013 Signs a management deal with Jay-Z's entertainment conglomerate Roc Nation. Begins recording a new album in Los Angeles.

Sept 2013 Confirmed as a new judge on *The Voice*, replacing Jessie J. Promises to be competitive.

Oct 2013 Begins filming blind auditions for *The Voice* at the BBC's new studios in Salford. Break-up with Andrés Velencoso made public. Spokeswoman for Kylie says it's amicable.

Jan 2014 An audience of 8.4 million tune in to watch Kylie's first appearance on *The Voice*. She reveals her new single will be called 'Into The Blue' and will be released in March 2014.

Acknowledgements

I am the proud owner of eleven Kylie Minogue studio albums and two greatest-hits compilations. It will soon be twelve. Surprisingly, perhaps, my least favourite is *Fever* from 2002 and my most played is *Impossible Princess*, the one that caused her so much anguish back in the nineties. It's been a huge pleasure plotting the progress of this very special artist through a marvellous 27-year career.

These are the people who have helped me most: Doug Booth, Spencer Bright, Peter Holt, Cassandra Hooper, Paul Marcolin, Jane Oddy, Rick Sky and Frank Thorne. My old friends Kevin O'Sullivan and Alison Jane Reid were as helpful as ever. Kevin is the best television critic in the country and offered invaluable insight into *The Voice*. Alison Jane is a terrific fashion writer. Check out her website www.ethical-hedonist.com.

A special thank-you to Dave Seaman, who as one half of the brilliant production team Brothers In Rhythm did so much to develop Kylie's music when she left Stock, Aitken and Waterman. Dave's new record label, Selador, is up and running, so please listen to *The Selador Sessions*.

I am grateful to the brilliant team at Simon & Schuster. They are Mike Jones and Carly Cook, who oversaw this project, Abigail Bergstrom, who, assisted by Mark Burgess, ensured everything ran smoothly; Anneka Sandher for her cover design; Jo Edgecombe for looking after production; Alice Murphy for marketing; and Rumana Haider, Dominic Brendon and Gill Richardson for handling the all-important sales.

Gordon Wise is a brilliant agent, ably supported by his assistant at Curtis Brown, Richard Pike. Thanks to Jen Westaway for ignoring the bar noise and patiently transcribing my tapes, and to my excellent researchers Emily Jane Swanson and Catherine Marcus. It's always a delight to work with Arianne Burnette, who once again has used her copy-editing skills to improve the original manuscript, and Madeleine Moore, who tells me she loved working on Kylie's birth chart and is now a firm admirer of the star.

Finally, thank you to Jo Westaway for her support and bringing me wine and chocolate.

You can read more about my books at seansmithceleb.com or follow me on Twitter @seansmithceleb and facebook.com/seansmithcelebbiog.

Select Bibliography and Picture Credits

William Baker and Kylie Minogue, *Kylie: La La La* (Hodder & Stoughton, 2002)

Jason Donovan, *Between The Lines* (Harper Collins, 2008)

Dannii Minogue, *Dannii: My Story* (Simon & Schuster UK, 2011)

Dino Scatena, *Kylie* (Penguin Books, Australia, 1997)

Simon Sheridan, *The Complete Kylie* (Titan, 2012)

Sasha Stone, *Kylie Minogue: The Superstar Next Door* (Omnibus Press, 1990)

Photo Credits

© Rex Features: 5, 7, 10, 21, 25, 30

Courtesy of Richard Young: 3, 11, 14, 16, 17, 22

Courtesy of The Sun: 1, 4

Courtesy of Brendan Beirne: 6

Courtesy of Edward Hirst: 12

Courtesy of Peter Carrette: 18

Courtesy of Nikos: 19

Courtesy of Brian Rasic: 20

Courtesy of SIPA: 23

© London Features International: 2

© Fairfax Photo Library: 8

© Corbis UK Ltd

© Bigpicturesphoto.com: 15

© LFI: 26

© WireImage.com: 27, 28

© Getty Images: 29, 31, 32, 33, 34, 35, 36, 37, 38, 39, 41, 42

© PA Photos Ltd: 40, 43

Scan Smith is the UK's leading celebrity biographer and the author of the number one bestseller *Cheryl,* the definitive biography of Cheryl Cole, as well as bestselling books about Robbie Williams, Tulisa Contostavlos and Kate Middleton. His books about the most famous people of our times have been translated throughout the world. His subjects include Gary Barlow, Alesha Dixon, Justin Timberlake, Britney Spears, Victoria Beckham, Jennifer Aniston and J. K. Rowling. The film *Magic Beyond Words:* The J. K. Rowling Story was based on his biography of the Harry Potter author. Described by the *Independent* as a 'fearless chronicler', he specializes in meticulous research, going 'on the road' to find the real person behind the star image.